The Extra-Marital Sex Contract

Dr. Jay Ziskin
and Dr. Mae Ziskin

The Extra-Marital Sex Contract

Nash Publishing, Los Angeles

Library of Congress Catalog Card Number: 72-95241
Standard Book Number: 8402-1307-7

Published simultaneously in the United States and
Canada by Nash Publishing Corporation,
9255 Sunset Boulevard, Los Angeles, California 90069.

Printed in the United States of America.

First Printing.

Authors'
Note

We wrote this book because we believe in marriage. Through our own marriage, we have been able to observe the contrast between what marriage can be, and how seldom it turns out to be that good—a fact we have seen among acquaintances, clients, and in our own previous marriages (one each). We have experienced our marriage as a loving, caring, mutual, exciting, and growing relationship. Each of us has contributed to the growth and development of the other as well as to the achievement of mutual goals and satisfactions. While we are comfortable and secure with each other, it is not the comfort of being in a "rut." It is, rather, the comfort of knowing that we belong together so that we can experiment and change, keeping our relationship vital with little fear of harmful consequences. We do not believe in avoiding all risks at the expense of foregoing an enhancement and enrichment of living. We see our relationship as one that reduces the anxiety that usually accompanies risk taking in any area.

It is our hope that others will be able to find the kind of joy in marriage that we have achieved. We feel that for many people this may require, as it has for us, a reconceptualization of the marriage relationship.

Contents

Introduction

There is hardly a more pressing issue in contemporary American society than the future of the institution of marriage. Problems of the economy, international strife, race relations, ecology, and crime touch the lives of all—but not on the intimate, personal, day-by-day, year-by-year basis that is involved in an enduring man-woman relationship. Typically, in America this relationship, which is at the very core of life for most people, is housed in the traditional structure of monogamous marriage. Yet the evidence is overwhelming that for large numbers of people, this structure has become inadequate. It is not surprising, therefore, that some variations of the structure have been attempted or proposed. One of these variations involves the extramarital sex agreement: an arrangement under which both spouses are free to have sexual relations with others than the mate, in an open manner, free of the connotations of disloyalty or cheating.

Until the present, little knowledge has been gathered concerning extramarital sex agreements. The subject has received, at best, only incidental attention from social scientists. Anthropologists have provided descriptions of nonmonogamous practices in other cultures, usually the so-called primitive societies. The University of Indiana Institute for Sex Research (Kinsey, et al.) has provided valuable but cold statistical data on extramarital sex. Gerhard Neubeck *(Extramarital Relations)* has updated the Kinsey data with studies of the phenomenon in greater depth. Writers, such as Morton Hunt *(The Affair),* have placed warm, living flesh on the cold, statistical bones. Similarly, John Cuber and Peggy Harroff *(Sex and the Significant Americans)* and Gilbert Bartell *(Group Sex)* have blended social-science methods with a humanistic approach to provide some insights into the dynamics and effects of extramarital sex. However, with the exception of recent publications concerning "swinging" which are devoted to only one type of extramarital sex agreement, there is a lack of in-depth analyses of such agreements.

With this book we hope to reduce this gap in our knowledge and to open the area for discussion. The extramarital sex agreement may be an idea whose time has come. Such arrangements are already here. True, where they exist, they are, for the most part, covert. True, treatment of the subject is almost nonexistent in the popular media of the news and entertainment fields. True, such agreements violate society's stated mores and even its laws. Certainly, such agreements appear to violate romantic notions of love and marriage, such as "forsaking all others." Nevertheless, a small, but growing number of people are considering or actually practicing this form of marriage. Of a sampling of 20,000 people who answered the questionnaires sent out by *Psychology Today* (July 1970, Vol. IV, no 2), 21 percent of the answers favored extramarital sex with the agreement of both spouses. A breakdown of these figures proves interesting in that they show nearly as many women as men taking this position. Are such individuals irresponsible, antisocial, "sick," or immoral? If morality is viewed as encompassing more than sexual behavior, these people appear to be as moral or ethical as most people, perhaps even more so. Evidence cited in the book suggests that, for the most part, they are healthy, well-adjusted, responsible, and productive people and, more often than not, they have reasonably good or very good marriages as we define a good marriage: one in which the spouses care about each other, enjoy doing things together, are interested in each other, are attractive to each other, and accept each other's faults with the knowledge that they are overwhelmingly outweighed by his or her desirable qualities. And, finally, they are able to communicate their feelings to each other, both positive and negative, openly and honestly.

In making our analysis of this practice, we have relied on several different kinds of information. Books and articles by others provided valuable information regarding the historical development of current marital modes, cross-cultural variations in marital practice, and the nature of extramarital sexual relations in present-day American society. Regarding the latter, we have found the previously mentioned books by Hunt, Cuber and Harroff, Bartell and Neubeck most helpful. We have also drawn on our training in both law and clinical psychology and our experiences in the practice of both of these professions. The news media have provided some material, as have discussions with friends and colleagues. However, without question, the most significant information came from the one hundred thirty-four couples practicing extramarital sex by agreement who granted us the privilege of in-depth interviews. These interviews were approximately two hours in length and were marked by a high degree of candor.

In evaluating the values and limitations of information obtained from a group of informants, it is necessary to know something about the nature of the population involved.

Geographically, the entire sample was drawn from the Southern California area, which in itself requires the exercise of caution in generalizing to other geographic areas. Some were from small outlying communities, but the large majority lived in the greater Los Angeles area, so it is mainly an urban population. The youngest was twenty-three years old, the oldest was fifty-eight. Nearly 80 percent were in the 35 - 50 year age group. The group was almost evenly divided between couples in their first marriage and those in which one or both spouses had experienced a prior marriage. The duration of the existing marriage ranged from two to thirty years, with the average at sixteen. The entire group was Caucasian and, with few exceptions, American-born. In terms of socioeconomic status, the group could be described as predominantly middle and upper-middle class. The lowest family income was $14,000 a year, while the highest was "in excess of $100,000," with the bulk of the family incomes in the $20,000 to $40,000 range. Slightly more than half had indicated some degree of religious affiliation, but less than 10 percent appeared to have any significant involvement with institutional religion. All had at least completed high school. Among the men, 70 percent had some college education, half had completed a bachelor's degree, and almost a third held advanced academic or professional degrees. Among the women, slightly more than half had some college education, about a third had bachelor's degrees, and almost 25 percent had advanced degrees. As far as their occupations were concerned, the majority of the men were in the professions or owned their own businesses. However, the sample included a number of salesmen, skilled tradesmen, and men occupying salaried executive or administrative positions. There were two artists and three writers. Most of the women were housewives, with only 35 percent employed full- or part-time. Some of them assisted their husbands in their businesses. About 20 percent were employed in professional work—teaching, the health professions, the arts. Three operated their own businesses independently. Twenty-two of the couples were childless. For the others, the number of children ranged from one to four. In some instances all the children had reached adult status. About fifteen percent had been involved in some form of psychotherapy or psychoanalysis; none were in treatment at the time of the interview. Incidentally, none were patients or former patients of ours. In none of the cases was the psychological assistance sought in connection with the extramarital sex agreement except for one, and then, not for treatment, but for consultation prior to making the agreement. All the men had some sexual experience prior to marriage. Forty percent of the women were virgins when first married. Of these, however, there were a considerable number in their second marriages, who had had a great deal of sexual activity in the interim. Politically, the group was approximately 50 percent Democratic, forty percent Republican, with the remainder scattered among the Peace and Freedom party, the American Independent party and "declined to state."

We have been asked how we managed to obtain this group of informants. We are always tempted to answer, "With great difficulty," but that is only partially true. It was quite easy to contact swingers through advertisements and going to swinging bars. All the people contacted in this manner did not participate in the study, but a sufficient number did. Swingers, therefore, make up about 40 percent of the group. Those whose extramarital sex agreements pertain to activities other than swinging were more difficult to contact. A few were acquaintances whose activities were already well known to us. They not only participated, but referred other couples to us. In some cases, other acquaintances, not themselves involved in such agreements but aware of our interest, referred couples they knew of to us. We also placed ads describing the study in underground newspapers, such as the *Los Angeles Free Press.* Most of the contacts came from such ads, either directly, or through referral from someone who had answered the ad. We assured each participant of absolute confidentiality and anonymity. Needless to say, we have changed the names and background information sufficiently to make identification of any specific individual impossible.

There are many cautions to be observed in dealing with data from such sources. To begin with, the number is too small to draw any firm conclusions. Secondly, they are "volunteers," which may make them atypical even among practitioners of extramarital sex agreements. Several were also proselytizers— crusaders eager to convert others to their position. Others seemed to need to defend their practices. In either case, one cannot be sure of the objectivity of their reports, as there is an absence of negative cases and unsuccessful outcomes. It seems highly implausible that there should be no couples who have tried this agreement with undesirable outcomes. Such couples are less likely to come forward for such a study than those who are enthusiastic about it. Finally, we made no effort to make this a "scientific" study. We did not use a standardized interview; instead we adapted the interview to each couple. We made no effort to quantify the data other than the background information in the preceding paragraph. No statistical analysis was performed; the nature of the sample would have rendered any such attempts at scientific precision meaningless. Thus, the data should be taken for what it is—a description of the experiences of a number of couples with the extramarital sex agreement. If it has any scientific value, it is as a preliminary to an investigation of the phenomenon.

One final point. It may appear to some readers that we are advocating the extramarital sex agreement. What we are advocating is that some serious thinking be done about the nature of people, of marriage, of sex, and the issue of whether or not the extramarital sex agreement has merit. Our opinion, for what it is worth, is that it is likely to be good for many people, bad for others, and of little interest to the remainder. But it is time to let the material speak for itself.

Part I: Marriage and Sex

1.
The Trouble with Marriage

What would happen if John and Betty sat down tonight, in the nicely furnished living room of their well-kept home in middle-class suburbia, and agreed that within the context of their marriage each would be free to have sexual relationships with others? What would happen if a sizable number of other couples entered into such an agreement? What would happen if such agreements became the norm, or, if not the norm, at least socially acceptable? Would these marriages be destroyed? Would the institution of marriage crumble? Would our society be destroyed? Would such an agreement harm the individuals or their families? Would it benefit them? What would married life be like under such agreements? What kind of sexual relationships take place under such agreements? Why would people enter into agreements of this nature? These are the questions to which the remainder of this book is directed.

Taking the last question first, some answers may be sought in the status and conditions of marriage in contemporary America.

UNTIL DEATH (DIVORCE, DECEPTION, DISCORD, DISCONTENT) DO US PART

From all of the media, from lectern and pulpit, from pundit to populist, and from beer hall to bull session, the word comes loud and clear—marriage, American style, is in serious trouble. It would be premature to predict its demise, but there can be no doubting that it is "sick."

Divorce

The most obvious and well-known manifestation of the disease is the divorce rate. Depending on whose statistics are being quoted, the figures show that there are somewhere between one and two divorces for every three marriages. Some of these are "mistake" marriages where the parties were ill suited to each other or not ready for marriage, and the mistake was soon recognized. Often these marriages occur among the young to get away from home, to "play house," for security, or as the only feasible or personally acceptable way of handling sexual needs.

Other marriages seem to start out on the right foot, but go awry. A phenomenon that might be called the "twenty-year syndrome" is becoming increasingly common. In many of these cases, to the shock and amazement of their friends, an apparently happy and well-matched couple announce the end of their marriage once the youngest child has grown up and left the nest. In some cases this results from the attrition and abrasion of many years of accumulated conflicts and resentments that inevitably occur in two decades of living and dealing with domestic and other problems together. In others, it is the result of the soul-searching and the evaluation of one's life that takes place in one's forties. The Swiss psychiatrist, Carl Jung, described this process lucidly. Jung pointed out that in earlier adult years people are busily preoccupied with establishing themselves occupationally, acquiring material possessions, and raising families. Somewhere in the forties, the culmination of these goals is achieved with varying degrees of success. For most people it marks the time when they have arrived at a fairly set position in life. It is then, according to Jung, that they begin to take stock, to examine their values, to weigh or evaluate their lives. For many, it is a period which might be described by the poignant popular song "Is That All There Is?" With the completing of major marital goals—establishing a home, raising children—many look at what is left of their lives and are unwilling to say "That's all there is." Seeing little hope of fulfilling themselves in the marriage, they make a break so that they may seek something more or something different, whatever it may be for them.

In other cases of the twenty-year syndrome, the spouses simply have not grown at the same rate. One may have matured and expanded far beyond the other so that, finally, they have little in common and little reason to continue the relationship. A variation of this problem occurs when one spouse has in fact grown and matured, but the other cannot see it. The matured spouse is a victim, then, of the other's "locked-in perception" of him, or her, as the youth or girl he or she married. This can eventually be deadly, as it was in the case of Peter and Ruth. Peter and Ruth were both nineteen years old, college students, when they married. Both were from wealthy families, and Peter went into his father's business. As he progressively took over the management, the business grew into an outstanding success. Along with this, Peter matured, becoming a deep, sensitive, and interesting man. But Ruth could never see him as other than the "boy" she had married—shallow and something of a clown. Worse, her perception was perpetuated by their friends, and Peter was condemned to play the role expected of him for many years. Finally, as might have been expected, he met a woman who had not known him previously and who was outside the "routine" context. She responded to him as the man he had become, and they had an affair. This experience, and the realization of what he was really like, forced Peter to face the dissatisfactions he felt in the marriage, dissatisfactions he had suppressed because of the importance the marriage held for him. He did not wish to give up the things he valued, nor was he willing to relinquish the joys of this new-found "self." Some men would have resolved the problem by maintaining both relationships. But this would have violated Peter's sense of ethics and responsibility. To the end of preserving the marriage, he consulted a marriage counselor who suggested that both Peter and Ruth come in and discuss some of their feelings. After several sessions it became apparent that Ruth was not going to change. Unwilling to be type-cast as the perpetual "juvenile" for the rest of his life, Peter felt he had no alternative but to obtain a divorce. So, despite the caring feelings that, quite obviously, still existed between them, and with an aura of wistful regret that touched all concerned in the matter (including one author as one of the lawyers), they were divorced.

Adultery and Deception

The second visible symptom of the "sickness" of marriage is the extent to which sexual infidelity exists in the United States. Precise and reliable information concerning the numbers of men and women who engage in adulterous relationships is extremely difficult, if not impossible, to obtain. The research problems involved in obtaining a representative population whose members can be counted on to be completely open and candid about such activities, are well known. Acknowledging these defects, past studies indicate that somewhere between 14 and 24 percent of women and roughly 25 to 50 percent of men have had extramarital relations. Most of these studies were performed in the 1940s and experts generally agree that the rate was probably higher than was revealed at that time, and is almost certainly higher now with the coming of the "Sexual Revolution." Morton Hunt (*Playboy,* August 1971) estimates that within another generation, probably four out of five husbands and two of three wives will have extramarital sexual relationships.

The "sickness" does not necessarily lie in the fact of such relationships but, rather, in the deception, the "cheating," that characterizes them. If, as the experts on marriage stress, honesty and open communication between spouses is the hallmark of a good marriage, the lying, cheating, and deception that accompany extramarital sexual relationships under present conditions detract from the quality of the marital relationship. It is true that many studies have shown that such activities can be carried on by some people without destroying their marriage. Nevertheless, it is difficult to believe that the quality of the relationship is not impaired. The necessity for deception shows the deceiver is aware that the activity might cause pain to the spouse. The guilt generated by knowledge of wrongdoing and dishonesty may impair the relationship in subtle ways. For example, some people become morose and depressed when they are carrying guilt inside of them. They are unable to enjoy life. Of course, such states affect the innocent spouse by virtue of the interdependency of the marital partners. When some people do something they feel is wrong, they tend to suspect their spouses of similar wrongdoing with consequent decrease of trust. Still others avoid guilt by denigrating the spouse to justify their own behavior. Such phrases as "my wife doesn't understand me" have become clichés. Further, the fear of detection or inadvertent disclosure of the misconduct creates a certain wariness in the relationship. Of course, in some cases, the adulterer actually is caught, with consequences ranging from disruption of the relationship through domestic discord to divorce and, even, to homicide.

And They Lived Unhappily Ever After

Less apparent than divorce or infidelity, but more insidious, are a multitude of marriages in which one or both spouses are unhappy but do nothing to ameliorate their discontent. The offices of psychiatrists, psychologists, and marriage counselors are filled with such cases; and these represent only the tip of the iceberg as the majority of such unhappy spouses do not seek professional help. These individuals go through life in frustration and misery, taking out their unhappiness on themselves and all around them. This illness of marriage affects not only the spouses, but often has a detrimental effect on children who are brought up in an unhappy or loveless atmosphere, or become scapegoats, or are used by the parents to provide substitute gratifications. For example, an unhappy mother may smother a child with excessive affectional, social, or achievemental demands which may interfere with the development of the child along its natural lines. Many children of unhappy marriages have found themselves on the analyst's couch as a result of their parents' efforts to achieve, through them, the satisfactions lacking in the marriages. Many a young man or woman has found himself or herself resisting marriage because of the unappetizing example afforded by their parents.

Get a House in the Suburbs and Die

A fourth symptom of the illness of marriage is the incipient rejection of this institution by the younger generation. While not yet widespread and still of undetermined duration, there is a groundswell of negative feeling toward marriage among young people. This disenchantment among the young may be expressed in their behavior or in their stated desire to put off marriage as long as possible, as though it were the end rather than the beginning of a good life. This may have been well expressed in a conversation of some young people we could not help overhearing in a restaurant. These young people were discussing life as young people commonly do. We could not forget the brief, desolate summation presented by one of the young men, " . . . So what do people do? They get married, get a house in the suburbs and die."

Increasing numbers of young people are living together as a means of avoiding marriage. One of the elements of the antimarriage feeling among the young relates to the value that the young people place on honesty. They see much that is artificial and hypocritical in present marriage practices. A number of them also straightforwardly declare that they do not see how one person could fulfill all their needs and desires over the span of a lifetime, and prefer not to enter into an arrangement that would force them to forego other love relationships or have them only surreptitiously.

Sex is only one of many elements involved in the success or failure of marriage. However, it is an important element, and its significance is increasing as people become more aware of themselves as sexual beings. In part then, the degree of success of a marriage includes the degree to which it encompasses sexual gratification. By sexual gratification, we do not merely mean the opportunity to copulate: We mean the opportunity for a full, rich, and exciting sex life.

MARRIAGE AS A SEX DEPRESSANT

Paradoxically, while marriage has been viewed traditionally as the doorway through which a happy and fulfilled sex life is best obtained, the fact is that at least for a large number of people marriage, which initially may meet this promise, rather soon becomes the agent for deadening the sex life. A good deal of humor has developed around this phenomenon. As an illustration, there is the old classic joke that if a couple put a bean in a jar every time they had sexual intercourse during their first year of marriage, and took one bean out every time they had intercourse after the first year, they would never empty the jar. Of course, this is an exaggeration, but there is truth to the idea it expresses. A brief look at some of the great loves—the "grand passions"—of literature and history is instructive on this point. These models of the "romantic ideal" love relationships are exemplified by such famous pairs as Romeo and Juliet, Heloise and Abelard, Tristan and Isolde. These loves share common elements that clearly distinguish them from most marital relationships. Foremost among these is the lovers' difficulty in making physical contact. Factors of distance, armed force, or socio-legal-moral constraints served to keep them separated most of the time. The second element is the absence of a shared domestic life. Juliet did not have to coax Romeo to mow the lawn or fix a leaky faucet when he would have preferred to play golf. Heloise and Abelard did not have occasion to quarrel over budgets or babies. Isolde did not arrive for her trysts with Tristan in curlers and flannel bathrobe. Envision Romeo and Juliet, if you will, not on the balcony or in the tomb, but after fifteen years of marriage, living in a three-bedroom tract home, sweating out the mortgage payments, dealing with the children, and wrapped up in all the rest of domesticity's drab, dulling detail, familiar with each other to the point of boredom, falling into bed unheeding of love, sex, passion, or intimacy, seeking only sleep, the refuge of the harried housewife and the exhausted provider. Picture Tristan and Isolde trying to make love with the baby crying in the next room and little Johnny at the door asking for still another drink of water.

It has been suggested that the waning of sexuality in marriage is not related to the marital status but is simply to be expected as a function of decrease in sexual drive with age. However, research suggests that it is not age that is the major factor in the decline of sexual interest. Studies of decline in sexual activity with age have generally involved married people and, thus, while some decline may be noted, it is not clear that the factors responsible are those of age rather than those of marriage. Other studies have indicated that sexual interest remained quite strong, well into advanced years. However, the most dramatic evidence comes from the upsurge of sexual activity that invariably accompanies the acquisition of a new sex partner. The tired businessman who finds his lost virility in bed with his new secretary is a familiar example.

What causes marriage to become the bane rather than the boon of sex? Sometimes a single factor in the life of the individual or the marriage is sufficient to depress sexuality, but, more often, it is a combination of factors, acting together or in sequence, that exerts this depressing effect. What are these factors?

Habituation

Habituation is a term psychologists use to describe the decrease in responsiveness to a stimulus which is presented with great frequency. In more familiar terms we say, "The thrill is gone." The gourmet whose favorite food is pheasant under glass would soon find his enjoyment of that delicacy fading if he had it at every meal. This does not mean that the response-evoking capacity of the stimulus is forever lost or remains at a constantly low level. A period of abstinence or of absence of the stimulus, generally can serve to revive the flagging response. However, it will often fail to return to its highest peak or, if it does so, the period for which it will remain there is of short duration. In marriage, the constant physical presence of the spouse tends to lower his sex-stimulus value. Sleeping together all the time is not the same as sleeping together for the first time, or the first few times. One of the authors can recall a conversation concerning marriage he had as a fifteen-year-old box boy in a grocery store with an older clerk, in particular, his disbelief when told that after a period of marriage there would be many times when he would find himself in bed with an attractive, available wife and feel no sexual desire at all. Overly impressed with the intensity of his own newly discovered sexual desires at that time, he was sure the older man must be joking. Experience has dissolved this disbelief, as we are sure it has for many other people.

While habituation alone may account for a significantly lowered marital sexuality in some cases, more often its effect operates in conjunction with other factors existing in the marital situation.

Routine

Related to habituation, is the quality of routine that so often characterizes married sex. For most married people, sex all too soon acquires a pattern, a regularity—in bed, in nightclothes, at certain times, in a stereotyped manner, at regular intervals, and so on. There is a taking for granted, a lack of challenge or suspense that tends to lower the stimulation and, consequently, the reward value. In nearly all human endeavors, the need to exert effort to reach a goal, with some doubt about the outcome, enhances the value of the goal. Sometimes the satisfaction is proportional to the effort required to obtain it. The excitement of the "chase" is a common human response. An athletic contest, where the outcome is scarcely in doubt, does not approach in excitement a close contest that is not resolved until the last moment. In this regard, sex is no different. Under mildly negative conditions—the hour is a little late, one feels a little tired—the spark of an incipient sexual desire is easily snuffed out by the knowledge that there is always tomorrow night or the next night. There is no pressure, no sense of urgency, no requirement to exert oneself to "strike while the iron is hot." How marked is the contrast between this limp sexuality and the hot-blooded pursuit of sex among the unmarried (or the married, with "someone else") which disregards time and circumstance and where the crescendo of excitement leaps over all barriers and obstacles.

Appearance

Marriage often leads to a diminished concern with maintaining one's appearance and sexual attractiveness. The pressure of courtship days to look your best simply is no longer there. The big and little things of physical attractiveness lose their imperative quality—a clean shave, makeup, and hair carefully tended, breath, deodorant, attractive clothing may not seem worth the effort. A few extra pounds do not matter so much. After all, this is for life, for better or worse, and one can, appropriately, let down a little. If the night is cold, it is not unreasonable to replace the black lace nightgown with the warm, but not very stimulating, flannel.

Domesticity

Domesticity, itself, can exert a stifling effect on sexuality. Dealing with the details of domestic life occupies much of the time of married couples together. Money problems, decisions regarding purchases, children, in-laws, social obligations, and so forth, take up more and more of the conversation between spouses and more of their time as individuals. Even in scheduled recreation time, these issues intrude themselves. An evening out which encompasses conversation regarding little Jim's need for braces, or fourteen-year-old Betty's first date, hardly constitutes the type of conversation that is an important part of the verbal presexual foreplay. Dealing with domestic issues is an appropriate and important part of marriage, and may very well contribute to the warmth and depth of the relationship. It may lead to that close and warm type of sex that develops in marriage, but it is not "sexy," at least not in the sparkling, turned on, toned up, excited sense that term conveys.

What Makes Jack a Dull Boy?

Aside from the interactional effects of domesticity, domestic life, itself, often exerts a deadening effect on the individuals involved. Domestic routine tends to make a person somewhat dull. It narrows the span of interest. More important, however, the interest in mutual explorations between spouses tends to diminish or even disappear with the passage of time. The intriguing aspects of the spouse become familiar, and there seems to be little of a deeply personal nature left to discuss. In some cases, a protective shell develops, not only to conceal parts of the self from each other, but even to shut out aspects of the spouse that might seem annoying or threatening. Quite often, extramarital affairs of long duration are sustained less by direct sexual activity than by the capacity of the lovers to remain interested, responsive, and reciprocally stimulating speakers and listeners. In some cases, in the comfortable rut of marriage, personal growth ceases, or drops to a negligible level. Thus, to paraphrase, marriage often makes Jack a dull boy and Jill a dull girl. This dullness inevitably seeps into the sexual relationship, diminishing the stimulation and the "zing" one hopes for, and without which something is missing in the sex life.

Marital Conflict

In some cases, sex interest is deadened as a result of marital conflict or neurotic interactions. Anger, expressed or suppressed, may lead to sexual disinterest, withholding, disparagement, or martyrdom. Some spouses express anger and conflict indirectly, by taking flight in excessive emphasis on household chores—the ironing or carpentry, for example—particularly at times when the other seems interested in sex. This maneuver is especially deadly as it hides the less than noble motives under a mantle of virtue—the meeting of obligations—and brooks no interference. How can a husband insist his wife drop these tasks, which must be done, and give preference to such a frothy activity as sex? Then, by the time all the chores are done, exhaustion has set in and sex is out of the question. Of course, as we know, if the motivation were to enjoy sex with her husband, other ways of handling these chores would have been found. Sometimes a spouse builds up resentment related to the responsibilities and sacrifices marriage requires of him, and then punishes the partner by focusing most of their interaction on these areas of marital responsibilities to the detriment of their sex life. These tactics frequently lead to retaliatory reactions by the deprived spouse, who then finds other ways of becoming extremely busy when the initially depriving spouse seems interested in sex. Thus, a circular system of sexual frustration is set up which can function on its own long after the precipitating events are forgotten, and which is broken only on infrequent occasions when there is synchronization of nonrevengeful or nonpunitive feelings on the part of both husband and wife. Under these conditions, marriage becomes considerably less than a sexual paradise.

An Oscar Every Time?

The recently acquired awareness of the orgastic potential of women has brought a new pressure into the marital sex scene. The capacity of a wife to fulfill her husband's sexual desires has long been a problem, as many a prostitute or mistress could confirm. However, this problem has been overshadowed by the growing emphasis on the wife's satisfaction. Now that we know she can have orgasms, there is the feeling that she ought to have them all the time. The husband feels inadequate if she does not. The wife may feel either sexually frustrated or inadequate as a sex partner in relation to her husband's need for her to climax as proof of his sexual capability. Thus, a demand is created requiring the husband to produce the orgasm and the wife to have it. While in some cases this has led to an improvement in sexual knowledge and technique, paradoxically it can also be self-defeating. In sex, trying harder can make the goal more difficult to achieve. In some cases impotence or frigidity are the result. In others, it may interfere with the spontaneity and letting go that is important in sex. There is less pressure in this regard in casual sex relationships—if it is good that is fine, if not, one can look for another partner. Also, in the casual relationship there is less need to be so concerned with the partner's needs. In marriage, with its permanent character, such a cavalier attitude cannot be maintained. Faced with this demand that it be "good," sex may be avoided except when the conditions appear highly favorable.

Stress And Fatigue

All of the above effects can be magnified by the stress and fatigue of modern living. Simply being tired from work or worry raises the threshold of response. This means that when one is tired it takes more than an ordinary amount of stimulation to generate an ordinary response. If this is viewed in relation to habituation, it is easy to see what a sexually depressing compound results. With habituation, the sexual stimulation of a partner decreases, while at the same time fatigue demands an even greater stimulus for sexual activity to take place. Of course, the same is true of fatigue in relation to any of the above factors. It seems little wonder that sexual activity decreases markedly as the years go by.

Privacy

Aside from the foregoing problems, there is sometimes simply the practical problem of privacy. Children are often the innocent culprits in this regard. When they are infants, a cry from the nursery may be sufficient to break the sexual mood. When they are a little older, there is the fear they will wander into the bedroom and catch the parents in the act. Even if they do not actually do this, the fear that they might is inhibiting. Teenagers may be even worse, because they stay up later at night and the parents must often wait until fairly late before the coast is clear. By then, what with being tired and the tasks of the next day edging closer, the idea is simply scrapped in the hope a more opportune time will come along. In addition, there is the need to be relatively quiet when sexually engaged so the children cannot hear what is going on. Resident in-laws pose similar problems. Of course, this does not prevent sex, but it certainly puts a damper on exuberant, free, sexual expression. This is particularly unfortunate in the case of those women or men who tend to become rather vocal at the moment of orgasm. (In spite of the foregoing problems, married people do engage in sex and even have orgasms!)

THE MERITS OF MARRIAGE

At this point, with such a listing of the faults of marriage, some readers may be tempted to ask, "Why get married at all?" Our answer is simple and blunt. With all its drawbacks, marriage still remains the best arrangement for a man and a woman to share a life together. To begin with, there is a solemnity of intent in the formalized, ritualistic declarations of permanence that are part of the marriage ceremony. Despite the protests of the more avant-garde that these are unnecessary, and despite the abundance of divorces and unhappy marriages, it still seems that there is some kind of deeper, more thoughtful commitment in the formalized marriage vows than in the simple act of moving in together. There are a number of consequences of this commitment.

In some ways, the very nature of the commitment that gives rise to some of the problems of marriage discussed above, also provides some of its advantages. Routine, taking for granted, permanence, lack of suspense all may have a deadening effect on sex. Yet this very lack of pressure to perform well or look one's best, and the opportunity to let down, are among the great comforts of marriage. There is a security and reassurance in the stability and permanence of the relationship that is difficult to achieve in any other arrangement.

In an age of rapid changes, and social, geographic, and occupational mobility, the continuity of the marriage relationship has obvious value in handling feelings of being completely adrift. The requirements of legal procedures for divorce provide some safeguards against impulsive or unthinking dissolution of the relationship. There is also the feeling generated by the solemnity of the commitment that nothing is being held back. It may not always be true, or it may not always work out that way, but in the beginning, at least, each spouse can feel that the other has thought enough of the relationship to take this serious step. The notion that marriage tends to preserve the family unit and protect children seems well founded. There is security for the child in knowing that the family unit is based on a stable, permanent relationship.

In a strictly practical sense, marriage also has value in terms of matters of property. Some mode for the disposition of property on the dissolution of the relationship is necessary, as well as upon the death of one of the parties. Some institutionalized definition of rights and obligations of members of the relationship is also necessary. The social order as well as the individuals concerned require it. Even the requirement of a medical examination has obvious social values, both in terms of protecting children, and, to some degree, controlling venereal disease. Furthermore, although it may seem banal to speak of tax advantages, social security benefits, and provisions for health insurance that are possible in marriage, in terms of a lifetime these are not inconsequential matters in our society.

Supervening all of these virtues is the basic goodness of the permanent man-woman relationship. In reasonably good marriages, the raising of children, the sharing of life's joys and problems deepen the affectional ties that formed the initial basis for the relationship. Love, in its fullest, warmest, most mature sense, grows in such a relationship. There is no greater value in life than the love of man and woman that can grow in this context.

Thus, as is the case with most human institutions, marriage seems to be an admixture of positives and negatives, good and bad. The remainder of this book is addressed to an evaluation of the possibilities of reducing one of the negatives—the problem of obtaining sufficient sexual satisfaction in marriage. We will consider an alteration of the rule concerning extramarital sex which might sustain and even enhance the institution of marriage without unduly endangering it.

2.
The Merits
of the
Extramarital Sex
Contract

In order to establish a rational perspective for the discussion of the benefits of extramarital sex, it is essential to deal with some preliminary issues. First, we would like to suggest that this chapter be read with as much objectivity and as little preconception as possible. We recognize how difficult it may be to put aside emotions and attitudes that have been conditioned-in by a society that has unquestioningly categorized sexual activities of married people with others than the spouse as "a crime," "sin," "evil," "cheating," and other similarly negative terms. For a great many people, it may be most difficult to view, dispassionately, any discussion of possible "good" in regard to such activities. Yet, this "good" is the issue to which this chapter is addressed. It is well to remember that what we have learned or have been taught may at times prove to be incorrect. For centuries people believed that the world was flat, a notion ultimately proven entirely incorrect. Galileo was forced by the Church to recant his adherance to the Copernican theory that the planets—including the earth—revolve around the sun, not vice versa. Despite the overwhelming authority of religious pronouncement, astronomers have presented incontrovertible proof that Galileo was right and the church, wrong. People tend to be resistant to new ideas. Yet, it is only through new ideas that the human condition can be improved.

Second, as an aid to reducing emotionalism about the subject, we will substitute the term "co-marital sex" for the term "extramarital sex" where a mutual agreement exists. Psychological research on verbal conditioning has amply demonstrated that we respond emotionally to the labels that are attached to people, objects, and processes. In our society, many people have been taught to associate negative emotions—shame, guilt, disgust, disapproval, fear—to the label "extramarital sex." Therefore, greater objectivity should be promoted by the use of some other term which is not as loaded at the outset with emotional overtones. The term "co-marital sex" seems more appropriate for the subject to be discussed here, as it appears to reflect more precisely the status of the activity *within* rather than outside the context of the marriage. Where the parties have incorporated it into their relationship by virtue of an agreement, an analogy may be drawn to the recent change on college campuses from the term "extracurricular activities" to the term "co-curricular activities." This change was made to reflect the conception that many activities which took place outside the classroom, such as fraternity or sorority membership, participation in student government, athletics, were viewed as enhancing and being within the context of the total educational process. Similarly, co-marital sex activities are viewed as enhancing and as part of the total marriage relationship.

Third, it is essential to dissolve a misconception about the sexual nature of women. This misconception, widely held, is that women are not interested in sex per se, but enjoy sex only in a love relationship, typically, marriage or some other ostensibly enduring relationship. Many sophisticated people with whom we have discussed the co-marital sex agreement have felt that it had obvious advantages for men, but expressed doubts that it would be of much benefit to women. They have based this position on the premise that women do not enjoy or have an interest in "casual" sex. As a generalization, this view of women is simply not correct. It is true that many American women have been thoroughly indoctrinated all their lives with the belief that this is the way they should be, that "nice girls don't do it" except in a love relationship. Because of this training they may reject casual sex and perceive themselves as not interested in it or even repulsed by it. However, evidence from women of other cultures who have not been subjected to such training and evidence coming from the many American women who have been able to resist or overcome such "brainwashing," strongly indicates that it is not a biologically given natural state for women. Jessie Barnard (formerly of the Department of Sociology at Pennsylvania State University) states her belief (in Neubeck, *Extramarital Relations*) that there is an increasing acceptance of casual sex among modern women. Bartell (*Group Sex*) states his conclusion upon making a study of women "swingers" that they do indeed enjoy sex outside of love. The eminent sex researchers Clellan Ford and Frank Beach (*Patterns of Sexual Behavior*), point out that in those societies that accept "adultery," women are at least as active as men in seeking such relationships. Cuber and Harroff (*Sex and the Significant Americans*) quote several of their women informants to the effect that they enjoyed casual sexual experiences. Twenty percent of the women in the "Cocktail Lounge Study" of Julian Roebuck and S. Lee Spray (published in Ailon Shiloh, ed., *Studies in Human Sexual Behavior*) indicated that they specifically sought the noninvolvement of sexual activity with the "emotionally safe" married men of that particular population. Anyone who has had contact with large numbers of today's emancipated young women knows that many of them have a very casual attitude about sex. Not unreasonably, they view going to bed with a man as a natural part of getting to know him. The views and experiences of our own informants are in complete agreement with all these views. Of course, this does not mean that most women are eager to jump into bed with any man any time. Women are as varied in their sexual tastes and dispositions as they are in other aspects of life. Most of our female informants indicated they preferred some kind of relationship, but this involved a quality of reaction and interaction which did not necessarily involve either love or duration. As one woman put it, "From time to time, I have met a man at a party or at a bar, and as we talked the conversation was stimulating and enjoyable. An awareness of sexual attraction grew, and we wound up in bed. There was no talk of love. Our conversation may have been serious or very lighthearted. We had no plans or expectations of each other beyond the evening. I have enjoyed sex on these occasions very much as a rule. I do not always have an orgasm, as some men are more exciting and skillful lovers than others, but I have nearly always enjoyed the experience. One-night stands are different from long-term affairs, sexually, but I have found that both are good. Sometimes, depending on my mood, I have found the sheer delightful playfulness and absence of demand or obligation in the one-night stand to be just the right thing for me at that particular time." There seems to be little doubt that many women are quite capable of enjoying casual sex.

Finally, the co-marital sex agreement needs to be defined: It is an explicit agreement between husband and wife under which sexual intercourse between husband or wife with persons other than the spouse is acceptable and is not in violation of the marital relationship. The agreement, or the activities involved, may take many forms, but the essence is the clarity, openness, and mutuality of the agreement.

CONGRUENCE WITH PSYCHOSOCIAL REALITIES

In a general sense, the principal virtue of the co-marital sex contract is that it provides for a married relationship which conforms more closely to psychological and social reality. As will be pointed out later, the principles or assumptions that form the basis for strict monogamy have little or no validity at the present time for many people. It is clear that a considerable number of people have sexual relationships with partners other than their spouses, and an even larger number would like to. Studies of extramarital relations place the figure between 25 and 50 percent of the population and these are relatively old. Most experts agree the figure would be even higher today and is likely to go still higher tomorrow. Other studies have indicated that approximately 75 percent of husbands and 25 percent of wives admitted to having fantasies concerning extramarital relations. There can be little doubt that such behavior and such desires are quite normal. This conclusion may seem to be in conflict with the romantic ideal of marriage, but it does represent reality. The co-marital sex agreement is in line with the greater openness and liberalization of sexual attitudes and behavior that currently exists. To paraphrase, it will allow people to preach what they practice (or would like to practice). It is in line with the contemporary, more natural and less somber concept of sex.

Realistic Expectations

To the extent that marriage is altered in the direction of psychological and social reality, the expectations of people entering into matrimony are likely to become more realistic with a corresponding decrease in the number and the magnitude of disappointments. With the advent of the co-marital sex agreement, it would be understood that each spouse might engage in other sexual relationships. The smudge of lipstick on a husband's shirt or the tell-tale aroma of an alien tobacco on a wife's hair will encompass neither shock, nor rage, nor fear. People will have no cause to question whether the marriage is crumbling or to look for some fault either in their spouses or themselves. The spouse engaged in such activities, or desiring them, will have no need to question the marriage or his own role in it. We have seen a number of people who were in distress because they were having extramarital affairs or felt a strong desire for them. Based on their training in the monolithic code, they felt there must be something wrong with them. This has been particularly true where the marriage seemed to be good and there was relatively little dissatisfaction with the spouse. Under these conditions, they tended to view their perfectly natural feelings as abnormal. An understanding of the normality of these feelings between the spouses, and the establishing of a philosophy for dealing with them, would eliminate much of the marital anguish and disappointment arising out of this common human propensity.

The Elimination Of Cheating

Obviously, under such agreements, the whole concept of "infidelity" would be erased. The term "cheating" would lose its present sexual connotation. Given that a considerable number of people are engaging in extramarital sex, and that it is likely that more will in the future, a number of beneficial changes can be envisioned. The individual can do what he does without feeling shame, guilt, or anxiety—certainly a healthier state of affairs. With the feeling that what he is doing is all right, there will be less need for defensive aggressiveness or denigration of one's spouse. Under present conditions, in contrast to those "philanderers" who seek the causes of their behavior in themselves, there is another group that needs to place the blame on someone else—usually the spouse. This is accomplished by focusing on the spouse's negative qualities, the my-wife-doesn't-understand-me, and, she-can't-keep-up-with-me-sexually syndromes. In some cases, in the manner of the self-fulfilling prophecy, a quite satisfactory spouse is goaded or manipulated into behaviors that then justify seeking satisfactions from other people. For example, a husband may put off performance of necessary household tasks, putting his wife in the position of having to make several requests in order to get the work done. If she makes the several requests, he can then appropriately describe her as a "nag" and point to this quality in his wife as the source of his need to seek sexual satisfaction elsewhere. Unfortunately, the denigration of the spouse, which has its genesis in the need of the wrongdoer to justify his actions to himself, becomes an independent, perceptual habit, and the limited purpose of the original accusation is lost. As the habit becomes fixed, a constant, negative attitude toward the spouse or the marriage hardens even to the point where the marriage is destroyed by what was initially no more than a defensive, psychological operation in justification of behavior that might be considered wrong. Certainly if the spouse has in effect said, "It's okay for you to go to bed with other people," there is no need for this destructive psychological process. Fewer spouses will find themselves going around in a state of bewilderment as to what it is they have done to become objects for so much negative reaction.

Similarly, the feeling of having been "wronged" by the dalliance of a spouse with another, would be eliminated. The behavior could and would be accepted, not only by the spouse who would, formerly, have been considered wronged, but by society as well. Thus, both internal and external pressures to react with rage and to take destructive action would be eliminated. This is particularly cogent with regard to the sexual affairs of wives. Until the present, the husband's "masculinity" has been severely threatened by such instances of his wife's behavior. Some societies have virtually demanded that the man take drastic punitive measures or lose his standing as a man in the society. Others have openly permitted such actions, while still others have more covertly condoned it as, for example, in the so-called "unwritten law" by which juries have refused to convict for homicide where a husband has slain either the wife or her lover or both. With a greater understanding of human sexuality and with the acceptance of the co-marital sex agreement, the husband's masculinity would not be called into question by the wife's affairs. There would be recognition that these in no way impugned the husband's bedroom capabilities nor other aspects of his relationship with his wife. While wives have been less prone and less pressured by society toward violent or destructive action in regard to husbands' affairs, the same reasoning would apply to them. The activity would be seen as an expression of normal desires unrelated to the adequacy of the wife or the husband's affection for her.

L'amour, L'amour, L'amour

When Freud was a young physician, before he had formu-
lated his famous theories, he visited Charcot, the leader of
psychiatric thought in France. It is reported that in response to
Freud's inquiry as to what caused neurosis, Charcot replied
"L'amour, l'amour, l'amour," which Freud apparently later
translated rather freely as "sex, sex, sex." Of course, Charcot
did not mean that love or sex caused neurosis, but that
psycological barriers and attitudes that interfered with the
acceptance of one's sexual self and one's sexual fulfillment
contributed to neurosis. Whatever the relation of sex to neurosis, we do not need such an eminent authority to make us
aware that sex is one of the very important areas of life.

There are many stimulating and exciting activities that
human beings can become involved in. For many people, few, if
any of these are more stimulating than sex. By sex, we do not
mean just the simple act of coitus. We mean to include all of the
aspects of sexual activity—thinking about sex, seeking sexual
partners, being attractive to and attracted by sex partners,
establishing the sexual relationship, and exploring varieties of sex
and sexual partners. There are few antidotes to boredom, few
activities that "tone up" a person as does sex. The psychiatrist,
Eric Berne (*Sex in Human Loving*) has described the "revitali-
zation" that occurs in many people following a divorce. They
become more interested in clothing and personal appearance,
there is a "new sparkle in the eye, a new lightness in the step."
Of course, as Berne points out, the same phenomena appear in
single people and in still married people with the approaching
prospect of a new sexual relationship. It is this expectant
vitality, this toning up, which seems to become lost in marital
sex and which can be restored by the freshness of co-marital
sexual activities. Our informants were nearly unanimous in
describing the increased "élan" in their lives as a result of
co-marital sex arrangements, and contrary to fears that have
been expressed, they have also described a marked improvement
in conjugal sex. Willard, an intelligent, responsible, highly
successful businessman, put it this way:

Mary and I had a good marriage. We loved and respected each other, but after twenty years of marriage and intercourse together maybe two or three thousand times there was just no real kick left in bed. We had done the usual experimenting and had tried 'most everything together. Not that sex was poor for us, it wasn't. We still enjoyed giving and receiving pleasure with each other, but it was on a fairly low plane of excitement, if you know what I mean. We had sex and we enjoyed it but the "pow" was missing. And I really think that many times we started with little desire, more with the feeling that it had been several days since we last had sex and we ought to do it.

I knew a lot of my business associates and acquaintances were playing around but I didn't like the idea of cheating on Mary. I wanted to discuss the problem with her, but, my God, how do you bring up such a subject? An opportunity finally came when a couple we knew quite well, also in their forties, broke up an apparently good marriage for no good reason that we could see. When that happened, I just sat down with Mary and told her what I was feeling. She was shook up, at first, but then admitted that she had been watching out of the corner of her eye for old age to creep up on her and sometimes wondered if she was missing something. [We are omitting the details of how they worked out the arrangements and a description of their feelings.] Anyway, we agreed that some new blood might be good for both of us. The change in both of us was dramatic. We both felt so much more alive. The really amazing thing was the change in our own sexual relationship. Naturally, we had both been worried about that.

As far as I know, I had the first experience. I was away on business and met a woman and went to bed with her. I don't know if I can describe my feelings. I seemed to get a feeling of release, an exhilaration as if I had just burst bonds that had tied me down. I suppose, at my age, it also did something for my ego. I felt virile in a way I hadn't felt in many years. The first night home, I found myself excited about Mary and couldn't wait to get her into bed. I think she felt my excitement and responded to it. It was the best sex we had had for many years. In fact, we did it twice, which we hadn't done for at least ten years. This continued for several months without any further extramarital affairs. We have been doing this for four years now and each time the same thing happens. We return to each other stimulated and exhilarated and, then, for a period of time we are sexually all wrapped up in each other. Not only sexually either, the whole relationship has more pizzazz. There is a sort of constant sexual charge in the background. We both just feel more alive.

This description was typical of many of the couples who were successful with the co-marital sex arrangement. They generally described similar improvement in married sex and an increased zest in living, in general. Mary concurred in Willard's statements and, in addition, indicated that while she had only two affairs during the four years, the knowledge of the possibility put a new sparkle in her general social contact with men.

If, as the evidence indicates, diminished marital sex interest is a "cancer" of marriage, the co-marital sex contract appears to be a promising cure.

A MORE TENDER TRAP

As a concomitant of the feelings just described, a reduction of negative attitudes toward marriage should and does occur with the co-marital sex agreement. Some feelings of constraint and of being tied down are inevitable in marriage. The institution requires a certain amount of yielding of personal desires in favor of the common good or the good of specific family members. This is not an evil. There is joy and happiness in the fulfillment of these obligations. They are a part of "love." For some people they are enough, but for others, they can become oppressive burdens if there are not sufficient satisfactions from other sources. For these people, it is a matter of degree and balance. If a high level of sexual excitement is not maintained, the burdens and obligations of the marriage generate a negative attitude towards it. In addition to the constraints imposed by family life, there is a feeling that the marriage is depriving the person of this source of gratification. As suggested by the quote above, the availability of added stimulation accorded by the co-marital sex contract can spill over and affect the general attitude toward the marriage by eliminating this one source of frustration and of feelings of being tied down while, at the same time, sustaining a more positive outlook on life in general. Anyone who has been married would agree that it takes reasonably happy individuals to make a reasonably happy marriage. If the marriage is not happy, it is more likely to be seen as a burden; therefore, anything that contributes to greater happiness of the spouse, reduces the weight of the "marital load."

The co-marital sex agreement also reduces the load the marriage must carry in terms of providing for the satisfaction of the spouse. There has been a tendency to look to the marriage for most of life's gratifications, as indicated by the cliché, "and they lived happily ever after." To a degree, this has been more true of women than men. Men have had their careers and "nights out with the boys" as nonmarital sources of gratification and enjoyment. Women have been more tied down by concepts of women's place in the kitchen and consequently have had fewer sources of fulfillment outside the family life. Granting the sex difference, many women and some men expect marriage to provide adequate satisfaction with life. Many of these have found marriage wanting in this regard and have become embittered towards it. The co-marital sex agreement provides an avenue for additional enjoyment and, thus, can become an agent for reducing such feelings of bitterness and disappointment.

Of course, sex is not the only outside source of excitement and pleasure, but in view of the erosions of sex in marriage this is an area in which frustration and deprivation are likely to be felt most keenly, reluctant as many people may be to admit it. It would seen to make sense, in the absence of strong deterrent factors, to make up the deficiency in the area in which it exists.

SEX AND THE MULTIPLE SELF

Personal growth, expansion of the self, and awareness of the self, are processes that occupy a prominent place in modern humanistic psychology. Among young people, particularly, but also among the middle-aged and older groups, "becoming" has emerged as a major aim of life. These people are no longer content to survive, or to "make it" in the conventional sense of material or career success. Too many have found that these are not enough, neither in their own experience, nor in their observation of others. They do not want to "get married, get a house in the suburbs, and die." They seek to "realize" themselves as fully as possible.

The sexual self is one very important part of the total self. Under past standards, many people had little opportunity to fully develop this sexual self prior to marriage, and, of course, after marriage they were limited to such development as might occur with their spouses. While some development of the sexual self may occur in marriage, it can be compared to a monochrome portrait of oneself. The awareness, the development, the experiencing of oneself sexually, are in part dependent on one's sex partners. Aspects of sexuality which might never surface with one partner, may come to full bloom with another. For example, Jeanette described a dramatic difference in herself in sex with her husband in contrast to herself with a lover. With her husband, she was tender, loving, considerate, comfortable, and sexually satisfied. She describes a different person in relation to her lover. "With Steve I am like a harlot, a tramp, an animal. I have no fond feelings for him. I don't even particularly like him as a person. But I have a volcanic reaction with him. I melt, and I erupt, and I am totally swept away by searing, gut-level, sexual feeling. I am just a different person with him." Walter, married young and divorced after fourteen years, said, "After the divorce, I discovered a great deal about myself sexually. I guess my wife and I were both pretty conservative. I felt some urges that just didn't seem appropriate with my wife, the mother of my children, or else seemed silly, like candlelight and wine. Now I find that I am capable of being a very romantic lover sometimes, and at other times very lascivious. Different women seem to bring out different things in me." Many people experience this kind of sexual growth after divorce. But what of those who do not get divorces? Should this kind of experience be denied them?

In addition, a number of people with co-marital sex agreements indicated that their co-marital sex experiences not only contributed to their sexual growth, but to a generalized expansion of self. Many thought they had become more vital and interesting people—more open, more tolerant, with greater depth and sensitivity as a result of some of the relationships they had. They felt that by knowing themselves better they could understand others better. Several reported beneficial effects on their marriages as a result of this greater sensitivity and understanding. Others claimed to have a richer marital relationship, not only sexually, but in many of its aspects. This would seem to be a likely outcome if, as many have indicated, the marital sex relationship was more satisfactory as a concomitant of co-marital sex. That is, as the marriage relationship became more rewarding and less depriving, increased positive interaction between the spouses occurred.

In addition to new discoveries about the self, a co-marital sex experience provides an opportunity for renewal of the self. The experience provides an opportunity for the person to reexperience himself as he was in the early days of his marriage. The logic of this process is self-evident. In a new sexual relationship the man and woman are in a situation similar to that of the early days of marriage. Weaknesses, inadequacies, unappetizing habits have not yet been revealed. The stresses and strains that inevitably occur in a relationship have not yet had time to accumulate. Thus, the stage is set for the old self to reemerge in the new relationship.

ANOTHER KIND OF LOVE

Some couples reported that once the marriage was relieved of the burdens of its role as the be-all and end-all of sexual experience, they seemed to have more freedom for positive experiences in the total relationship. Some reported great relief at being able to drop a kind of artificial role playing they had found necessary. Husbands no longer tried to fit what they perceived to be a wife's expectations of a great lover, and wives no longer felt they had to try to be their husbands' sex goddesses and give Oscar-winning portrayals of great passion. Of course, they might continue such role-playing with lovers; but that is different from having to maintain it week in and week out, on a permanent basis, in the context of the more complex and wide-ranging relationship of marriage. With the removal of the demands and frustrations in this area, both wife and husband were able to become more aware of the many good things in their relationship. In a few cases, the sexual relationship virtually ceased, but the parties found much reason to remain married in terms of deep attachment and trust, commonality of interest, and just plain comfort in the familiarity of the long-standing relationship. They found they were able to be more honest and authentic in their relationship. Harold and Martha are both college professors. Harold describes this kind of experience as follows:

When Martha and I were finally able to face the fact of our lack of sexual interest in each other, we both experienced a sense of relief. It turned out that for several years we had both been giving performances that would give credit to a Broadway cast. As Shakespeare said, "What fools these mortals be." In fact, when we realized what we had been doing and started describing the artifices we used, we broke up laughing. We agreed that each could seek other sexual contacts—although in practice, this turned out to mean me. Martha is forty-eight and has a dozen interests that excite her and, apparently, has little interest in sex. However, we both felt that we had a lot in our marriage that made it worth keeping. We are both trained to be objective, and we found no reason to break up the marriage because I was going to have a fling once in a while. I would rather live with Martha and share my life with her than with any woman I have ever met and she knows it. We had always enjoyed each other's company, but it is even better now that we can be together without wondering if we are going to have to play "passion's puppets" before the evening is over. We are much more relaxed together and this has allowed our relationship to blossom. We are friendlier. I really think that some of the frictions we had before involved some kind of subconscious effort to avoid sex.

Harold and Martha were typical of several couples who reported similar benefits in the non-sexual aspects of their marriage, once they faced the reality of diminished or vanished sexual interest in each other and abandoned the pretenses they felt were required of them. It was as though their relationship, in which sex originally played a major role, had developed into another kind of love based on an appreciation of the total qualities of the other as a person. Devotees of the "romantic" school of love might challenge the "love" aspects of such relationships. But is not love as variable as people? Does it not have phases and undergo changes as people do? Is not "caring" for the other more the hallmark of love than passion? Is not enjoying and relating to the other an important element of love? Are not giving and receiving the essence of a love relationship? Martha expresses these sentiments: "I have no doubt that we love each other. It is in constant evidence through all of those big and little things you do for someone you love. It is apparent in our desire to be together and the way we enjoy each other. Perhaps, it is the little things that are the biggest proof. For example, when we are walking, we often hold hands or Harold puts his arm around my shoulder. This to me, is warmness, closeness. It is a way of saying 'we are together and you matter to me.' I have seen this occasionally in very old people, who, I am sure, are quite beyond sex, but not beyond love." And regarding Harold's sexual activities,

> I think that loving someone means that you want him to have what he wants. I hope that doesn't sound noble and unselfish—that isn't what I mean. I think it has to be mutual. He also wants me to have what I want. Maybe love is finding some kind of balance in this. Let me give you an example of what I mean. Not long ago, I was working on a project that was very important to me. There were meetings to attend, deadlines to meet, and just a great deal of time involved. I could never have done it if Harold had not assumed a lot of responsibility for household matters, such as grocery shopping and the children, and things like that, for almost a year. This meant that he gave up some of his productive time for me so that I could have what I wanted. Both of us have done this sort of thing for the other from time to time. Now that we have discovered—what would

you call it, "non-sex?"—between us I understand Harold's desires in this regard and feel he should satisfy them. I think I might resent it if they took a lot of his time away from me, but, fortunately, this has not happened. These seem to be once in a while things. I think he spends more time on committees than on women. Maybe that helps make it work—the fact that he seems to keep things in reasonable proportion. As far as the sex part goes, I am more grateful than jealous. The other women are providing something for him that had become a bit of a chore for me.

It might be illuminating to compare the restricted conventional code to the co-marital sex contract in terms of morality. As Martha indicated, loving someone means wanting that person to be happy and fulfilled, to have as much of what they want as possible. This is what the co-marital sex contractors seem to be trying to accomplish. "Enjoy" is what they say to each other. In contrast, under the "code," they say to each other, "I own you, I possess you, I do not permit you to have what you want. If you have or even want sex with another person I call you bad. You must totally suppress these desires." Which is the superior morality?

3.
Sexual Modes in the Co-Marital Sex Contract

The forms of sexual activity which occur under the mantle of co-marital sex contracts are many and varied. Some couples limit themselves to one type, while others engage in several. In some, the activities are a joint enterprise, as in swinging; in others, the activities are carried on independently. Even in the latter type, there is some degree of sharing, in some cases by virtue of discussion of the events. As with any other choice, the type of sexual contacts selected depends on the tastes and desires of the parties involved, although practical considerations also have an influence. These types can be divided roughly into four categories: swinging, independent, partial living apart, and the one-way contract.

SWINGING

In modern usage, "swinging" has become the accepted term for activities formerly called "swapping" or "switching." The essence of swinging is the joint and mutual nature of the activity. In swinging, a married couple deliberately and consciously seeks out additional partners to have sexual relations together. The basic aim is sexual action, although other social relationships may also be involved. Basically, swinging occurs in three modes which, at times, may overlap. These modes are: group sex parties; two couples; and the threesome.

Group Sex Parties

Group sex orgies have existed since ancient times as religious rituals. Indeed, the word "orgy" is of Greek derivation and refers to the secret rites in honor of a deity, often a god of fertility. Secular sex orgies recently enjoyed a spurt of activity in America. Modern commercial methods have made their contribution to this renaissance; that is, in much the same way that there are country clubs for golf and tennis clubs for tennis, there are sex clubs for sex operated on a commercial basis. The existence of such clubs, which advertise in a relatively open manner, reveals the extent of the sociosexual changes that are taking place. In addition, there are also private groups which operate less conspicuously.

The private party revolves around an "in" group. Often there is a leader who supplies his home and runs the show. These are parties which, with the exception of the sexual activity, are like other parties. There are refreshments, there is music, and conversation; sometimes there is a theme, such as a Halloween party. For obvious reasons, they are not likely to be costume parties, although the members of one well-to-do group, who could afford costume rental, described, with considerable salacious hilarity, the added excitement, not without attendant difficulties, of disrobing when wearing eighteenth-century garments. Another group gave a "Come as your suppressed desire" party, to which one man came as an over-sized penis by wearing a sheet of flesh-colored plastic appropriately painted, and a somewhat flat-chested woman wore nothing but a bath mat she found in a "gag" shop, made up of foam rubber molded and painted to resemble several, more than adequate, female breasts. We mention some of these variations to indicate that, in general, these parties are lighthearted, humorous, "fun" affairs. Generally, the people know each other rather well, although from time to time a couple drops out or another couple is added. Singles usually are not welcome at couples' parties, although in some cases single males with special qualifications such as unusual sexual stamina or skills are accepted as group members.

Usually, co-marital sex contract couples do not start their co-marital sex activities in these large groups, but progress from two-couple swinging to either a three- or four-couple party or directly to the larger group—sometimes a group consisting of as many as forty or fifty people, but, more typically, between twelve and thirty.

While variations exist, there is a more or less stereotyped pattern to these parties. After most of the guests have arrived, there is a period of roughly an hour of social conversation, possibly some dancing, and drinking. It is noteworthy that drugs are usually prohibited and drinking is minimal—perhaps because these sexually sophisticated people are aware that too much alcohol reduces sexual capacity and enjoyment. It also seems quite clear that they do not have inhibitions which need to be dissolved in alcohol. After the social hour, people start pairing off and disappearing into various bedrooms, sometimes one couple to a room sometimes more. Sometimes this is a matter of choice, sometimes multiple use of rooms is necessary. For those whose tastes run to the multiple, one wealthy "leader" has an orgy room with a huge custom-built circular bed, covered with imitation leopard skin.

Sexual activity occupies the major portion of the evening. Frequency of intercourse and changes of partners vary according to the tastes, moods, and physical states of the participants. Some prefer to pair off with one partner for the evening, having intercourse one or more times. Others prefer to move from one partner to another. As a generalization, it can be said that these people are free and adventurous concerning sex. They like to experiment and will try almost anything in terms of variations, except that most groups avoid anything that is painful or degrading. That is, except for a few rare "kinky" groups, sadism, bondage, and the like are out. However, sex between two or more men and one woman, two or more women and one man, or two men and two women is not uncommon. Oral genital contact is, of course, commonplace.

As a rule, at private parties guests are expected to participate. An occasional "begging off" is allowed regular group members. One might ask why go to the party if you are not going to take part, but sometimes the wife or husband who is not interested at that time simply accompanies a spouse who is. However, anything more than rare abstinence, would result in exclusion from the group. One is not, however, required to have sex with any person who requests it—there is freedom of choice as to partners. Obviously, if there is no one in the group who seems desirable, there is no point in belonging to it. Initial advances may be made by either man or woman. While a slight majority of the women tend to wait to be chosen, many seem quite comfortable in the role of the "aggressor."

Most groups will allow a new couple to attend one party as prospective members without any obligation to participate. Frequently, however, they are required at least to disrobe as a measure to discourage police or those who might come out of purely voyeuristic or curiosity motives. If the couple attends a second time, it is understood that this is a signal of their willingness to participate.

As the activity is illegal, precautions are taken, usually in the form of careful screening before a couple is invited. Excessive noise is discouraged, as is discussion of the group with outsiders. With all the precautions, occasionally a group is "busted." But this is rare and the members do not seem to go around in fear of it.

Typically, the evening winds up with a buffet supper, more social conversation, and planning of the next party.

As with any social group, there are occasional bickerings and petty jealousies. Everybody does not always like everybody else. We had the impression that there was, if anything, less of this than in most social groups, and it did not seem to be related, particularly, to the sexual activity. We found no evidence of psychological disturbance in the members of groups with whom we had contact. There is, of course, the usual gamut of personality types that one finds in most groups—the boisterous, the quiet, the deep, the shallow. In the groups we attended, the members were all solid citizens and considered respectable members of the community. One group, for example, included a former PTA president, a psychiatrist, a business executive, and a free-lance writer. Those who had children appeared to be responsible and concerned parents. As an amusing aside, at one party we witnessed a very naked lady engaged in a telephone conversation with the baby-sitter to check up on things at home while being lasciviously embraced from behind by an equally naked man. We had to admire her capacity for dual concentration.

Most of the participants felt this group-sex activity had been beneficial to their marriages and to themselves as individuals.

Another type of group-sex arrangement is the more or less commercial type. There are several such groups in most large cities. Some present themselves as philosophical societies, oriented toward achieving greater sexual freedom, while others offer only swinging social activities. They give parties once a week or more and, of course, attendance is by invitation only. There is a membership fee ranging from twenty-five dollars to seventy-five dollars per couple for which the members receive "newsy" letters, including dates and whom to call for information about parties. In addition, there is a charge for attending, to cover costs of food and other necessities. The charge, typically, is five dollars per couple. Those who wish to drink must bring their own.

In the main, these parties are quite similar to the private group parties. There is a social period, followed by a sexual period, followed by another period of eating and socializing.

One principal difference is the greater turnover in the member-ship. In contrast to the private groups, there is a greater infusion of new people. There is, therefore, less group feeling and less familiarity. Consequently, there is more of an atmosphere of getting acquainted. At these parties, there is no requirement to participate. They seem to stress the idea that sexual freedom includes the right not to engage in sexual activities. However, if a couple were to attend frequently without participating, the operator of the group might politely indicate to them that they ought to drop out.

Although some efforts are made by the operators of these groups to screen prospective members for acceptability and compatibility, the risks of encountering undesirable or incom-patible people is higher than in the private groups. The com-mercial nature of these enterprises requires sufficient numbers to pay the overhead and return a profit and this, inevitably, influences the screening. At least, in the instances we could observe, we found the participants in the private groups to be more polished, of somewhat higher socioeconomic level, and generally more attractive than those in the commercial groups.

Both types of groups occasionally organize swinging vaca-tions to various places, such as Las Vegas. Members feel such trips add to the fun. As a variation, some groups have weekend parties at a local residence.

In addition to these organized affairs there are opportunities for impromptu parties. Most large cities have cocktail lounges or nightclubs that become known as "swinger" hangouts. Out of an evening of drinking, dancing, and conversation, a party may develop involving several couples. Most often they will be at least slightly acquainted with each other through previous casual meetings at the bar. It is virtually impossible for a total stranger to get an invitation to such a party. Occasionally, the bar operators will make some provision for introductions. We were not able to finagle our way into one of these parties but did have an opportunity to discuss them with a couple who had been to several. They are similar to the organized parties except that there is much more feeling of spontaneity, which would seem natural enough. They are riskier because there is no type of formal screening.

While in most group-sex arrangements the couple remains together in the sense of being in the same house, there is the so-called "car-key" variation. In this version, the group meets with the intention of pairing off, with each couple then departing to a motel or whatever accommodations are available to spend the evening together. Some method of pairing off according to chance is usually employed to avoid jealousies and to insure "equal opportunity." The theory is that if you do not get someone you want this week, you probably will next week. In the car-key method, for example, the men place their car keys on a table and the women pick one, the owner of which becomes their partner for the evening. Except for a brief initial period prior to the drawing, this is much less a social event than the conventional party.

In group swinging and, to a slightly lesser degree, in other forms of swinging, emotional involvement is a no-no. It is perfectly appropriate to praise sexual attributes of a partner, but words of love are forbidden. The emphasis is on sex for its own sake.

Two Couples Swinging

Swinging involving only two couples differs from group swinging in several ways. The most obvious differences are the lack of organization and party atmosphere. It contains many of the elements of sexual pursuit in single life. To begin with there is the need to establish initial contact. Then there is the "getting to know each other" phase to determine interest. Then there is what might be termed a seduction phase, although seducer and seduced are often the same. Thus, while there are some couples who swing more or less on sight, more typically the process unfolds over a period of time more like an affair. As reported to us, there appears to be more anticipatory toning up, more of the feeling of expectancy and of intrigue that is involved in the unknown and the uncertain found in dating.

Occasionally, swinging occurs spontaneously between two couples who have been friends or acquaintances. More often however, it requires a deliberate effort to find swinging partners. The most common methods employed for this purpose are the personal ad in an underground newspaper, or visiting the swinging bar to effect a pick-up. Most couples prefer a getting-acquainted period, which may be no more than a couple of hours of conversation, followed by swinging at the first meeting or which may extend to several purely social get-togethers before sexual activity is initiated.

Some couples prefer a great deal of variety, rarely swinging more than once with the same couple. Others, seek a more extensive relationship both in terms of time and quality of involvement. Some of these relationships last for many years and involve genuine friendship as well as sex. While there is some risk of emotional involvement in this situation leading to switching, not only for sex, but for marriage, this seems to occur rarely. Most couples swing together, that is, in the same house. Some couples, in fact, insist on being together in the same room as they like to view the sexual activity as something they are doing together. As one waggish informant put it, "the couple that lays together stays together." Some have literally described this practice as a way of having sex together, viewing the other couple as instrumentalities for their sexual stimulation and gratification.

Less typical are couples who swing separately. The two couples meet, perhaps for dinner or some other brief social interchange, but at some point the swinging partners go off to different sites. Some, after the initial meeting and after having established the relationship, do not meet again as couples. One husband takes the other wife out, as on a date. These separate swingers indicate that they prefer the privacy of the situation, and, in addition, avoid the interactional problems that may come up in a four-person situation. That is, in the four-person process there may be a tendency to be concerned and watchful to be sure that the spouse is making out all right which may put a damper on the proceedings, or sometimes the possibilities for jealousy or other irritations are greater when all are together than when they split off into couples. Some also report that the similarity to dating, in this situation, enhances the excitement.

Some couples who practice separate swinging keep the sexual activity private—they do not "kiss and tell." Other couples appear to enjoy discussing their experiences with each other as a form of sharing. This seems to be a counterpart to those couples who wish to be in the same room during the activities. These after-the-fact discussions allow for privacy in the sexual activity without altogether excluding the spouse. It should be remembered that these people are sexually emancipated and do not consider sex to be dirty, wrong, demeaning, nor sacred, and inviolable, nor do they have the usual uneasy attitudes generally found among those with more traditional attitudes. In addition, they have a high interest in sexual matters and, perhaps, slightly stronger voyeuristic and exhibitionistic interests than the average person. Therefore, while a more conventional person would find it strange that a husband or wife could enjoy a spouse's description of sexual activity with someone else, it seems quite understandable among swingers. People who are interested in art, discuss art. People who are interested in social action, discuss social action. People who are interested in sex, discuss sex. Quite often, these swingers report, the discussions have a sexually stimulating effect which they enjoy.

Threesomes and Moresomes

A type of swinging that has received less attention than the conventional forms is the threesome. While this type of activity may occur within the context of group or couple swinging, it is usually only in the nature of a side excursion or a variation. However, there are a number of couples for whom it is the preferred mode, and in some cases, the only one.

The threesome encompasses sexual activity between two men and one woman or two women and one man. Characteristically, two make love to one simultaneously. In the two-man situation the men jointly kiss, fondle, and manipulate the woman as part of the foreplay. One may concentrate on the genitals, stroking or sucking them, while the other may concentrate on the breasts. Then the woman may alternately "french" each of the men or may "french" one while having coitus with the other. Positional variations are commonly practiced. Sexual contact between the men is relatively rare. A similar aversion to male homosexual practice is to be found among swingers.

The two-women-one-man threesome frequently follows a similar pattern with joint foreplay followed by the man "frenching" both women or "frenching" one while having coitus with the other. Various sequences or combinations are practiced. The major distinction is in the sexual activity between the like sexes. We dislike to use the term homosexual for this activity as its connotations seem inappropriate in this heterosexual context; bisexual is the term more commonly applied to it. Quite often, sexual contact between the women is not only acceptable, but desired—by the man as well as the women. While the reasons are not well known, it is clearly established that many normal men are turned on by the sight of two women making love to each other. Perhaps in the threesome situation, it also reassures the man that satisfaction is available to both women in the event he should fall somewhat short in this potentially arduous enterprise. The women, once they have discovered that it does not mean they are Lesbians, appear to get a great deal of enjoyment from this activity, either as prelude, intermission, or finale to the heterosexual act.

Because of the dearth of information on this practice, and, because among our population of informants only six couples practiced the threesome exclusively, our impressions must be quite tentative. Nevertheless, we were struck by two particular aspects of the threesome. First, the married couple are involved with each other in the sexual activity—this must be considered marital sex in anybody's lexicon. There may be moments of more concentration of the spouse on the other person, but taken as a whole, the main focus is on the couple. The third person is an added element to their lovemaking. Secondly, we were struck by the gourmetlike attitude towards sex. Our informants were not looking for simple sexual discharge or sexual outlets, as the cold Kinseyian term puts it. They seek sexual experience in capital letters. They are the mountain climbers of sex, pursuing ever higher pinnacles of sexual stimulation and enjoyment. Sex, for them, is an art form with the two men or women as the artists and the third person as the medium through which their art is expressed. Success lies in achieving maximum sexual excitement in that person.

Given the limited number of hands, mouths, and sex organs of any one person, these informants point out that on a purely physical basis, the stimulation afforded by two "lovers" is greater than could be provided by one. More important, they say, is the psychological effect of being the center of such attention, being allowed to be at least for a portion of the time, the passive recipient upon whom are lavished the sensual caresses. Further, along this same line, is the excitement one feels at turning on two members of the opposite sex at the same time.

In addition, threesomes contain many of the exciting elements of two couples swinging—the meeting, the feeling out, the process of getting to it—in short, the chase. Typically, the threesomes are casual or short-term relationships, but occasionally a ménage à trois evolves. The three may take up residence together for an extended period of time, in a genuine three-way loving relationship.

The overall impression we received from our informants was that their marriages had benefited, not suffered, from swinging as a form of co-marital sex. This conclusion is in line with similar findings by others (Bartell, *Group Sex;* Pomeroy, in Neubeck, editor, *Extramarital Relations*). Similarly, in line with prior findings, we did not find that as a group, swingers were irresponsible, or psychologically sick people. Their lives appeared to be well within the normal range in all respects other than swinging.

INDEPENDENT CO-MARITAL SEX

In contrast to the joint character of the sexual enterprise in swinging, some couples have explicit arrangements that allow them to carry on sexual activities completely independent of each other. This independence refers only to the sexual activity itself. Obviously, there is a great deal of dependence upon the spouse in terms of the cooperation needed to handle the logistics of the situation, especially if the couple has children. The major categories of this type of arrangement are: dating, separate vacations, and relatively durable affairs. Dating and separate vacations, along with partial living apart (to be discussed later) may come as close as it is possible to do in achieving that most desired of human conditions—the best of two worlds. These arrangements allow one to eat one's cake and have it too, by incorporating some of the pleasures of single life into the warm and secure context of marriage.

Dating

In this type of arrangement, each spouse is free, within limits, to date other people much as though they were single. The limitations, and these are characteristic of all three modes of independent co-marital sex contracts, are that these activities must be carried on without interfering with or neglecting marital and parental responsibilities. Granting that human judgment is seldom perfect, nevertheless, what these arrangements seem to call for is the exercise of good judgment and a sense of proportion. These limits will be discussed more extensively under the topic of Problems under the Co-Marital Sex Contract.

While there are some studies and estimates of the number of people engaged in extramarital sex, there are no comparable studies of the number who have explicit agreements for this activity, and it is impossible to make an estimate. Cuber and Haroff (*Sex and the Significant Americans*) mention such arrangements but give no indication as to numbers. In contrast to swingers, who are relatively easy to contact through clubs and advertisements, it was quite difficult to make contact with couples of this type and we feel fortunate to have been able to reach as many as we did.

In marriages where the wife was not employed, the most common arrangement seemed to be for her to have her dates during the day, with evening dates relatively rare. In view of the husband's occupational requirements, he had more freedom with regard to evening dates. This varied somewhat according to the occupation. If the husband owned his own business or had a fair degree of control over his time, he too, might date more during the day than in the evening. Where both are employed, the logistics are more difficult. In that situation, coverage of parental and domestic responsibilities has to be worked out. Some couples arrange a schedule of free time, while others simply require checking on the availability of the spouse. With sufficiently affluent couples, domestic help relieves this problem somewhat, although considerations of the welfare of the children still require a reasonable amount of parental presence. Requirements of the normal social activity of the marriage must also be considered. That is, sufficient moderation is required to see that dating does not swamp the marriage relationship. Among our couples, the frequency of dating was generally left to the discretion of the spouse, although one couple specifically established twice a month as the limit. However, in actual practice, neither dated that often. Actually, the number of dates in our group ranged from two to twenty a year. Sometimes there would be little flurries of dating, usually with a single dating partner, with several dates in a two- to four-week period, but in the long run, the average seemed to hold up.

In some instances, the dating evolved out of some other kind of relationship. The husband might date a woman he had come to know through business or social activities, while the wife might eventually date a man she knew through social or civic connections. Some couples indicated they preferred to avoid dates with mutual acquaintances because of potential complications and because of some concern that a competitive situation might develop, or just because it might be awkward socially. Others did not seem to have these concerns. Some couples felt the pick-up approach was safest with its minimal involvement. In this approach, the spouse, when he or she felt the urge, would go to a bar and if a suitable contact was made, go to bed with that person. Of course the risks of venereal disease or becoming entangled with an undesirable person are increased in this approach. However they are no more than many single people take all the time. Again, judgment is the key to success. Some go to the trouble to use an alias and give false telephone numbers to avoid entanglement.

Some of the individuals we talked to dislike the idea of going out to "look for it." They prefer to have freedom for sexual engagement if it happens to come up. One woman described this type of experience, under the agreement, as follows:

> I was on my way to a meeting of the — [a local philanthropic organization] in the early afternoon. While I enjoy working with this group, frankly I was not looking forward to this meeting which I knew would take up a lot of time with boring committee reports and speeches. As I was stopped at a red light I happened to glance across at the car next to me and saw the driver staring at me with "that look" if you know what I mean. He was a rather good-looking man and when he boldly motioned toward the curb, I was quite intrigued. We stopped, and he invited me to have a drink with him. We spent the next couple of hours at one of the better bars in the Valley. He was a newspaper reporter and we had a most delightful conversation. After that we went to his apartment and had a rollicking good time sexually. By 5:30 I was home preparing dinner, a happy woman.

THE SEPARATE VACATION

The separate vacation exists among some married people even without any sexual implications. Many people have found it revitalizing. It is not usually taken instead of family vacations, but in addition to them, and is a totally different kind of experience. On the typical family vacation, little is changed for the parents except the locale. Parental responsibilities are omnipresent. The need to interact and consider the needs of the spouse come along on the trip. The usual family roles must be played. The separate vacation provides freedom from all these responsibilities. For most people who practice this life-style, a two- or three-day holiday is sufficient, although some couples arrange for more extended periods.

For co-marital sex contract couples, such vacations include the added spice of sexual adventure. Of course, many non-contracting couples also manage to include this type of indulgence. The distinction is that if they do, it is a violation of the marriage although it must be assumed that in some such cases there is some sort of understanding of at least a covert nature. It would be a naive spouse who was not aware that the opportunity would at least be considered by the vacationing spouse. Under the co-marital sex contract the freedom to indulge sexually is explicit.

Most commonly, such vacations are not taken simultaneously by the spouses especially where there are children. This helps in dealing with the logistics of family life. The remaining spouse "minds the store" while the other is on vacation. The favor is returned at another time. Weekends are the easiest to manage because then the husband is usually able to be home. Where domestic help is available the timing makes somewhat less difference. Of course meeting these obligations sometimes ties the remaining spouse down for that period of time, but our informants uniformly felt that the benefits of the arrangement were worth the temporary constraints. In some cases where the husband traveled fairly regularly on business, it was understood that these would be his "vacation" opportunities.

In the pattern we found most frequently, the vacationer would go to a nearby resort; for example, in Southern California, Palm Springs and Las Vegas are just a few hours away. In these resorts, there are a large number of people "on the make," and contacts are easily found. Several of our informants report a feeling of greater attractiveness in this type of situation. Resort clothing, greater attention to dress and grooming, the general good-time atmosphere and, often, elegant surroundings, and the attention received, all seem to contribute to this feeling. Several also report that the factors of increased time and distance from family permit a more luxurious enjoyment of sex than dating allows.

While most couples operate in the pick-up mode on these vacations, some individuals find this an excellent way of bringing to fruition an affair which had begun to develop in the home locale. That is, the vacation may provide the opportunity to conclude, in a Palm Springs bed, a flirtation that had begun in a Los Angeles living room. Some individuals either go on a vacation with an established or potential lover or arrange to meet the lover there. Loretta describes this approach: "When I find I am becoming interested in a man who has shown an interest in me, I begin to drop little hints about the trip I am planning in a couple of weeks. If he doesn't get the idea, he's not the man for me anyway. I try to allow enough time for him to make any arrangements he needs to and I manage to let him know I will be alone and where I will be staying. When I'm in my hotel room and the phone call comes, or when I see him approaching in the lobby or in the bar, I get a thrill. It's like the scene where Ingrid Bergman walks into Humphrey Bogart's bar in *Casablanca.* It's an electric moment. I prefer this to a quick dash into a motel. We can take our time. The build-up is wonderful and we have time to spend together afterward. It is just like a miniature affair. I think this arrangement is one of the wisest things Jim and I have ever done." Larry had different motives for the vacation: "I don't like to fool around in town because you never know when you are going to run into someone you know. Jean isn't the problem because we have this understanding, but in my position, I don't want to be involved in any scandal, or even gossip. So, when I have something going, I take the lady to San Diego where I don't know anyone. Aside from the absence of risk, I just feel more comfortable. I can go anyplace I want to and I'm not always looking over my shoulder to see if there might be someone there who knows me."

THE DURABLE AFFAIR

Dating and separate vacations are similar in that the sexual relationships are casual or of short duration and carry little deep personal or emotional involvement. In fact, it is almost always a condition of the co-marital sex contract that deep relationships are to be avoided. Under this concept, it is falling in love, not going to bed that constitutes infidelity. Of course, accidents happen, but then they also happen where there is no co-marital sex contract. In respect to deep attachments, then, the durable affair differs from other forms. In these, it is not only expected, it has often already happened. That is, quite often the agreement arises only after the affair has been acknowledged and faced. If, for whatever reasons, the couple concludes they wish to preserve the marriage, the affair is accepted and, at least in some cases, the other spouse is accorded the same privilege. In our sample, we found few cases in which there was an agreement to permit, in advance, a long-standing love affair. Because the agreement arises out of an existing, unwished for reality, it would seem less a sought-after style of life than a making-the-best-of-it accommodation. It seems to be primarily an alternative to divorce or separation. In contrast to the other types of co-marital sex activity, this type does seem to diminish the marital relationship rather than enlarge and vitalize it. There seems little doubt that this is so because the relationship of a spouse to a lover is different from the relationship with a bed partner. In the casual arrangements we have described, the relationship between the spouses remains central. Each occupies the position of central importance with the other. This centrality is impaired in the durable affair. The best the husband or wife can hope for is an equal place, and even this does not usually work out in practice. Often, the other woman or the other man is the true love object. However, this does not always require that the marriage be terminated. In some cases, people have built a certain kind of life together that they wish to maintain. Sometimes the best interests of children seem to call for preservation of the marriage if it can be worked out. Sometimes the spouse's qualities as a parent and trusted friend, or the husband's income-producing ability, or the wife's homemaking talent, may similarly provide a basis for the continuation of the marriage. In this situation, the husband or wife who becomes the third person in such a triangle may prefer to retain the marriage and satisfy the missing emotional needs by taking a lover or by substituting other types of gratification, much as in marriages without co-marital sex, but where "love" has long since left the marriage.

When it is recognized that the marriage is failing to provide sufficient fulfillment to one or both spouses, some prefer this type of arrangement to the casual sex approach.

> Of course when I found out about it, I was shocked and hurt, but when I thought about it, I felt it was a good alternative for us. We had not been what you would call romantic lovers for many years. Sex was infrequent, and, frankly, from my point of view, was a wifely duty. I had wondered if Frank was playing around with girls at the office or something like that. I felt quite sure he was lying when he gave me reasons for not being home and of course I was concerned about whom he might get involved with — you know, some girl who might try to make trouble or wasn't clean. So, in a way, when I found out about Judy, it was a sort of relief. I know that she is a fine person and that no one is going to get hurt except maybe Judy. I wouldn't like to be in her position, it seems so fragile. But after Frank and I talked the situation over, and it was clear that he also wanted to maintain the marriage, I felt pretty secure. Isn't there an old saying "The devil you know is better than the devil you don't know"? I think Frank and I are more comfortable now. He doesn't have to lie to me in order to be with her. He just says he won't be home and I know where he is. As long as he can manage this and still meet his obligations to us, I'm satisfied. I suppose it's not the best state of affairs—I didn't mean that as a pun—but it seems to be the best possible for us. I doubt that I could find another man who would be as suitable for me as Frank.

PARTIAL LIVING APART

Undoubtedly, the most unusual plan we encountered was the two-home arrangement. We are, perhaps, somewhat accustomed to the periods of separation between well-known movie stars while one is shooting a picture on location. The two-home situation is different from this in that it represents an ongoing way of life: The couple maintains two homes—one is the family home, and the other an apartment occupied from time to time by the husband. In one instance of this, business was only one of the reasons for the apartment. Bill is a public relations consultant who practiced in San Diego before moving to Los Angeles. He retained a small but lucrative clientele that made it worthwhile for him to more or less commute between the two cities. He spent more time in Los Angeles, but usually spent three or four days in San Diego a couple of times a month and, occasionally, would be there for a week or more at a time. As he conducted his business from an apartment there, the cost was tax deductible and the expense was no greater than a hotel would have been and it certainly was much more convenient.

Both Bill and Marsha were free to date others during the periods of absence. Each had been married once before, and had had two children in their teens from the prior marriages. They were sexually libertarian and, definitely, hedonistic.

We were particularly impressed with two aspects of this relationship. Both spoke with intense emotion of the joys of being reunited after brief separations (a point also mentioned by some separate-vacation practitioners). There was an élan in coming together again. Perhaps the old adage, "absence makes the heart grow fonder" has validity. Secondly, when the family was together, it was really together. They engaged in frequent family activities such as camping and boating. They seemed genuinely to enjoy being together, and the marriage and the children were not felt as burdens.

While there was an economic rationale for the arrangement Bill and Marsha have, they felt that having discovered it, they would continue it even if Bill gave up his San Diego practice. For those who find the co-marital sex contract an attractive concept and can afford it, the idea appears to have merit. It is not necessary to maintain an apartment out of town, one in town would do as well. For people who enjoy life, one life can hardly seem like enough. If they can, in effect, lead more than one life at a time, they do indeed have the best of both worlds.

THE ONE-WAY CONTRACT

The one-way contract refers to the situation in which one spouse is sexually free, but the other is not. In actual practice, it boils down to a formalization of the double standard because, at least in our data, it is always the husband who has the freedom. It is only in the honest acceptance of the husband's behavior by both spouses that it differs from the double standard informally practiced by a substantial number of American husbands. Many men, for various reasons, cannot tolerate the idea of another man having sexual relations with their wives. This attitude may be related to early training concerning women or to men's ideas of masculinity.

As this type of contract is obviously a good deal for the men, it is most necessary to explore the motives of the wives in this type of arrangement. Whether the agreement was contemplated at the inception of the marriage or arose later, either because of an acknowledgment of the husband's desires or because of the discovery that he was already doing it, the most common attitude was one of weighing the values of the marriage and accepting the philandering as an inevitable price that had to be paid for it. This is not remarkably different from those instances in which a wife discovers her husband's infidelity and there is a big scene, after which he promises to "be good" and she accepts this and they go on. Many such wives do not have great faith in the execution of the promise.

In the one-way contract, there seems to be a tolerant acceptance of reality. June's description may be informative:

> After Bob and I had been going together for a while, I knew I wanted to marry him. I could go on and on about the details, but the short of it is that he is just about everything I wanted in a man. His big fault is that he's nuts about girls. I'm not sure that's a fault in a man, but it usually is not on the list of most desired qualities in a husband. We broke up several times because he would go out with other girls, but the important thing was that he kept coming back to me. Finally, when we got serious, we talked about this. He insisted that he loved me and I believed him. I still do. But he told me honestly that he doubted that he could be faithful and he didn't think we should kid ourselves about that. Sexual conquests are very important to him—maybe that's part of his idea of being a real man. I heard someplace that's supposed to be a sign of

insecurity in a man. If so, Bob has it deeply hidden because I've never seen it. Anyway, after that conversation, I sat down and had a long talk with myself. There were other prospects for me, but when I thought about them in comparison to Bob, I couldn't see them. So, it boiled down to a question of what I had to give for what I could get. When I looked at it that way, the answer seemed pretty clear. I think part of it was knowing that these "lays" didn't mean anything to him as people. He liked the idea of making it with a girl. Usually it was just once or a couple of times with one girl and that was it. I felt that I was different and pretty special to him. The way he kept coming back to me seemed to prove it. So, when we got married it was out in the open between us that it didn't mean he was going to quit getting laid.

I don't regret it. I wouldn't kid anyone that I like this aspect of it. I don't. Still it has its good side. For one thing, Bob keeps himself very sharp. He wears nice clothes, keeps up his general appearance and keeps himself informed about things. It's different from a lot of men I know. They get married and pretty soon they develop the potbelly and forget how to shave. Bob's hobby forces him to keep himself very attractive so in a way I benefit from it too. His playing around is no big secret among our friends. Sometimes they get on me about it. One friend in particular, Amy, bugged me about it quite a bit, trying to get me to do something about it. Her husband was 20 pounds overweight and getting bald. I wanted to tell her that I'd rather have my share of Bob than all of her husband, but of course, I didn't. I just kidded her along, telling her that it didn't bother me. You know what it's like sort of? Did you see the movie *La Strada*? You know, Anthony Quinn was a carnival man and he sort of buys this pretty but dumb girl from her parents and takes her on tour with him. He abuses her and takes advantage of her, but she is transformed when she is with him. She is radiantly happy. When he leaves her back at her parents' farm, she dies. That's extreme, but it's kind of like that with Bob and me. I feel alive with him and I think I'd be dead without him. Whatever he's got that gets other women gets me too. I'm luckier than they are because I have him most of the time.

We asked June if they had ever discussed the same privilege for her. "I wasn't really interested in it, but once I did bring it up just out of curiosity. He said, 'Absolutely not,' and explained that it was different for men than for women. He said that he could never tolerate the idea of another man laying his wife. He seemed very jealous and possessive. I must say I kind of liked it." This brief description might be sufficient to start psychiatrists and clinical psychologists speculating about the possibility of personality disorders in this case. However, any such glib diagnosis should be tempered by the knowledge that June and Bob are engaging in fairly common practices and attitudes distinguished from others only by the fact that they are being open and honest about it.

TO EACH HIS OWN

Usually when people think of extramarital sex it is in terms of heterosexual relationships. Very likely this is due, at least in America, to the general contempt and revulsion toward homosexual acts. If these acts are considered to be abnormal, it is assumed that people who enter into heterosexual marriage, being normal, would have no such interests. Yet a longer view of the history of man tells us that neither assumption is correct. The prevalence of homosexual behavior among males, married and unmarried, during the period of the glory of Greece is well known. Both Freud and Jung postulated masculine and feminine components in the makeup of normal individuals of both sexes. With some diminishing of intense negative attitudes toward homosexual behavior that is currently taking place as part of the sexual revolution, some increase in such behavior may be anticipated. At least so far as women are concerned, the evidence from studies of swingers indicates that many women who enjoy sex with a man also enjoy it with a woman.

It is necessary to distinguish between homosexuality and homosexual acts. Homosexuality refers to a condition where one prefers or practices sex exclusively with partners of the same sex. A homosexual act is simply a sexual act between partners of the same sex either or both of whom may be basically heterosexual. It is in the latter sense that the term is used here.

Our sample does not include any couples who have an agreement for co-marital homosexual sex. As indicated, the studies of swingers show this type of activity is fairly common among women, but not among men. We have no doubt, however, that such arrangements exist. One of the authors can recall one such instance from his early days as a lawyer in which the heterosexual or bisexual husband continued his homosexual relationships after the marriage and the wife agreed to this. That situation ended in divorce, but we cannot say what role the homosexual behavior played in reaching that terminus, as in those days the situation was seen only through legal, not psychologically trained eyes.

If one accepts the concept of the co-marital sex contract, homosexual activities have some virtues for those who enjoy them. The most obvious is the complete elimination of any possibility of pregnancy. Another virtue is the reduction of any competitive threat. Of course some rivalry might exist between the wife's husband and girl friend, but it is of a different character. The husband, for example, does not worry about the size of the girl friend's penis and no direct comparison between lovemaking abilities is possible because of the sex differences. The sex act is simply a different act. The probabilities of leaving the spouse to marry the friend are obviously remote.

Of course, at present, while this avenue is somewhat open to women, it is still culturally and legally closed to men.

THE NAME OF THE GAME

With the exception of the durable affair, the theme that ran most consistently through the various modes of co-marital sex activities was that of play. The general attitude was that sex is an enjoyable pastime and that variety should not be denied married people solely because they are married.

We do not mean to indicate that the co-marital sex contract is a good arrangement for everyone or that everyone should try it. There are many people for whom it would bring more difficulty than happiness. There may be circumstances that may make it undesirable. Nor do we mean that marital responsibilities and other considerations of the relationship between the two people most involved should be disregarded. We are convinced, on the contrary, that such an arrangement can only be of benefit to people whose concern and consideration for each other and for their families are at least average. As we look at some of the potential problems of these arrangements in the next chapter, it will be apparent that a high degree of responsibility and mutuality is essential to success with the co-marital sex contract. In most instances, it is not the answer to a bad marriage although it might make one more palatable if circumstances prevented its dissolution. Its benefits appear most likely to accrue as a form of enrichment in the relatively good or even very good marriage, whose constituents, perhaps because of their complexity, seek still more.

4.
Problems of the Co-Marital Sex Contract

If the course of true love never runs smoothly, as poets and playwrights have indicated, it would be unreasonable to expect life under the co-marital sex contract to be troublefree. The potential for frustration, disappointment, anger, and worry found in most interpersonal relationships are present. In addition to these problems, some of which may be unique to the co-marital sex contract, there are a number of practical problems. The success of the contract depends, to a large extent, on the degree to which problems arise and the manner in which they are handled.

GREENER PASTURES

A wise old Greek philosopher, upon being shown the vast treasury of a king of legendary wealth, is reputed to have said to the king, "All this gold is very nice, but someday someone may come along with better weapons and take it all away from you." As things turned out, that is what happened. In the co-marital sex contract, it is difficult to entirely erase the worry that a paramour may come along with "better love" and steal a spouse away. Conceivably, this might happen on the basis of nothing more than excellent rapport in bed. However, this does not seem likely, particularly where the spouses have a reasonably good relationship and there is adequate access to the paramour. Most people are aware that sex is just one part of a relationship and are unlikely to trade a good spouse for someone who is merely a good lover.

The situation is more threatening where the relationship with the paramour has a good deal more to it than only sex. If a spouse begins to enjoy being with a lover more than with the mate, even without sexual activity, over a long period of time, trouble may be brewing. Of course, some paramours do not want to steal their lovers away from their spouses—they prefer to keep the situation as it is. Others might like the idea, but have a strong ethical stand against breaking up a family. More commonly in the co-marital sex contract, it is understood that things are not supposed to reach this point. Most of the couples in our sample had discussed this issue with each other and had agreed to avoid deep love relationships and to break off an affair if it threatened to become something deeper. Still, with human beings as they are, accidents do happen and people do worry about them.

To some extent, the risk is related to the co-marital sex mode employed. It seems to be lowest in swinging, where the men-women relationships are almost exclusively sexual. In fact, in most swinging circles, it is a faux pas to speak of love or to meet with a swinging lover outside the swinging context. Also, because sexual gratifications are received from several "lovers," attachment to one is less likely. The fact of sharing the experience with the spouse tends to further dilute the relationship with other swingers. Of course, this is even more true of the threesome, where the spouse plays an integral role in the sexual activity.

The durable affair appears to be at the other end of the risk spectrum. Deep attachments seem more likely to build up in a long-term relationship. However, this may be counterbalanced by a building up of irritations and a diminishing of sexual excitement over long periods of time similar to the marital situation. In our data, as well as that of others, the breaking up of a marriage to marry or live with a lover is rare. Once the arrangements had been worked out to the point where, on balance, they served the interests of all concerned reasonably well, people seemed content to leave it that way. Where a breakup occurs, it is our impression that a deteriorating marital situation is at the source. The presence of a lover is not a major causal factor, except as the availability of another relationship to move into may make it easier to make a marital break.

Dating lies somewhere between swinging and durable affairs regarding this risk. Some weight must be given to the type of dating that occurs. The strictly casual type—the pickup, or one-night stand, or the separate vacation—offer little threat. These activities are usually seen for what they are, little sexual escapades or brief romantic flings with no basis for further or deeper involvement. The short-term love affair is closer to the durable affair with one aspect that may make them even more threatening. These affairs characteristically involve more than just sexual fun. There is a deeper and broader relationship. Unlike the durable affair, no comfortable "rut" is established to perpetuate the status quo. Nor is there time for the negative aspects of the relationship to develop. For these reasons, the relationship and the feelings are frequently more intense. The excitement remains at a high level; the desire is stronger. The participants are aware there is no future for the relationship, so that, in most cases, it burns out after a brief period. However, if such an affair occurs during a period when the domestic situation is temporarily down, for one reason or another, or even if one of the participants is feeling low for reasons having nothing to do with the marriage, the brightly burning affair can appear to offer an answer. Under these conditions, there seems to be considerable temptation to "chuck it all" and run off with the lover. Fantasies arise of an idyllic existence in a sunny villa in Italy or South America, out of the rat-race, living off savings, making love in the afternoon, giving up ambitions, because with a love such as this, who needs more? Such fantasies are the stuff of which impulsive divorce decisions are made. Who has not had a time in his life when he could identify with Max, a forty-five-year-old owner of a small manufacturing business.

See, everything seemed to be closing in on me when I met Lisa. My business looked like it might go down the drain when they cut back on the aerospace program. My seventeen-year-old daughter got arrested for smoking pot. Marge and I were bickering a lot, probably because I was tense and hard to get along with, worrying about these things. Well Marge and I had an understanding that I might fool around once in a while. There had been other times—a couple of my secretaries, pickups on business trips, things like—they never amounted to anything. But Lisa, that was something else. I picked her up hitching a ride. I never did anything like that before. Who knows what trouble you're going to run into? She was twenty-one—not a hippie really, but maybe like a gypsy. Very natural and free. Like, one time we were out having a spaghetti dinner and, damn if she didn't take her finger and scoop up the last of the sauce. For a second I was as embarrassed as hell, and then I was glad she had done it. You know, she was hungry and this was food and it just made a lot more sense than being polite and leaving a little bit on the plate. She was real! She was always broke, although she did work from time to time. She would never take any money from me, although she loved gifts. When we went to motels she would steal the roll of toilet paper. When I told her I would buy her a case of it, she asked what for? she was getting all she needed from the motels. That's the way she was . . . natural . . . elemental.

Well, we had a ball. She was so different from anyone I had ever known. All she seemed to care about was just surviving and enjoying life. Except, she seemed to be crazy about me. I'll never know if it was just an act, but, if she was trying to take me, why didn't she ever take money when I offered it? Anyway, I started to have these wild thoughts about running off someplace with Lisa and leaving all my problems behind. I started checking about places in Mexico and South America where you can get by for very little money. I figured out how much I could take and still leave Marge and the kids provided for. I never said anything to Lisa or Marge. I suppose, deep down I knew I wouldn't do it. But for a couple of weeks I was in seventh heaven daydreaming about it. You know, never wearing a tie again; sexy siestas with Lisa; sitting in the sun eating grapes that Lisa would have scrounged up—or probably stolen—boy, it seemed great. And, if things had gotten a little bit worse I might have done it. But I picked up a little unexpected business and things started looking better there. My boy won the Outstanding Player award in the Little League. I started to relax, feel I could handle things. I was enjoying my family again. And I knew I could count on Marge. Lisa—well, we might have had a great year or two, but then, the way she was, she might meet another guy anytime and walk out on me as though it was the perfectly natural thing to do. Still—if things hadn't turned around, I just might have figured on grabbing a hunk of happiness while I could.

Sometimes, things do not turn around in time, and the need for drastic change coupled with the excitement of a new love overwhelms the marriage. However, we may properly ask whether the co-marital sex contract is a causal agent in these instances. It is well known that such incidents occur in the absence of any co-marital sex contract. The conditions of internally or externally generated discontent which lead to such breaks, and potential, if not already existing, new loves to ease the break, exist for many people. In fact, for some, such as Max, it seems that the legitimate opportunity for a brief escape into a new love affair may make it possible to ride out the temporary crisis of discontent. Further, in some cases, the absence of the co-marital sex contract may contribute to a breakup. For example, in some cases, a spouse who is engaging in a clandestine affair may have to exaggerate its quality as a love relationship in order to justify his or her behavior. This seems to be particularly true of well-brought-up women. If they are sleeping with a man, they reason, they must be so much in love with him that the only logical step is to get a divorce and marry him. Divorce is clearly not more prevalent among swingers, the practitioners of extramarital sex studied by Cuber and Harroff, nor among the co-marital sex practitioners of our study than it is in the presumably more conventional population. The trend of the data is in the opposite direction.

Thus, it appears that the co-marital sex contract does put the marriage into some risk of dissolution if the spouse becomes overinvolved with the lover. The risk appears to be no greater, and may even be smaller, than it is in conventional marriages, and appears to spring mainly from factors that are independent of co-marital sex contracts. The risk is also related to the co-marital sex mode practiced, being higher in some modes and lower in others. Finally, counterbalancing the risks is the potential of the co-marital sex contract to provide a cushion at times when the marriage or the partners are experiencing distress.

While the foregoing appears to be generally rather valid concerning the co-marital sex contract, it says nothing about individual cases. Further, as we know, the actual reality and a spouse's perception of it can be quite different. Thus, while a real threat might be minimal, a spouse might worry about it a good deal just the same and the marital relationship is likely to suffer. The most common, and apparently effective, means of preventing such worry, or of diminishing it should it occur, is large and frequent doses of reassurance between the spouses. Roger talks about this:

> We had only been doing this a little less than a year at the time, and maybe that makes some kind of difference. Anyway, when Beth got involved with Keith, I found that I became quite concerned about losing her. He seemed to have a lot more to offer than I did—money, position and, on top of it, he was a handsome, charming guy. Fortunately, one of our strengths is that we've always been able to be quite open and talk to each other about anything that bothered us. So, I just told Beth right out that I was worried. I didn't particularly elaborate on the reasons, I certainly didn't want to build up Keith, or sell Beth on the idea. Her response was so quick and spontaneous that it really put my fears to rest. She told me that she was really quite happy with me and that while I had my faults, I also had a lot of things she liked and that she felt our life together was good and she was not about to give that up. She felt that we had established strong bonds between us

and that these meant more to her than anything a new relationship might provide. Well, I not only stopped worrying, I actually felt just great about it. The funny thing is, that she might never have said anything like this to me, so directly. You know how people are—when things are going okay you don't tend to talk about them particularly. I think that since then we've both been much more sensitive about this kind of concern and as a result, we each make a point to talk about how pleased we are with each other and how good we feel the marriage is. So, in a way, it turned out to be a good thing. You're always hearing how important it is to discuss problems. Well, somebody ought to write a book explaining how important it is to talk about the good things, too.

As suggested by Roger, this type of worry tends to occur with the highest probability in the early stages of practicing this style of marriage. For most couples, after there have been two or three affairs and they see no evidence that the spouse is about to pack up and leave, they settle down into a fairly comfortable state. As another informant put it, the fact that the spouse, after having a number of affairs has always returned, provides him with evidence that there is really nothing to worry about.

NUMBER ONE AND OTHER NUMBERS

Aside from fears of actual loss of the marriage, attitudes towards exclusivity and the romantic ideal are matters of concern. The essence of the romantic ideal is exclusivity—the notion of the one and only—the wish to feel that one is fulfilling the needs of one's spouse so completely that he or she does not and could not, have any romantic or sexual interest in anyone else. It seems to us that this notion springs from the desire to avoid the subjective pain that may occur when the loved one evinces an interest in someone else. There is the feeling that if he or she wants to make love, why doesn't he do it with me? This may raise questions concerning the genuineness of the love, one's own adequacy as a lover, and all the fears related to the possibility that someone else is preferred. The existence of such an interest in another, may be experienced as a blow to one's feelings of being in all ways an excellent partner and capable of satisfying all of the spouse's needs.

Yet we would question the necessity and the reasonableness of such reactions. Of course, we recognize the power of traditional concepts in perpetuating such views; however, we feel that such reactions are based on a misperception of the nature of people and of the good man-woman relationship in and out of marriage. There may be couples who truly have no interest at all in relationships with outside members of the opposite sex. Cuber and Harroff (*Sex and the Significant Americans*) describe such relationships to which they attach the label "total" marriages. However, they point out that such relationships seem to be exceedingly rare, and we would agree with that finding. Such psychologically true exclusivity does not really exist for the overwhelming majority of people. We feel that it is far more common and, perhaps, even more natural for spouses to lack such a complete disinterest in others. The extent of known infidelity, with the high probability that it is even more widespread than is known, strongly supports this conclusion. The fact that infidelity is so prevalent in the face of powerful social, moral, and legal constraints, lends even greater weight to it. The data indicating a desire for extramarital sexual activity even when the desire is not put into action, lends still further support to this position. It is the normality of the existence of these desires that demonstrate the irrationality of the exclusivity notion. If variety is the spice of life, and we believe it is, why should it not extend to the sexual sphere? No one whose favorite food is filet mignon would be satisfied with a steady diet of their favorite dish, granting even that this steak can be prepared in different ways to provide variety. The time will come when he will feel an irresistible desire for roast duck, or Southern fried chicken, or broiled lobster or, perhaps, even just a plain hamburger with onions or a grilled-cheese sandwich. Of course, this does not mean that the hamburger is preferred to the filet, quite the contrary. Over the span of a lifetime, the filet is quite likely to remain the favorite. Let us extend the analogy. We enjoy dining out with the Smiths. They are our favorite couple to dine out with. If we were going to be marooned on a desert island with some other couple we would unhesitatingly choose the Smiths as the couple. Still, from time to time we find that we would enjoy dining out with a different couple, the Joneses, or the Browns, or whoever. We still prefer the Smiths; it's just that after several evenings with them we find a change refreshing. We notice that we don't enjoy dining with the other couples as much as we do with the Smiths and often remark how nice it is to return to them after an excursion with another couple. The Smiths, incidentally, do not consider it a disloyalty or an impairment of our relationship with them or a reflection on them in any way if, occasionally, we dine with another couple. We enjoy boating and tennis. We enjoy boating more than tennis. If we had to give up one, we would give up tennis. Sometimes, however, we feel more like playing tennis. Fortunately, we don't have to give up either and thus can enjoy both.

We are not saying that sex is the same as food or dining out with friends. We do feel, however, that the human desire for variety extends to sex as well as to other activities. We feel that once this desire for sexual variety is recognized as the normal human attribute that it is, many of the surplus meanings attached to extramarital sexual activities diminish or disappear. With this kind of understanding, it becomes clear that sexual activity with a paramour does not represent a preference for that person over the spouse, but rather an expression of a normal and to be expected human desire; it becomes clear that it is no reflection on one's own sexual attractiveness or capability to give satisfaction and enjoyment; it becomes clear that it does not represent a loss or diminution of the relationship or the love on which the relationship is based. When this kind of understanding is fully incorporated by the spouses, the problems that many people feel are inevitable in this area, simply do not exist. If one or both spouses find they cannot fully accept this perception of co-marital sex activities, we would strongly warn them not even to attempt the co-marital sex contract. The couple must be able to appreciate that these activities are not based on any deficiency in either partner, but on a normal and healthy and positive desire for additional experience.

SAME PLAY—DIFFERENT CAST

Psychologists have long been aware that a specific act may be the product of positive, healthy motives, or that it may spring from negative or neurotic needs. This principle is applicable to the co-marital sex contract. Dr. Albert Ellis (In Neubeck, editor, *Extramarital Relations*) has compiled a list of both healthy and disturbed reasons for extramarital sexual relations. In the healthy category, he includes the desire for sexual variety, love enhancement, which he terms "romantic pluralism," experiential drives, adventure seeking, sexual curiosity, situational, social, and cultural inducements or approval, and sexual deprivation due to the illness or absence of the spouse. Ellis's list of disturbed motives includes: low frustration tolerance, hostility to the spouse, self-depreciation, ego bolstering, escapism, in general, and marital escapism where the marriage is totally unsatisfying, sexual disturbance (namely impotence or frigidity in sex with the spouse) and inordinate needs for excitement.

Admitting lack of sufficient knowledge to make firm judgments, at present, Ellis gives a speculative description of standards of what he terms healthy adultery. In brief, he believes the healthy adulterer is nondemanding and noncompulsive, accepts his extramarital desires without guilt, carries on his extramarital activities without unduly disturbing his other relationships and activities, faces problems, is sexually adequate with his spouse and is generally tolerant of himself and others. While Ellis was discussing adulterous activities under the restrictive code, the points he makes are generally applicable to the co-marital sex contract. Where the motives for the contract are unhealthy or disturbed, the arrangement is unlikely to be successful. For example, a co-marital involvement may provide a valuable respite from dealing with temporary marital or other life problems. However, if the purpose of such an activity is to escape from long-standing problems instead of coping with them, two negative outcomes are probable. The first, of course, is that it will not work. After each escapade, the problem will still be there. The second is that when one marriage partner uses co-marital sex to escape from coping with problems, which are then left unresolved or become the burden of the other, the latter is likely to become quite irritated over the irresponsibility involved in the behavior.

Hostility toward the spouse is unlikely to be expressed through the co-marital sex agreement where the motive is punitive or vengeful, as it would be in the case of hostility. Such a goal is incompatible with the mutuality involved in a genuine agreement and is much better met by a hurtful kind of activity such as cheating. Going to bed with another person with the full agreement of the spouse is simply unlikely to cause the spouse any pain.

There may be another sense, however, in which the co-marital sex agreement can be used as a vehicle for the ex-pression of hostility. What is involved here is an overall hostility towards women, in general, not towards the spouse in par-ticular, combined with the notion of a woman being "had" sexually which many men in our society still cling to. The case of Bill and Linda may seem paradoxical in this regard, because they have quite a good relationship and quite a good marriage. Two or three times a year, they engage in a threesome with another man in a manner which differs from the more typical practice of this form. They go to a swinging bar which caters to both singles and couples, and, if things go well, manage to get picked up by a single man who ultimately invites them to his apartment for a drink or a cup of coffee. Linda does not wear her ring and they do not present themselves as a married couple. At this stage, Bill's interest is primarily voyeuristic; that is, he wishes to watch the process of "seduction" take place. To provide gracefully for his non-participation, and to maximize the opportunity for the other man to operate, Bill shortly after arriving indicates that he doesn't feel too well and goes to lie down in another room for a few minutes. In five or ten minutes, he returns to the living room and usually finds that Linda and the other man are quite engrossed in heavy petting. He then busies himself with some activity such as pouring a drink, lighting a cigarette and so forth, which gives him an opportunity to observe the events as they develop without creating a feeling of awkwardness concerning his abstinence. Bill described his reaction:

This scene of a guy "making" Linda gives me a block-buster reaction. I really can't explain it, but it's different from the kind of excitement we have in bed together. Maybe it has something to do with the guy, you know, "getting it" from a woman. I was never very good at that. I mean I had some affairs, you know, but they were more the going steady kind of thing. I was never much good at—well, like I'd hear guys talk about—picking up a broad and getting a piece, and that was something I was just never much good at. So maybe I do it now vicariously through the other man. I know I feel as though I am somehow taking part in it. Also, I think there's an element of suspense because Linda is free to stop at any point she wants to and, sometimes, she decides the guy doesn't appeal to her and she doesn't go through with it. So I never really know if he's going to make it or not.

Yeah, I think that's an important point. Maybe you can make something of it, you know, when married people make love, there just isn't any doubt about it—no question of will she or won't she. So, there isn't really any suspense of that kind in married sex. So, I think we get some of that into our sex life this way. Like, well okay, I'm watching and I can feel my own excitement mounting as I see that he's getting more intimate, his hands are getting bolder and sometimes I can see that Linda's beginning to get aroused. Then there's this sort of critical point. I know I have often noticed that I am scarcely breathing until it happens. It's when the guy starts pulling her panties down—that's the critical point. If she lets him get her panties down, then I know she's going to go all the way, you know, he's going to make it. I hit a peak of excitement at that moment. I think that's the highest . . . well, no, there's one other peak that's like it—that's when I finally see her naked on the bed or the couch with her legs apart and there's that one moment when his penis first goes into her. I sort of imagine his feeling of, oh, well, you know, like conquest—making a conquest—and I think I feel some of that also. I get a terrific charge out of it—I really do.

Bill's description strongly indicates the presence of an element of hostility in this situation. The language he employs— "broad," "getting a piece," "conquest"—and the aspect he emphasizes such as getting her panties down, suggest that he perceives Linda as being in an inferior position—being dominated and having something "done to her" by the man. Yet, there is no doubt from other interview material and from observing the interaction between Bill and Linda that Bill is very fond of Linda and harbors little animosity towards her. However, other data concerning Bill's developmental history indicate that he was subjected to domination by both a very strong mother and very strong older sister and, further, that he frequently and painfully experienced a put-down in his attempts to "get a piece from a broad." Thus, his strong reaction to this particular scenario seems to be much more related to a generalized hostility toward women rather than to a specific hostility toward Linda. He is enjoying the sense of the male dominating the female without actually doing it himself and, thus, he is not harming the loving and equalitarian relationship that he has with Linda. We would speculate that this activity provides a harmless vehicle through which Bill can work off some of this generalized hostility. Interestingly, Linda reports that Bill is exceptionally loving for several weeks following such an event. Linda also indicates that she enjoys the activity on a different basis than Bill.

> I think, for me, it's mostly just the adventure side of it. You know, it's certainly out of the routine and if the man is attractive and sexually interesting to me, I enjoy it in a sexual sense, but I think another thing that's important is that I know how the whole thing turns Bill on. I know how much of a kick he gets out of it and I think that also is something that I enjoy. We usually go home and have sex together afterward and we usually both are in a very high state of excitement and it's really great. And then I also know that for weeks Bill is going to be in this marvelous mood, enjoying life tremendously and very affectionate, not getting upset about things that often make him quite angry at other times. So, I enjoy it for my reasons and I guess he enjoys it for his reasons, but as long as we both enjoy it, I'm for it.

Generally, the other "disturbed motives" on Ellis's list appear to be matters of individual personality disturbance and are unlikely to be found in people who can successfully practice the co-marital sex contract. They are simply characteristics of particular individuals which are likely to be expressed in some way with or without co-marital sex.

WHO'S COUNTING?

Disparity of co-marital sex opportunities or successes poses another problem. If John has many more affairs than Jane, she may be envious and resentful. If Jane's experiences seem to be much more gratifying than John's, he may have similar feelings. This does not occur where the disparities are small or where they are in line with the expectations of each spouse. For example, one spouse may want only an occasional experience, while the other might seek fairly regular activities. However, where the desires are approximately equal, but the realization of them is quite different, problems may arise. The spouse who is having few successes may request more opportunity to balance the scales. Even such efforts may not succeed—one spouse may simply be better at the game than the other.

Of course, this type of problem seldom arises where the marriage relationship is genuinely loving and giving, or where the couple has had the foresight to anticipate this type of situation and have made their peace with it in advance. One husband described this approach: "We knew this would prob-ably happen. It's the old law of supply and demand. In our society there are always more men out looking for some action than women. Go to a bar and you'll always see, maybe five guys out to pick up a woman for every woman who is available. Sally is not a raving beauty, but she's attractive enough. No question, she can score every time she goes out. I have to find an available woman, beat out the competition, make the right approaches, and all of that. Sometimes I make it and sometimes I don't. So, I look at it this way: I like being free to enjoy another woman if

I want to. If we had a conventional marriage, I couldn't do that without going through the whole cheating bit. So, I figure that if Sally makes it three times and I make it once, I'm still ahead of the game. Part of the fun is just in the game anyway." Many couples in our sample had similar attitudes. They felt that co-marital sex was a good thing and if one had more of it than the other, they still felt they were both gaining by the agreement.

The problem is somewhat different where the disparity is not in the winning or losing, but in the opportunity to play the game. For example, the work or family responsibilities of one may leave him with less time for the pursuit of co-marital sex than the other. Some couples deal with this problem by establishing schedules—Tuesday for John, Thursday for Jane, or four weekends a year for Bill and four for Betty. However, the more common approach is to avoid this kind of structuring and simply rely on mutual responsibility and concern for each other, lacking which the arrangement is likely to fail in any event.

WHAT HAVE I DONE?

Because of their early training in our cultural standards, some spouses have difficulty shaking off feelings of guilt. Despite mutuality in the agreement, and a supposedly rational approach, these deeply ingrained emotional attitudes may persist. Mike describes his guilt feelings as follows:

We had talked about swinging for months before we tried it. Debbie was naturally reluctant and I had to pursuade her. Finally, we went to one of these group parties and got initiated. Afterward, we talked about it. Debbie had enjoyed it and we both felt really good about it. But a couple of days later, it hit me; I started wondering what kind of man I was—getting Debbie laid by another man. I felt low and indecent, just crummy. The thought kept popping into my mind "What would my mother and father say if they knew about it?" It took months for me to really digest the fact that of course, they never would know and even if they did, that I was a big boy now. It's funny, during our discussions before getting into it, I thought that I was pretty broadminded and that Debbie was more hung up about sex. I just hadn't realized how hung up I had been on all the crap about sex and love. Debbie was a gem. She assured me that she had no regrets about it and wouldn't mind trying it again. It finally sunk in that there had been no harm done. That's when we started up again. I'm okay now, but I really felt bad for awhile.

There is no assurance that feelings of guilt can be avoided in an individual case. Most couples approach their first venture with trepidation. However, strong negative reactions such as Mike's were not typical. One woman describes a milder reaction:

The only time I felt anything like guilt was right after the first time. In fifteen years of marriage, we had been strictly faithful to each other. So, when this man came inside of me, I felt something had been changed—something had been lost. It wasn't really guilt that I felt, I think something more like regret. I told Harry how I felt and he was very reassuring. He told me that he didn't feel anything was changed between us. He said that he just considered it an extension of our own sexual relationship. I think maybe I had been concerned about how he might feel about me afterward and when I saw that he still loved me, I stopped worrying about it. I haven't had any of those feelings since then.

The only prescription that can be given is to know one's self and know one's spouse. Unfortunately, this is not a prescription that can be filled at the corner drugstore. One clue that can be used is the existence of a general tendency to feel guilty. People who are prone to feel guilty in other matters, or to be very critical of themselves, are likely to experience some of these feelings in regard to co-marital sex. This is particularly likely to be true if the person is over thirty and has been brought up in the old sexual morality. Of course, when the practice achieves common social acceptance, the problems of guilt should be reduced or eliminated.

WHAT DO YOU TELL THE CHILDREN?

Handling the co-marital sex arrangement in relation to children is a delicate issue. One of the purposes of the agreement is to be open and honest and avoid the lying and deception that may occur in the absence of such an agreement. While openness between the spouses may be easy enough, the problem of candor with the children remains. The problem has three basic aspects. One of these is the concern children have regarding the stability of their parents' relationship. This is related to the security needs of the child. It is believed that where the parents' relationship is perceived as shaky, the child may become anxious about his own welfare in the event the relationship should dissolve. Of course, problems of this type abound in marriages where there is no co-marital sex agreement. However, as a child becomes old enough to be aware that extramarital relationships are not ordinarily supposed to be practiced by married people, awareness of his own parents' activities in this regard may touch off fears of this type. A second aspect concerns the attitudes the child will develop towards marriage and commitment. (That is, will the child view marriage as a flimsy relationship?) The third aspect relates to the effect on the developing child of the parents' violation of the existing mores. (That is, will knowledge of the parents' activities encourage the child to be socially deviant?) With the growing emphasis on individuality, some authorities would not necessarily consider this an evil.

The couples in our sample were somewhat divided on this issue, with a little less than a fourth favoring candor, although some of the remaining couples said they would favor it if there should be a change in the direction of social acceptance of the practice.

Several arguments can be advanced in favor of candor: The value of an honest relationship between parents and children is well known; parental hypocrisy, if it should be discovered, can impair the child's respect for and trust in his parents. Many of the couples in our sample who favored candor, felt that the children would soon learn that the fact that parents "liked" other members of the opposite sex did not mean they did not love each other, or that their relationship was threatened by other relationships. They felt that this, coupled with the high quality of their relationships with the children would amply provide for the child's security needs. Because they believed in this type of marriage, they wished to allow their children to view it positively and to avoid some of the hang-ups they had had to grow up with and overcome. They felt they could deal with the problem of violations of social mores by explaining, if necessary, that the social order was changing and that many other people shared their views. They felt they could explain that no one was hurt by their activities and that many authorities have recommended that adults be permitted to regulate their own sex lives as they choose, as long as they do not hurt anyone.

The majority simply felt that the issue would be too difficult for children to handle and that the subject was too complicated to explain adequately to a child. They recognized the potential problems if the children should find out about their activities, but felt the probability that this would happen was extremely low. They felt that if they were discovered, they would at that time offer explanations similar to those suggested by the minority.

Unfortunately, there is a dearth of research information with which to evaluate these different approaches. Our interviews did not reveal any unusual degree of disturbance among the children of the participants. However, our only source of information was the parents themselves, and the research may be open to some question on that account. Further, any attempt to assess the effects on children of knowledge or concealment of the co-marital sex arrangement would necessarily involve a longitudinal study covering many years before any critical conclusions could be drawn. Therefore, this issue must remain open at present. Of course, if the co-marital sex arrangement becomes an open, socially accepted practice, the problems should diminish or disappear. Evidence from those cultures where co-marital sexual activities are accepted or condoned does not indicate that there are harmful effects on the children in such a milieu.

YOU PLACE YOUR BETS AND TAKE YOUR CHANCES

The vast majority of the couples in our sample displayed little or no concern over the possibility of pregnancy or venereal disease. The women, except for those few who knew they were sterile, used the pill or an intrauterine device, and a very high proportion of the men had had vasectomies. Given such precautions, they simply felt that the possibility of an unwanted pregnancy was too small to concern themselves with. In the event of such a pregnancy, they were each quite prepared to have an abortion. Regarding venereal disease, they seemed to feel that they practiced sufficient discrimination in the choice of sex partners that the likelihood of infection was small.

A few couples did indicate some concern about these matters—more so in regard to venereal disease than pregnancy. Their attitude in regard to continuing the activities in the face of these concerns, as indeed was the attitude of the majority, was that life is filled with risks and the more deeply and widely you live, the more risks you must take. Therefore, on this basis, having weighed the relative disadvantages, they felt they would prefer to take the risk rather than give up this enjoyable activity. Generally, they felt that they were sufficiently knowledgeable to detect the presence of venereal disease should it occur and were aware that these diseases have usually been treated successfully. One couple went somewhat further in terms of their concern, and had a monthly checkup to make sure that they had not been infected.

While it seems too good to be true, in view of national statistics, it is a fact that none of the people in our sample had contracted a venereal disease, nor had there been any accidental pregnancies. Of course, statistics based on the nation as a whole often are not applicable to such small and nonrepresentative samples as this one.

TOO MUCH OF A GOOD THING

Problems of excesses in co-marital sex activities to the detriment of the marriage were rare in our sample. When such problems occurred, they tended to arise in the early stages of the arrangement and were resolved through a process of trial-and-error experimentation until a manner and level of activity appropriate for the particular couple were found. There were few cases of a spouse's prolonged deprivation of marital sex due to the co-marital sexual activities of the other spouse. Of course, there were some cases where one might return from a co-marital sexual adventure physically and sexually exhausted so that for a period of a day or so further sexual activity was out of the question. However, these dry periods were short-lived. Almost uniformly, the couples in our sample report that over extensive periods of time their mutual sexual activity was at least as great, and in many cases, greater than it had been prior to entering into the co-marital sex arrangement.

Swingers, particularly those who swing at group parties, are the most prone to sexual excess. This appears to be due to the variety of sexual partners available at group parties. Women reported intercourse with as many as ten different men during a single evening, while the highest figure reported for a man was six women. But these were not typical. More commonly, relations with one, two, or three partners at a swinging party was the rule. Some swinging couples, once they are into the activity, will swing as often as two or three times a week. Outside of a very hardy few, however, this pace tends to taper off with the passage of time.

Problems of excessive sexual activity occurred much less frequently among those couples who practiced the independent modes of co-marital sex. Very likely, this is due to the fact that in contrast to the ready availability of partners in swinging, this mode is more dependent upon finding partners who are both interesting and interested. In a few cases, this led to a more than desirable amount of time devoted to the pursuit of partners. However, because of the good communication between spouses involved, the activity was reduced to reasonable proportions. The same was true when a husband may have been spending more money than the family could afford in the pursuit of a particular lady-love.

The general lack of problems involving excesses in this activity seems attributable to two major factors: One of these is that despite the fact that many of these people may appear to be totally unbridled hedonists, they are not. Hedonists, they are, but they appear to practice a disciplined form of hedonism which allows them to keep their pleasure-seeking within bounds that are reasonable in terms of their own situations. The knowledge that this pleasure will continue to be available to them, helps them maintain a reasonably controlled expression of their desires. A second factor, which has already been noted but which cannot be overstressed, is the degree of concern and consideration for each other that these husbands and wives have. They value their marriages and are aware that inappropriate behavior by one or both could be damaging to it. They are aware that the co-marital sex arrangement entails the possibility of risk to the marriage and, perhaps because of this, bend over backwards to act in a manner calculated to minimize the risk. Openness of communication between the spouses is a valuable tool in checking potentially detrimental behavior. For example, in one instance, when a woman perceived that her husband was in the early stages of getting involved with a woman she disliked very much, she was able to tell him directly that she would be very hurt if he had an affair with her. Aware of her feelings, her husband immediately desisted from any further involvement with that particular woman. What is also important is that the wife knew that he would respect her feelings in this regard, and that he knew that she knew. We are impressed by the fact that it is this caring, this concern and consideration for each other, this respect for the needs and wishes of the other that are the essential ingredients of a successful undertaking of the co-marital sex arrangement; but are they not also the essential ingredients of any good marriage?

Part II:
Case Studies

Part II of this book contains interviews with various couples involved in co-marital sex contracts and activities as told in their own words. The interviews were informal and unstructured, following no specific or consistent pattern. In some instances, the interviewer played a more active role in the questioning than in others; in most cases, however, the interviewer remained relatively inactive, instructing the couples to tell the story in their own way. However, a general request was made that the couples try to touch on their motivations for co-marital sex activities, on how they got started in it, the nature of their activities, the kinds of problems they encountered and how they coped with them, and how they feel this activity has affected their marriage and themselves as individuals. Most of the case material presented here is roughly organized around these issues. The cases were selected with the aim of presenting some examples of the more common patterns described in the chapter on Modes; thus, they include swinging, threesomes, independent dating, and separate vacations.

Most of the interviews were conducted with the husband and wife together. If some readers find the degree of candor surprising, it should be borne in mind that for the most part these people are almost necessarily quite open regarding sexual matters, and that they maintain a high degree of openness and free communication between them. In a very few cases, either at the request of the interviewees or because cues operating in the initial telephone contact suggested its desirability to the interviewer, the interviews were conducted separately.

In most cases the interview material has been edited in the interest of relevance and brevity. Also, in most cases the material has been somewhat reorganized to fall roughly into the key issues described above, such as motivation, type of activities, and so forth. Except for this minor editing, the material consists of the words of the couples as they spoke them.

5.
The Separates

MONOGAMY IS FOR MOUSY PEOPLE: ALICE AND MARTY

Alice and Marty have an arrangement for independent co-marital sexual activities. Marty is a 35-year-old newspaper staff writer. He is tall and good-looking, something of an Ivy League intellectual type. Alice is 32 years old. She is petite, blonde, and extremely attractive, with an excellent figure and a bright, alert appearance. She has been a free-lance writer, has written a column for a newspaper, and is, at present, employed as a copywriter in an advertising agency. It is the first marriage for each, and they have been married for ten years. They have three children, two girls aged nine and five, and a boy aged seven. Both hold bachelor degrees—Marty in journalism, Alice in English. Their income is in the range of $20,000 to $40,000 a year. Both were raised in strongly religious Catholic environments, but neither is a practicing Catholic now.

Alice was a virgin at marriage, while Marty had had consider-able sexual experience. They have had their arrangement for the past five years, beginning in Rio de Janeiro and continuing in the United States. They are highly extroverted, and so voluble that in their eagerness to speak, they often overlapped one another. They also have a tendency to shift rapidly from one topic to another conversing more with each other rather than with the interviewer. During the interview, numerous gestures of affection passed between them, such as touching and holding hands. While sometimes there were indications that they might be shallow or superficial people, overall, we were impressed with the intensity of their interest in each other and the quality of their relationship.

Motivation

Marty: Well, now listen, we're not missionaries, we haven't converted people, we don't talk about it. But just as far as the two of us are concerned, I'm just not a monogamous guy. I love Alice madly. I'm devoted to her. Like for a Christmas present I gave her two weeks in Rio and then I was miserable the whole time she was gone. I spend two days away from her and I begin to break out. With our working hours, we tend to be separated anyway. She works during the day and I'm on the night staff, so, frequently, when I get home from work she is asleep and when she gets up I'm asleep. But we arrange to be together as much as we can. Like we'll have lunch dates in the middle of the week just so we can see each other. As I say, we're madly devoted to each other, but you know I'm just not mono-gamous.

Alice: I really can't think of anybody, who in the deepest, darkest crevice of their little old heart is monogamous. I just think that the situation has been conditioned and imposed on people over all the centuries.

Dr. Ziskin: A lot of people seem to adjust to it.

Marty: Maybe. I really don't know.

Alice: Also they don't have the opportunity to live their life any differently either. We were just in an ambiance that made it so easy to fall into. You know all those tacky things you hear about women seducing meter readers and milkmen, well we were just in a situation where I would meet really interesting men who traveled the world, painters, writers, financiers, whatever. And that makes a difference, which is just one of the reasons why I am opposed to swinging and I may be wrong but I always see them as Lockheed engineers with white socks and ladies with teased hairdos.

Another thing I think is important is the fact that when I was married I was a virgin. I had been brought up in a very strict environment. I think the fact that we moved to Rio had a great deal to do with it because the circle that we traveled in was just so completely different from the American scene or surburbia.

Dr. Ziskin: Different in what way?

Marty: I was in our bureau in Rio for many years. It's a very sophisticated and cosmopolitan environment. Parties at the embassy, presidential receptions, weekends at country estates.

Alice: And men are expected to have mistresses. It's almost required that you have a mistress. There's a kind of social milieu that is set up that almost dictates in a way that you have extramarital relationships. This is praticularly true for men. They're more strict with women. The people we met were sort of an international community, and I think that if you're in a large cosmopolitan city and not in your own home town where everybody knows what your business is, it creates an atmosphere where having extramarital relations is just expected and it's easy.

Dr. Ziskin: I understood about the men having mistresses, but I'm surprised about the women being this free in Rio.

Marty: It's not a traditional Latin relationship, but you see Rio is a very cosmopolitan, international city. Women in our circle were not the average ordinary Latin women. They were women from wealthy families, educated, and they had traveled a lot. One of the things we remarked on after we got there was that every time you went to a party it seemed you had to speak three languages just to follow the conversation. They were interesting people who controlled their own lives instead of letting the setting they were born in control them. And they tended to have their own standards in that circle as opposed to the traditional Latin women.

Dr. Ziskin: So it was the setting in Rio that caused you to make changes in your marriage?

Marty: Well, there were a couple of other things involved too. I had had occasional girl friends on the side anyway as many men did, you know. I'd go away on a trip and so forth. I never thought of it as doing anything that would particularly harm my marriage. Then, later on, at a party or someplace, I began to notice that she was obviously out-and-out flirting with men. At first I had the traditional natural reaction to be kind of jealous. But before I said anything to her I began thinking: Now that's pretty silly, you've been to bed with other women and it doesn't affect your marriage and if she found out about it you would have said it doesn't mean anything. It's something completely separate from us. It's a different thing. It doesn't touch us. So if that were to apply to me, why shouldn't it apply to her? And it would be kind of selfish and a little illogical to apply one standard for my behavior and another for hers.

So, it was obvious to me as time went on that she was getting restive, itchy, uneasy, and a little bored. I thought it was having a detrimental effect on her character. She was getting a little grouchy. I never understood men who would chase after and eventually marry a woman because she was a glamourous, attractive woman, and then do everything they could to turn her into their mother, a frumpy housewife standing over a stove. And then they'll go out and look for another woman because their wife bores them. There may be something natural about this because so many guys seem to do it, but I don't understand it.

Now, another thing I want to throw in here, incidentally is that I think my wife is a very, very good-looking girl.

Dr. Ziskin: No question.

Marty: This is less than gallant to say but she wasn't always. She looks a lot different now than when I married her. She was, to be blunt, an unattractive teenager.

Dr. Ziskin: That's hard to believe.

Alice: It's true. I think this is important too, inasmuch as I was, you know, short, fat, and funny-looking all through school and college. And I wasn't overwhelmed with people dying to go out with me. As a consequence I didn't do much dating and I suppose in a childish way, you know, some psychologist might say I'm making up for all those years that I didn't do a lot of dating, which may have some truth to it.

Marty: Around age twenty-five or twenty-six she took off a lot of weight. Her facial features changed and she started getting kind of better-looking by the month. It was astonishing, the change.

Dr. Ziskin: Was that before or after you started the separate dating?

Both: Before.

Marty: It was a combination of a lot of things. All of a sudden we lived in a different milieu, in a much more cosmo-politan, sophisticated atmosphere than we were brought up in and all of a sudden she turns from a sort of chubby, average-looking little girl into a very, very good-looking woman. And in a Latin atmosphere, where men are throwing themselves at her. After being the girl who sat home on Saturday nights in high school, all of a sudden she blossomed out.

Alice: Well, of course, Latins are just so aggressive about sexuality and flirting and dating.

Dr. Ziskin: I take it then that this kind of attention that you were getting was something new for you?

Alice: Oh, yes. But you see we didn't set out to save a failing marriage, or a marriage that was shaky.

Dr. Ziskin: Your marriage was good, but you felt that this was a kind of enrichment.

Alice: It's just, well, why not?

Marty: Yeah. Why not? Part of it is simply that we are so sure of each other. We've been married a long time. I can't imagine her running off with another man. Can you image me running off with another woman?

Alice: No, and I think it's like a number of men I've been out with. They always have such obvious flaws, I mean I know that I'm thoroughly enjoying this twenty-four hours, or eight hours or whatever, but I couldn't possibly stand to live with them for a weekend or whatever, probably much less for the rest of my life. There are a lot of people that you can really enjoy but you couldn't possibly stand to be around them for twenty-four hours a day.

Marty: I've never met a woman who attracted me in any way comparable to the way Alice does, but as I said, we're just plain not monogamous. I'm the kind of husband that a lot of women divorce. Alice is the kind of wife that a lot of men would shoot. (*Laughs*) But you know we live together very, very happily.

Dr. Ziskin: How was your sexual relationship at that time?

Marty: Sort of good, I think.

Alice: Yeah, maybe a little immature.

Marty: You were obviously getting bored.

Alice: Yeah.

Dr. Ziskin: Was your sexual relationship as good then as it had been earlier?

Marty: Yes.

Alice: It was fine. I'm trying to remember, but I can't ever recall us falling into a big slump.

Dr. Ziskin: By that time you had children. You were more into the domestic type of living then. Do you feel that had any effect?

Marty: What you mean is did being a housewife make Alice a little less sexy. Yes, that's true.

Alice: Yes, it's true.

Marty: She's less interested in sex if she is just hanging around the house watching the kids.

Alice: Right. I think what makes the difference too, is working. I hadn't started doing my column yet and was the classic housewife.

Getting Started

Alice: It was at my husband's suggestion. (*Laughs.*) I was going to Acapulco to cover the film festival. It was at this point that he suggested that as long as I was up there if I wanted to have a good time, you know—"I could do whatever I wanted"— I was very shocked. That was when we had been married, what, about five years.

Marty: A little over five years, I think. I did this because I think she would have anyway if I had brought up the subject or not. If I never said a word to you about it, you probably would have gotten around to it by yourself eventually, right?

Alice: I can't say. I don't know because I really was shocked.

Marty: She was obviously restless and I figured, what the hell, sauce for the goose, sauce for the gander. I remember we were in a Chinese restaurant in Rio and I just said, "You're going to Acapulco and I'm going to be off on a story so, you know, do whatever you want." As I recall though, you didn't do anything in Acapulco.

Alice: No, I didn't meet any interesting people.

Dr. Ziskin: What was your reaction when you said you were shocked?

Alice: I was. I distinctly remember it. I was so taken aback because I had been brought up in such a very moralistic, conservative environment.

Dr. Ziskin: Did you feel it had any implications for you or about you, like, did you question whether Marty loved you?

Alice: Oh, no, no. I suppose one of the two things important about our relationship is that we both have a lot of confidence. Not only in ourselves, but in the other person and in our relationship. And the whole underlying thing is that we're not jealous. I mean I'm never jealous, never have been, and you aren't either. It's such a dumb emotion. Such a waste. I mean it is not an intelligent way to feel, to be jealous.

Dr. Ziskin: So the shock was just at the idea?

Alice: Yes.

Dr. Ziskin: There was no sense of rejection.

Alice: No. No.

Dr. Ziskin: No concern that you weren't important to him or anything like that?

Alice: No. No. But he is more adventuresome than I am. A man is more prone to pick up on these things. But once I do, a-hoo. (*Laughs.*) It's true though, once I made up my mind that it was an okay idea, then I had no moral thought about it. I don't think of it in moral terms.

Dr. Ziskin: No qualms the first time? No bleak morning-after?

Alice: No. No. No. Quite the contrary.

Marty: We never have gone into this ourselves. How did you decide what you were going to do?

Alice: Well, with my Catholic background, I have a great charitable streak. (*Laughs.*) On more than one occasion I've slept with people because I thought it would be a nice thing to do for them. Which is the way it was on the first occasion. This fellow had just separated or divorced from his wife.

Marty: The agreement we had made was that we were both of us free, but said we would not talk about it. In fact, we would conceal it from each other. She was free and I was free, but that we would operate quietly on our own. This affair I do know about now, but it came out a long time afterwards.

Alice: Anyway, he was really charming, a lovely person and very attractive. So I don't know, I think my instincts were more charitable than sexual at the time. (*Laughs.*) And I've done that on other occasions—not that I haven't enjoyed it. (*Laughs.*)

Dr. Ziskin: That's what I was about to ask, if that was the only motivation?

Alice: Oh, yes. Oh, no. I suppose if I had to figure out precisely what my motivation was at the moment, that was a good deal of it.

Dr. Ziskin: Okay, so you did it and you found that the sky did not fall down.

Alice: Oh, no. We haven't seen each other since, but we're good friends. Marty and I send him Christmas cards and things because he's a friend of both of us. And I'm sure if I ran into him again and he's as cute as I remember. . . . (*Laughs.*)

Dr. Ziskin: Okay Marty, and when you first found out that something had actually happened, whenever that was. . . .

Marty: She was pretty well into things before I suspected that she was probably doing something. I thought she was getting kind of grouchy and uptight. She stopped being grouchy and uptight. I certainly knew in the back of my mind she was into things, but I never knew who or where or when.

Dr. Ziskin: What I'm trying to get at is, though oftentimes we anticipate how we're going to feel about something and we think we're going to feel okay, then we find out that whatever it is has happened, and we find out we don't feel okay. I'm asking if that happened at all?

Marty: It was no big shock. First of all, we had intellectualized the whole thing at least a year before, and we talked about it one night quietly and, in our heads, everything was straight. It took a year and a half before we actually found out how to live that way. We did a little groping at first. Our first understanding was quite different from our eventual one. When it finally did come, it was no big shock. As I say, I had had time to adjust to it. We had discussed the alternatives. We talked about what it meant and what it didn't mean long before. The first one I really knew about for sure was that French artist. One of a group of people we had out for a weekend. There was a glance between the two of them across the room and I just knew instantly she'd been to bed with him. It was just the way she looked at him and the way he looked at her. It was just all there and I might not have said anything to her except that we were all pretty high and Alice and I had gone to bed. I just said something like, "You've been sleeping with René haven't you?" And she just kind of giggled and said, "Yes, I have." And there was no great shock. I suppose it was the fact that I'd known in the back of my head for months, for well over a year, that she was free to do anything she wanted.

The next morning we were having breakfast and he was sitting across the table from me. I deliberately went through a sequence of thoughts like—"If my wife wants to go to bed with this guy and not see him again, that's okay, it doesn't mean anything."

Activities

Marty: We did something before you got here because we didn't know what you'd ask. We just made a list as best we could recall of how many people we had slept with since our marriage. It came to twelve for me and seventeen for Alice.

Alice: But I'm sure you've forgotten somebody. (*Laughs.*) I don't think of myself as promiscuous in the traditional sense of the word. I don't do it for any of the reasons that I've read that make women nymphomaniacs. I don't hate men and use it as revenge or anything like that. It's strictly just a very fun thing.

Marty: I tend to get more into fairly long-term affairs. I think Alice tends to have relatively brief affairs. I had this one mistress for a long time and she and Alice knew each other. And she knew Alice knew about her. She came over to the apartment once for about a month and took care of the kids while we were gone. I think that was when I got one of the nicest compliments I've ever had. We were leaving on a vacation, a six-thousand-mile motorcycle trip and Alice said, "This is why I love you darling. Now that's real class. You leave the kids with your mistress and take your wife on a vacation!" On the other hand, I can't imagine spending a whole week with Olga. Every now and then we lived together for two or three days at a time, and we still maintain a sporadic relationship; in fact, I was out with her last month. She's a stewardess and I've seen her in New York, Montreal, and out here. In some ways she is the perfect woman of the world, international playgirl with apartments various men keep for her in all major cities of the world.

The funny thing is that she's always censuring Alice's conduct. I don't know if I ever told you this. She saw you downtown one day and, later, when I was having lunch with her she said, "I saw your wife today. Do you realize how short she wears her skirts?" She was always complaining about Alice but they weren't personal friends then. Then there was this couple, friends of ours, I had known the guy for quite some time before I met his wife. We're both motorcycle buffs. One day we'd been out riding around and he invited me over to his place. His wife was just walking in from the front of the apartment house. She'd been shopping. I took one look and it was one of those instant lust affairs. One look and everything was set but the time and the place. In fact, on a date several weeks later, she asked me when did I decide to put on this furious campaign to sweep her off to bed. I said, "Remember when your husband and I rode up in front of the apartment house, as I was putting down the kick stand on the bike? I was thinking, I've got to get that girl into bed with me." And I asked her when she made up her mind to say yes. And she said, "When I shifted the groceries to my left hand."

She and Alice became very good friends. Very close friends. At the same time Alice realized that she was also sleeping with me regularly, and I don't know how George reacted, do you?

Alice: No, I don't think he knew.

Dr. Ziskin: Marty's relationships seem to be long-standing. Are yours more like one-night stands or a couple of times, something like that?

Alice: No. No. Like they're still good friends of mine. It's just that we are such mobile people—like if Marco came to town here, I'm sure we would go out. If I go back to Rio I would go out with him again. With some men though, I lose interest quickly and I don't want to go out with them again. Then there have been others I've gone out with on and off for three or four years, very occasionally. Most of the men I go out with, I date them again. That's just about everybody that I can think of. They're good friends of mine so I would, naturally.

Marty: I always got the idea that you would have an affair with some guy for maybe a month or so and then it would taper off because you found somebody else. We really hadn't gone into this.

Alice: Well, I think that's about right. Although I do keep up some of the relationships.

Marty: You keep multiple balls in the air.

Alice: Yes, I would consider them all very dear friends and I would see them again.

Marty: We really ought to talk about Glen.

Alice: Oh, dear. Oh, yes. That was one adventure into weirdism. (*Laughs.*) It's just that the three of us made love. He's a very good friend of ours. I've gone out with him in Rio and he really is a good friend. Marty sees him in New York when he's there. The two of us have stayed with him in New York.

Marty: Glen and I had been friends long before he met Alice.

Alice: He's been very sweet. It's just that he's very swingy. Jet-setty. Leaping around the world. This one instance we referred to, was when we were staying at his apartment in New York and the three of us made love.

Marty: What happened was, I knew that Alice had been sleeping with Glen. I've known him a long time and he's one of the grandest guys I know and he's very charming.

Alice: He really is.

Marty: Anyway we were staying at his apartment and I knew they had slept together and I was wondering if I should leave. So I asked Alice if I should just kind of go away. She said no. But then the whole thing was so obvious, I knew she'd been to bed with him and I think he knew that I knew and again we were all pretty high, so the two of us took her to bed.

Alice: Yes, it was fun. (*Laughs.*)

Dr. Ziskin: You don't sound as if you have any interest in repeating it.

Alice: Well, it's the circumstances. Not like the swingers, they're so structured. That really bugs me, it's sort of like joining the PTA. This was just very casual and informal and it just came to pass.

Dr. Ziskin: So that if that happened again you think you would enjoy it?

Alice: Yeah, it's the circumstances, the mood, the company and everything else.

Marty: Everything flowed together very well.

Alice: And it was very natural.

Marty: It was very different from what I would have expected. I would suppose, had I never done it, getting involved in troilism with your own wife and a good friend would seem kind of perverse or wickedly erotic, and it wasn't. Was it for you?

Alice: No, I remember going to breakfast the next morning, the whole thing was delightful.

Marty: It was very friendly. It's difficult to explain. It wasn't sexy, it was friendly.

Alice: Yes. You mean breakfast.

Marty: The whole thing. It was a different kind of thing.

Alice: I thought it was very erotic but not in a wicked, perverse way.

Marty: Right. You know, we were all good friends and we went to breakfast the next morning and we all felt very close. You probably wonder about my masculine feelings in this situation. You know, here we were sitting at breakfast together and just a few hours before I'd actually seen him having sex with my wife. Well I didn't have any masculine feelings. For us, sex is just a very natural thing and it had been a lot of fun, very enjoyable and it just wasn't anything else.

Dr. Ziskin: Most of these affairs appear to have developed mainly out of other social relationships, like meeting somebody at a party. Do either of you sometimes feel restless and say I'm going out for a while, have a couple of drinks, or whatever?

Alice: Once I did it and it was terrible. No, I'll never do it again.

Marty: You hit a sore spot. She told me about it when she did it.

Alice: That's the only time I feel bad about. The guy was such a creepy person. I got picked up in a bar. I have a very conservative streak, but, on the other hand, I have a journalistic sense of curiosity. It turned out to be a real creepy Latin. I mean a horrible macho, bah. A terrible guy. He took me to the South American version of the hot bed motel, just a cubicle with a curtain actually. It was very dull and boring. Many Latin men don't accept the fact that nice women have sexual feelings, so they don't expect you to be responsive or have an orgasm or anything like that. In fact they look down on you if you do. So it turned out to be one of those kind of wham-bam kind of things and it was just horrible. So I would never do that again. I cannot imagine myself going in a bar and getting picked up. I just can't.

Marty: I don't think I've ever set out specifically to go out and pick up a girl. I've never done that since we've been married. Sometimes when I'm out of town on an assignment I wonder about it, but you know, if you're in a town you don't know you can wind up with some pretty funny little birds.

Problems

Marty: Well, one that we've already mentioned was whether or not we should talk to each other about these affairs. As we said it became inevitable.

Alice: Because it's very convenient. I mean we don't go into great, gory details all the time except like I would say or he would say—I'm not going to be home tonight. He or I might even know who the other is going out with by name, though not necessarily in person.

Marty: I hear her describe guys like she'd say—I met a guy— you know—what he was doing—what he was in.

Alice: It takes a lot of tension off. Like for example, I was in Rio last month and I met a very charming man who invited me to go to London and so I probably will go. I mean I can ask Marty and say, "I'd like to go to London, do you mind?" and he'd say he didn't mind. So now it's changed from not saying anything to—you know, we do talk about it.

Marty: We thought earlier that was the way to do it. Simply not to speak to each other about it. What you don't know can't hurt you. That kind of thing. We found out it got impossible to maintain. When she was coming home at seven in the morning it was obvious that she had spent the night with another man. If I didn't come home for a day or two, she knew.

There is a little difference between us here; I tend to get a girl friend and then, in effect, have an affair for a long period of time. I think you go through more men over shorter periods.

Dr. Ziskin: Let me dwell on that for a moment because there's been a lot of controversy about it. Many people insist that women cannot enjoy casual sex.

Alice: They're so wrong on that. (*Laughs.*) They really are.

Dr. Ziskin: Why?

Alice: Because I have a number of friends who, I mean we do a great deal of screwing around and as I say the motives are not some great passion, that I want this guy to marry me, you know, quite the contrary. When I was in Rio as I say, a couple of weeks ago, I was down for two weeks and the first guy I went out with I had known when we lived there before. We went to bed and I enjoyed it. It wasn't fabulous, but I enjoyed it as I always do (*Laughs.*), but then I didn't want to see him again because he wasn't as interesting as I remembered him. But we're good friends and I talked to him on the phone a few times and then a few days later I met this fellow from London who was very charming, and that was a very nice relationship for three days. But then he had to go off to Venezuela. Then just a couple of days before I left, an old friend of ours called me up. He had been calling and I didn't feel like going out with him. And then we had a party and he came in and he was really cute. He said look what you're missing. And I thought you're right (*Laughs.*), you are very right. So I went to bed with him and had a marvelous time. And he's just a very dear friend. I mean I can think of sex as very friendly, that this is a very friendly thing to do. Then again, the men I tend to go out with think sort of the same way. I mean, they don't want to marry me, I don't want to marry them. I don't want to get involved in any heavy thing and it's like—I don't know—going bowling or whatever—you know—just something that's fun to do.

Marty: There was another kind of problem that came up with this particular guy the first one I knew about. The French painter. I disliked him. Not because he was sleeping with Alice but because I thought he was a creep and mean to her. The guy just struck me as a kind of wrongo. At first I had a kind of protective instinct. I knew this guy was a wrongo. He was a mean, selfish little creep. I would have disliked him whether he had anything to do with my wife or not. And my reaction was that this mean, selfish little creep was going to hurt my wife. My first reaction was to try and talk her out of it. You know—say, "You're having an affair with this guy, why don't you taper it off? Because he's the kind of guy who will beat your teeth in or something," and my next reaction was she's a big girl, she's growing up late, she's got to do it on her own and she's a big enough girl to go out and have affairs and she's a big enough girl to do it herself. Stay the hell out of it. She doesn't tell you whom to go out with. So just stay the hell out of it and, sure enough, I was right.

Dr. Ziskin: Marty, do you get any of the, well, I guess we could describe it as a conventional male feeling, no anger, no qualms about your adequacy, your masculinity?

Marty: It's been going on for years and she keeps coming home, so, if anything, that's a compliment. I think it would bother me if some guy used it as some kind of put-down to me. I can remember the only time. Well, it never really came to that but it was close and it was with the same French artist that we told you about who was such a wrongo. We ran into him at a party after the affair had broken up. He was high and started making all sorts of innuendos. There were a lot of us standing around the buffet table and I think I really felt a moment of panic there, because I think he was the kind of guy who just might blurt out to somebody, "Say, you know Marty's wife is a great lay." I almost expected him to do that and I was trying to think of how I would react. I remember I was practically panicky because I didn't know what to do. I didn't know whether I should hit him or just walk away or really—well, I didn't know what to do in that kind of situation.

Fortunately, it didn't go that far, but as I say, I think this is the one thing that might be a problem to me if it ever happened. But it isn't the kind of masculine thing that I think you're talking about, it's more just—well, not knowing what to do in that kind of situation. I guess maybe it's like we know where our heads are regarding this and we're very comfortable with what we're doing. But still it's not something, at least not at this time, where you want it to become a subject of conversation in front of you at a party. I guess I would feel ridiculous trying to explain to people, you know, don't make anything too much of it because we have this arrangement and we're very happy with it. And that sort of thing.

Alice: Well, I don't think that's likely to happen. I think that, in general, the kind of men I get involved with are just not the kind of men who would do that. René was one of the first and it was just a mistake, that's all.

Dr. Ziskin: How do you feel, Alice, when he mentions money that he spends on other women, and he's obviously spending time? Let's take them one at a time, how about the money?

Alice: I don't care.

Dr. Ziskin: No problem?

Alice: No. I must say in a different sense I feel guilty sometimes, like if I'm with a fellow, I often think—Oh, dear, I hope they're not spending a lot of money taking me out to expensive restaurants they can't afford.

Marty: I always got the idea that you loved spending money.

Alice: Oh, I do, I do.

Dr. Ziskin: She's just concerned about whether the men can afford it.

Alice: Like sending me a ticket to London. I mean he's a millionaire. I don't care. I know he can afford it. For him it's like a bus ticket to San Diego, but if it were some impoverished, starving artist, I wouldn't want him to take me out and spend a lot of money on me. So I feel a little guilty occasionally. Not about taking up their time or their sexual prowess, but I don't like them to spend a lot of money they can't afford. I don't mind Marty spending money. If he sends a girl a ticket to London, then I might have a few qualms about that. (*Laughs*.)

Dr. Ziskin: It's okay as long as he uses good judgment?

Alice: Which he has. Good judgment but not much money. (*Both laugh*.)

Marty: We were just talking about the fact that when we lived in Canada, after Rio, there was much less of this kind of life.

Alice: We just couldn't seem to meet any interesting people.

Marty: It definitely did have a bad effect on us.

Alice: Yes, it did. There was no doubt about it.

Marty: She got irritable and grouchy and cried.

Alice: There was something else—this was when we were living in Rio. That was the only time I got mad. I was really furious. Marty was sick in bed because he had just gotten back from Honduras and picked up a bug. Lisa came over to visit and I thought she came over as a social visit as a friend, but she ended up—I mean the two of you were behaving very badly. It was the social aspect of it, it wasn't the sexual thing that bothered me. I just thought that in the social sense they were acting very badly.

Marty: There were a lot of roles to keep straight. The fact that we all knew about it didn't make any difference.

Alice: Yes. You were going to bring up what we discussed earlier about the complications and when to bow out. Because when I left the house I was mad. As I say, not because of the sexual thing, but because I considered their behavior bad form. It was like inviting a couple over, whoever they are, and they don't even talk to you, they just start necking. But it does create a problem when you are in a social situation and you know that your husband's girl friend is there or one of my lovers is there and knowing just how to handle it. This is the only problem I can think of.

Marty: I don't think there is any real problem. Say I have a girl friend there, or you have a lover. The problem is to do it our way as opposed to the swinger's way. Like let's say, we go to a party or a reception, whatever, and I'm there with my wife and we're relating as a couple with other people, but we're also there looking for girls and she's there looking for guys. Now, the point is I have to be able to gauge, judge at what point I shall say, "Gee, I have to go back to the office," or at what point she'll say, "I'll catch a cab home." For instance, I would never throw her out, even if I met some girl I was interested in. I would never say—you know—get lost. She's never said anything like that to me. But if she disappears, obviously she's got something going and she does the same thing for me. Even as well as we know each other, it's hard for me to tell when she's met some guy that she likes. Maybe he's a nice guy and she's talking to him and they're establishing some kind of sexual thing. I think it's just as hard for her.

Dr. Ziskin: What happens if you miscalculate?

Alice: We can talk about it and I can come over and say "Would you like me to bow out?"

Marty: But we usually don't. I'm trying to think of the times we've done that. There was a night at the press club when I asked you if you wanted me to leave and you said no. All right, I think you did want me to leave, didn't you? But you said no. Didn't you want me to leave?

Alice: No. But if you hadn't come in it would have been all right. (*Laughs.*)

Marty: In other words, we really do go out of our way to be polite to each other and considerate of each other.

Dr. Ziskin: How do you handle this with the children, if you handle it at all with them. You have a somewhat different situation than most people where your lives are different, it's not unusual for either of you to be away. Maybe you don't have a problem.

Alice: I don't think it's a problem either because again the house has always been full of single people, men and women. People crashing in like Niagara Falls. I think the children just have always accepted the fact that we have a lot of friends around and when Mommy goes out with friends to a movie or whatever they're with friends of ours you know. Then I don't think that they have any feeling that there is any kind of sexual thing going on.

Dr. Ziskin: Have you given any thought to how you might handle this; you know, they are getting older.

Marty: The children really don't know that we live this way. What do you think Alice? Like when Mary is thirteen.

Alice: I don't know why she would pick up on anything. I think I'm very discreet. I suppose the fact that we're away from home so much helps.

Marty: How can you tell? I don't know, maybe we're underestimating them. When they hit puberty they may know what's going on.

Alice: I suppose that will make a difference. I hadn't thought about it.

Marty: The children obviously don't know we're any different from anyone else. They know that Mommy goes out, she has friends, she goes places, she works. I would think for many years they would continue to accept that you do a lot of moving around, not necessarily that you're going to bed with other people. Okay, let's pose a hypothetical question. Let's say Mary's fourteen, and she comes to you some day and says "Mother you're disgraceful, you know, running around with all those guys." Or she comes to me and says, "Daddy, it's terrible. My friend saw you and your girl friend on the street. How can you do that to Mother?"

Alice: I can't imagine our kids being that stuffy. I don't know. I suppose kids can be more puritanical than their parents. On the other hand, they may not be. They may say, "Gee, I just realized what you're doing and I think you have the right idea."

Marty: I think when they're older that might happen. I think if they found out when they are nineteen or twenty. Nobody really cares so much about this any more. Also we've generally been pretty open with our children. We don't have any hangups about clothes for instance. The children accept that as completely natural. But they don't know that you go out with other men. They don't know that I go out with other women.

Alice: So I don't know. I really don't know.

Dr. Ziskin: Do you have any problems with the children at this point? Do they seem normal, healthy?

Alice: Oh, yes.

Marty: Delightful kids.

Alice: They're just fantastically normal. They really are charming, charming children.

Dr. Ziskin: What about logistics. Like now Alice is thinking of going to London for a couple of weeks so this kind of leaves you with the responsibility of the whole household. Is that okay with you?

Alice: He just went away for two weeks with his model.

Marty: I sent you to Rio.

Alice: That was my Christmas present.

Marty: I miss her terribly and get very lonely without her around.

Dr. Ziskin: Is there any special feeling when she comes back?

Marty: Yeah.

Alice: Oh, yeah. (*Both laugh heartily.*)

Dr. Ziskin: Okay, there doesn't seem to be any doubt about that. Do you have any concerns about pregnancy?

Alice: No. No concerns. The pill certainly makes a huge difference.

Dr. Ziskin: What about venereal disease, any concern there?

Alice: That's another reason why I wouldn't go around picking up people at bars. I must say it's crossed my mind with some of our friends, but they're all very clean, intelligent people.

Marty: Between the two of us there's what—twenty-nine various people during the course of our marriage and neither of us has ever gotten anything, we've never even had crabs.

Effects

Marty: I understand people take up these different life-styles and then they go out to convert others. We don't. We're not missionaries. I can't recall us converting anybody or trying to. I think we've changed some people. We've had an effect on them but we've never tried to convert anyone. One of the reasons is that we just don't do it to make our marriage better. I understand that's the common rationalization. If you swing your own marriage gets better. I don't think that. You think it makes our marriage better? I think it just doesn't have any effect.

Alice: Well, it does. I mean if I'm bored, then I go out. I haven't been sitting home bored getting drunk. You know it has an effect on my personality, which in turn has an effect on our marriage.

Marty: It has an indirect effect. She will probably keep up her looks more, knowing she might want to meet some guy.

Alice: Then too, I wasn't aware of my sensuality completely until I started going out. Somehow that makes you more sensually aware. You know, suddenly you become more sex-oriented. Like when you go to a party you start checking around to see if there is anybody interesting. Even if you don't go to bed with anybody, there is a kind of toning up to it. That's the whole idea.

Marty: Oh, yes. You see I partly suggested this because I hated to see her turn into some kind of grouchy housewife. And the reaction when she actually got into it was exactly what I expected. She kind of, I don't mean to say she revamped herself completely, but she kind of held herself together a little bit better than most women do.

Alice: And the trouble too, with being just a housewife is that you get awfully inward directed at all the wrong things. You know, keeping the cupboards immaculate, and stuff like that. Whereas when you're out working, meeting interesting people who are doing things, then you just have to generally shape up all the way around. So just staying home does have a very depressing effect on your whole life not just your sexuality.

Marty: I don't know how this would work in a woman but I find—well, okay, let's say I meet some girl. I ask her out. I take her to lunch. You make a point, you know, of what you wear, you make a point of where you take her. You take her to a nice place, buy her flowers, send her a cute gift, you make an effort—you know the traditional bit to charm her and get to know her and get to understand her. And when you get to understand each other you go to bed and it would sometimes occur to me that I would put on this effort for a woman who is not a fraction as important to me as Alice is. And I would ask myself when is the last time I paid as much attention to myself, bought Alice flowers, took her to a nice restaurant and out dancing just to kind of interest her. And then I would find myself doing just that.

Dr. Ziskin: Let me ask a question. Was your own sexual relationship continued while this other? . . .

Alice: Oh, yes, it was never interrupted.

Dr. Ziskin: Diminished? Increased?

Marty: If there was any effect I supposed it would be increased.

Alice: Yes, it certainly doesn't diminish it. I don't know, maybe we just sort of roll along at our own natural pace.

Dr. Ziskin: Let me touch on another area here. Some of the men that I have talked to have indicated that there's a special kind of excitement in going to bed with their wives after they have been to bed with another man. Do you have any reaction of that type?

Marty: Yes. Yes, definitely.

Dr. Ziskin: How would you describe it if you can?

Marty: I don't know. It's a turn-on if I know, if I'm aware of it. It's sexually exciting. I can't think of any other way to describe it. Now this doesn't just apply to my wife. I'm not much interested in timid women. I'm not interested in timid people of any kind. The girls that I go out with have to be fairly experienced, active, have active sex lives. I like people who get a hold of their own lives and make their lives conform to them instead of being led around by the nose.

Dr. Ziskin: Well, about the feeling particularly. You know, maybe it's just been less than an hour and she comes home fresh from the arms of another man.

Marty: There's still an aura of . . . yes, a number of times we would have sex afterwards, especially when I'd come home from work at three in the morning and she'd get home about four and there was—I don't know—there is an odor women develop about them when they've been sexually involved, and she would slip into bed and I would be able to smell it. I knew where she'd been anyway. Now that is very erotically arousing, very, very.

Dr. Ziskin: Has this worked the other way, Alice?

Alice: No. It's nothing that ever crossed my mind.

Marty: I'm trying to think if I ever came right from one girl to you. Yes.

Alice: But it's never. . . . No, I don't find that erotic.

Marty: I find it erotic coming from one girl—okay in less than an hour and going to bed with you.

Dr. Ziskin: It sounds as though it works both ways for men then. If the woman has just come from another man or if the man has just come from another woman. The man finds it, well not necessarily better, but it's a different kind of eroticism.

Marty: Alice would come home and she would be more excited let's say, than if we were just going to bed together, if she had already made love to one guy. Just the way she walks, the way she moves, the way she talks, a certain way of laughing, she would come home obviously experiencing him first and having me right after. She'd get aroused with one and then come home and make love to me. Am I right?

Alice: Yes.

Dr. Ziskin: What do you think the effect would have been on your marriage if you hadn't had this arrangement?

Alice: I would be a very frumpy, horrible, icky housewife. I know it. No, I really would be just a complete frump because the other side of my personality is that I'm a real slob. Well, really it's true. I could always schlep around, you know in a classic Princess Peggy housedress or something, and just become a vegetable.

Marty: What would I do?

Alice: You would probably divorce me.

Marty: I'd hide pornography in my brief case or pinch secretaries on the elevator or something. It's an important enough outlet for both of us. It's difficult to say exactly what it would be like without it but I think it would make a difference in some things.

Alice: Still I would have been very monogamous if I had been married to somebody else who was monogamous.

Marty: If you demanded monogamy from me I'd give it.

Alice: But you've done the classic Professor Higgins thing, really. You have created me as you wanted me to be.

Marty: I don't think I made you, just made some openings. But you're right, married to somebody else, you would have been different. Married to somebody else, I would have been different.

Dr. Ziskin: Would you recommend this for other couples?

Marty: Well, as I said, we're not missionaries and we don't go around trying to sell this. I don't know, if a couple knew we were doing it and came to ask us about it, I guess we'd tell them how it's been for us. But then they'd have to make up their own minds.

Dr. Ziskin: What do you think is the key to making it work?

Marty: I think two things. You have to get rid of all the crap you've learned about nasty old sex and the other thing which is really important, is consideration. I think if the two people have consideration for each other they can do almost anything they want to.

EVERYTHING IS NOT ENOUGH: DON AND LOUISE

Don and Louise have an arrangement that permits independent sexual activity. They are a couple that comes close to having everything in terms of status, interesting careers, money, and a superb relationship. (This couple was known to us prior to undertaking this study. We have a close acquaintanceship of many years standing and we were aware of their activities. In fact, it was our knowledge of them that, in part, led us to do this study.) Their relationship is loving, mutually exciting, and secure. They have a great deal of respect for each other. While they are not wealthy, they are quite well off financially. Don is a full professor of philosophy at a major university, with a national reputation in his field. He is the author of three books and numerous articles. He was married once before for ten years. He is a powerfully built, fifty-year-old man, who maintains himself in excellent physical condition. His close-cropped, jet-black hair, just touched with gray, gives him a virile appearance, considerably in contrast to the usual sterotype of the college professor. Louise is a very attractive, forty-five-year-old brunette, who looks considerably younger. She is well groomed and dresses smartly, vivacious, alert, and equally at home in the ponderous proceedings of committee and project work and the gay, bantering atmosphere of the cocktail party. She is a full professor of sociology, also at a major university. She is very active in professional organizations in which she has held several offices. She also was married once before, at a very young age, that marriage lasting two years. She has an unusual background in that during the period following her divorce, and prior to her marriage to Don, she worked as a secretary, as a fashion model, and as a dancing instructor before returning to college to further her education.

They have two children, a boy of fourteen and a girl of eleven. Neither has any involvement with religion. Don was raised in a family which was not religious, but Louise has a rather strong religious background. In terms of education, both hold a degree of doctor of philosophy in their respective fields. Their income is in excess of $40,000 per year, consisting of their faculty salaries, royalties from Don's books, consultant fees that Louise earns and income from real estate. They have been married for fifteen years. Louise was a virgin at the time of her first marriage, while Don had had fairly limited sexual experience at the time of his first marriage. Louise had a great deal of sexual experience between her divorce and remarriage; Don had a brief period of considerable sexual activity subsequent to his divorce which was, perhaps, cut short by the fact that he met Louise within a few months after his divorce.

They have been practicing the co-marital sex contract for five years.

Motivation

Don: It just fits naturally into our basic philosophy of life. If I may borrow from a beer commercial, "You only go around

once in this life and you have to grab all the gusto you can get."
We have very consciously set out to live as deeply, widely, fully,
relentlessly as we can. We view life as a marvelous opportunity
... a gift to be used to its fullest extent. It is my personal
ambition to have used myself up totally by the time I die. To be
entirely consumed by life. That, of course, is an ambition in
which I cannot possibly succeed, but I will be satisfied if I feel I
have taken a reasonably good swing at it. In my case, I think
this stems partly from the reaction I had when my first marriage
broke up. Prior to that time I had been a very conservative
individual, leading a very careful, cautious life—very conventional and clinging desperately to what I had—almost without
realizing that what I had was very little. Then the marriage blew
up in my face and caused me to do a great deal of thinking
about life, and made me much bolder in reaching out for it. I
realized there is no real safety or security anywhere, and that
the protection we hope to derive from the cages we put
ourselves in is an illusion. These cages do not protect us, they
only confine us.

I think Lou realized this at a much earlier age than I did and
that's why she terminated her marriage after a couple of years.
As she describes it, there really wasn't anything bad about the
marriage. She was married to a conventional, average, nice
fellow whose ambition was to get an administrative civil-service
position where he would have the status of having two phones
on his desk. Lou projected their life together over the next
forty years and knew it wouldn't be enough for her and, having
more guts than I, resolved to take her chances on finding
something richer. I think I can say quite frankly that, despite
the floundering and failing she went through for several years,
she has given me the inspiration to do battle with life as I had
not done before.

Well, I'm beginning to lecture and I think what you really
want is something more specific about our sexual arrangement.
I still have to give you more background. As you know, you can
hardly ever get a simple answer from a professor. I think it's
important to make clear that our motivation was of a positive
nature. By that I mean we were certainly not suffering from a

poor sex life. We have always found each other very exciting
and very satisfying sexually, as well as in other ways, and we led
quite an active sex life together for about ten years. We still do,
but somewhere around the time we'd been married ten years,
give or take a little, I think we found that our sexual activity
was beginning to diminish a little and, that while it was still
good and still exciting, it wasn't quite the "wow" thing it had
been. I hasten to add that I'm convinced that the vast majority
of people would have been very happy to have a sexual
relationship such as we had at that time. But, as I said earlier,
we are greedy. Perhaps to be perfectly honest, I should say I
was greedy. I think Lou was pretty well satisfied to go along as
we were. Probably my age had something to do with it also.
Although I think if I had known earlier what I know now, I
would have gotten into this much earlier.

At any rate, I was forty-five and it's a time in life when you
do a lot of thinking. You do a lot of evaluating and you have to
make a lot of decisions about what's important to you . . . what
you want to do with the time you have left. I knew that I
wanted to have more sexual experience, more variety. I also
knew that I would not cheat on Lou under any circumstances. I
think one of the great things we have is a very honest
relationship. And there isn't anything in the world that would
have been worth the price of lying to Lou. I should probably
mention here that I did cheat in my first marriage. Maybe a
dozen times or so, and fortunately for my conscience, I learned
that my wife had also been cheating. Given the perspective of
time, I think I can fully understand that. We really didn't have
much together. I'm bringing this out to point up the fact that I
would not have cheated with Lou and, had we not come to the
arrangement we have, I might have had to endure some
frustrations, but I would never have gone about it in a deceitful
way.

Well anyway, as I said, I was forty-five, the sexual revolution
was already under way and, as you know, from our occupations
we tend to be quite open to new ideas, to new ways of thinking
about things. I had begun to have these thoughts perhaps a
couple of years earlier and took a lot of time to really get it

worked out in my own mind. I became more and more impressed with the fact that there really wasn't any good reason for us not to have a degree of sexual freedom. Our relationship was very strong, very secure. Of course I recognized the possibility of some risk in getting involved with other people. But, as I said, we have a life-style based on looking at the values rather than the risks. So, I broached the subject with Lou and, of course, her first reaction was conventional and feminine. She made it clear that she thought I was crazy.

Frankly, I didn't have a very clear idea of what it was I wanted at that time. I had just the feeling of wanting somewhat more variety, more adventure, something like that. As I recall, what I proposed at that time, was maybe looking into swinging, which was just then beginning to get some recognition. Anyway, based on Lou's reaction, I dropped the subject for a few months, but then I brought it up again.

Louise: Well, I was quite shocked when Don dropped this idea on me and I think I was pretty angry. I took it personally. I felt he was being quite unreasonable and well, frankly, I felt that I was an attractive woman and I'm pretty good in bed and I just felt he ought to be satisfied. I was satisfied and really didn't have any particular desire to extend our sexual sphere.

I think also, aside from all the usual reactions to this sort of thing, I had had some experiences with married men during my years as the "gay divorcee" and I always had a bad feeling about it. You know, I had some empathy for the wife. Although, I would say, regarding those experiences, that they were with men who had married at a time when they had little to offer and, at the time of my contact with them anyway, their wives were quite unattractive. These men had become successful in life and I could at least understand their desire for sexual experience with a more attractive woman. So, again, I think that played into my reaction, somewhat, in dealing with Don's suggestion.

Don just didn't have that kind of excuse. It took a lot of pursuasion to convince me that this idea was in no way a reflection on our relationship. And, it was just part of, as Don puts it, the total life-style in which we reached out for more and more experiences. Besides, I didn't really think I had any desire for it, so it looked like pretty much of a one-way thing to me although, of course, Don had made it very clear that it would be on an equal basis. Still, I couldn't see much benefit in having a privilege that I didn't care to exercise. However, as we discussed it I began to realize that that wasn't entirely true and that while I had not been particularly interested in any extracurricular activities, it was at least possible that I might have such an interest in a situation that was more open to it. I could recall one instance—I'm around people a great deal in my work and meet a lot of new people—and I recall this one instance when I was having a conference with a man about one of the projects I was working on, and I did recall feeling some sexual attraction, particularly when I became aware that he was indicating some interest in me. The way I remember that situation is that I became alarmed, because I certainly didn't want to get involved that way, and I felt some relief when I got out of his office.

Then, the more Don and I talked about it, and the more I thought about it, the more I became aware that I was reacting to a lot of things I had just accepted and had never very carefully evaluated. I had just accepted them and, of course, mainly the idea that when you marry you don't have sex with other people. Then we couldn't really find any good reason why we shouldn't if we wanted to, and it was clear that Don wanted to, and it was at least possible that I might want to. I've occasionally been out of town at professional meetings without Don and I could recall some flicker of feeling that it might be fun to have a flirtation, play around a little, maybe even go further. I think though, I was much more concerned and fearful than Don was. But once I've made up my mind about something I don't usually let fear stand in my way. So we agreed to try it and see how it worked out.

Getting Started

Don: Then we went through this awkward period for several months in which, having agreed that we would do something like this, neither of us knew exactly what to do. I was very curious about swinging and we finally made contact with another couple, and tried that, and it was enjoyable. I think mostly for the, well, just the idea of the experience, itself. We did get a kick out of it, and yet we didn't feel it was really what we were looking for or, I suppose, what I was looking for.

Louise: Well, I really didn't get much of a kick out of it. The man was good-looking, and a nice enough person, but he just wasn't the kind of man that turns me on. The funny thing is that I had three orgasms with him, but felt absolutely nothing beyond the physical sensation. He was very skillful—I think there is a term for it—the bedroom mechanic. He did manage to get me physically aroused, but I had no feeling of psychological involvement. I wasn't starved for orgasms, I have enough of that with Don who is quite a skillful lover, himself, and I have a lot of feelings with him. So, for me, except for being kind of interesting from the standpoint of clinical observation, it was a sort of a nothing.

Don: Yes, but it was valuable to us in another way. I mean, it meant that it was done. You know, I had been with another woman, Lou had been with another man, and we found that there was absolutely no damage to ourselves or to our relationship. We knew then that we could have this kind of freedom.

Louise: Well, professor dear, I think you are over-simplifying now. I don't think you remember that we talked about some of the feelings I had. I think afterward, I didn't feel quite good about it. You know, the man had come inside me and I felt different. There had been no one but you for those ten years and when that happened, I had a feeling of somehow being changed, and I was quite sure that you must feel differently about me, too. It took a great deal of reassurance on your part before I was satisfied that everything really was all right.

Don: Yes, that's right, I had forgotten that, but it was really only a few days before you got over that. Anyway, we decided that swinging was not for us and we agreed that each of us would then simply be free to have whatever activity he or she desired on their own.

Activities

Don: There's a difference between us here. I am more prone to seek some kind of sexual experience when I am in the mood for it, where I think Lou doesn't go out looking for this but just lets it happen, if it happens. Sometimes it happens that way with me too; that is, I meet someone in the course of my professional activities, whom I find interesting, and then I go on a campaign to get her interested in me and get her into bed. And I have a more or less brief affair in the sense of something that may go on for, oh, perhaps three or four weeks—something like that. Then it just burns itself out.

More typically, though, I go the pickup route. There are three or four bars where I stop in occasionally on the way home from work—often enough, I guess, to be considered at least a semi-regular. These bars are in the Ambassador-Wilshire district. You know, in the high-rent office district, and they are frequented by a lot of the young women—some not so young—who work in these offices. They're quite intelligent— legal secretaries—people like that. It's fairly easy to get acquainted—much different from when I was a young man and most nice girls had a lot of scruples about being picked up. Things are much more open and casual today and many of the girls really know that they come to the bar with the idea of meeting men. Bartenders can be a big help in this if they know you because they have a pretty good idea after awhile which girls get picked up and which girls really only come in for a cocktail and don't want any involvement.

I personally don't take advantage of that kind of assistance very often because I like to see if I can handle things on my own. Part of what I like is the element of challenge and suspense. It adds something to the whole scene. So if I meet someone and there's enough interest there, we'll usually have a drink or two together, or we might meet two or three times in the bar before anything else develops. But sooner or later, we'd probably leave the bar and go someplace nice for dinner. Of course, I always call Lou to let her know that I won't be home. She understands what's happening and then I'm free for the evening and more often than not we wind up in bed. I always let them know early in the acquaintance that I'm married. I do that as a matter of ethics and it doesn't really seem to make any difference. In fact, a couple of them have told me they prefer relationships with married men. Sometimes, after dinner at home, I get to feeling restless and I can just tell Lou that I'm going out and then I'll go to a bar and try to pick up a woman.

The way I'm telling this, it sounds as though I am extremely active in it, which is not accurate at all. I do this sort of thing maybe four or five times a year. I think that the main thing for me is the variety it offers plus the excitement of the chase, but mostly it's the idea of some sexual variety. I think I'm a great appreciater of women—each one is different and the experience is exciting.

Louise: As Don stated, I don't particularly go around looking for sexual experiences. I really just don't have it on my mind. I think most women enjoy a certain amount of flirtation and attention and the big thing the arrangement does for me is to allow me to have this kind of contact with other men without the feeling of having to keep my guard up—not to go too far. So I'm quite relaxed and comfortable and, if at some point I feel as though I'd like to go to bed with the man, I do. Actually, this doesn't really happen very often. I think in the past five years, there have been just six men that I went to bed with, although I've had some pleasant experiences with men that didn't end up in bed.

The majority of my experiences have been at times when I was away at a convention or conference. These things are always held at the better hotels. They have very nice bars and draw a very nice class of men. So, it's not uncommon for me, after the day's activities of the convention, to go into the bar—it's pretty standard behavior—and I may get involved and talk with someone from the professional group, or quite often there will be a man who is not part of the professional group who will start to talk to me. If he's an interesting man, we may wind up having dinner together and, as I said, occasionally, if I'm interested enough we go to bed. I think what it is with me is mostly a kind of lark where I'm free to let it go wherever it will. I am not under any big pressure to have sex, but I'm free to—well, just be myself.

I have only had two affairs that were not of that type. One was with an artist who was painting my portrait and it just seemed to grow naturally out of the contact while I was sitting for the painting. That was a very enjoyable experience. He was a very sensual man and his enjoyment of me was quite thrilling to me. Also, he was a good deal younger than I was and I think I was quite flattered by the passion he evinced. I quite distinctly recall thinking to myself afterward: "Hmm, not bad for a 43-year-old woman." The only other experience I had outside of conventions was with a real-estate broker. We were buying some income property and I had to meet the broker at the escrow to wrap up some final details. I am much better at business detail than Don. He's marvelous in having his head soar through the heavens of abstract thought, but he has no patience for any degree of details of everyday life. So, I had done most of the negotiating on the deal and had a number of contacts with the broker. We finished our business at the bank a little before noon and he invited me to have lunch with him. I had no more classes that day and it seemed like a nice idea, so I did. Lunch turned out to be very enjoyable. He was a most interesting man—very successful—self-made with little formal education, but he had managed to educate himself a great deal through books and he was very well-read and much more knowledgeable in the arts and humanities than many people I've seen walk away from commencement with their diplomas.

We started lunch with Martinis and, in fact, never did get around to having lunch. The conversation was quite stimulating and I found him very attractive. He was charming, with a delightful sense of humor, and while he had acquired a great deal of polish, there was just a touch of crudeness about him that I found appealing for reasons that I am not really aware of. By the third Martini, I was feeling rather giddy and lightheaded and, when he invited me to see a new, ultra-elegant apartment building that he was handling, I just went along. The building was not occupied. There was just a furnished model that they were going to start to display the following weekend. Of course, at that point I knew that he was going to try to seduce me and I must say I was really enjoying it. He was very skillful, very sharp and had an excellent sense of timing. He knew just how far to push and when to ease up. You know what I think also? The situation appealed to my sense of adventure. It was certainly an off-the-beaten-track kind of thing. There we were, alone in this not quite finished twenty-six-story apartment building. I think we were in a furnished apartment on the twentieth floor. It had a gorgeous view of the city and when he took me in his arms and started making love to me, I found myself turning onto it. It was just a great lark. I thoroughly enjoyed it.

It got to be a little sticky after that as he apparently was quite interested in me and he kept calling and wanted to see me again. But I had no interest in really getting involved with him. I had enjoyed what happened for what it was and I finally had to just explain to him that he was misinterpreting the situation, that I was really very happy with Don and not looking for any big relationship with anyone else. I'm afraid I probably hurt his ego because I finally had to tell him that while I had enjoyed the afternoon, I just wasn't interested in pursuing it any further. Well, I think that just about covers the nature of my activities.

Problems

Louise: I think the biggest problems for me were at the beginning. I really was quite worried about the whole thing. I was terribly worried about what it meant—like was it the beginning of some kind of destruction of our relationship. I was afraid it might lead to more extensive involvements with other people and I could see where that might dilute the importance we had for each other. On top of that, you know, you can get carried away in these relationships. So, that worried me a great deal, but I think the proof was in the practice. We've been on this arrangement for five years now and I can't see where it has in any way diminished the importance or the intensity of our own relationship. So, I think I've put that pretty much to rest, although I still have a twinge from time to time, especially if Don describes an experience with someone and I can see he found her quite interesting or exciting. I think I still get a little worried over what it might lead to.

Another problem that we had to deal with was whether we should discuss these things with each other or not, but as it turned out, there really isn't much you can do about it. I think you have both the desire to know and the desire not to know about it, but you can't help knowing that something is going on, particularly if Don calls and says he's going to be out for the evening. I know he's not concocting some story about where he's going and I know what he's doing. I think my feeling is that I would rather know about it than conjure up images about it in my own mind of what she might be like, or, you know, something like that. Reality is always easier to deal with, I think. Then, too, I think, we both just feel better about it. I know that somehow I feel better if I tell Don; if I say, you know, I was up in San Francisco at a convention and met an interesting man there and we went to bed.

We vary in the extent to which we talk about things. Sometimes the affairs themselves are interesting and it becomes a kind of shared experience. I'm still troubled, I think, with some jealousy—not so much specifically about the sex itself as the idea of his being interested in another woman.

I'm jealous in another way, too, and we really haven't been able to do anything about that. I'm jealous of the time Don spends with other women, even though it's quite little. Still, with the kind of busy schedules we keep, we don't have a great deal of time together anyway. So, I am jealous of his time. I wish he would spend it with me. However, I even have to qualify that because at least some of the times I would be busy during that evening anyway. So it really doesn't amount to a great deal. I don't think Don has this problem with me because at least so far, whatever I have done has been at times we wouldn't be together anyway.

Don: Well, I think that's true, but it's true of a number of activities we have which obviously take us away from each other, I'm jealous of some of your board meetings. In all of these cases, it's a matter of having to make choices and you have to give up one thing in order to have another. I could imagine just doing nothing but spending all of my time with Lou and I think I would enjoy that, but then I think there are all these other things that I want to do. I don't mean just the sexual things. I mean all the different things I'm interested in. This does mean giving up some time together and so this is the price we pay for having a large number of activities. As I'm talking about it now, I think it's probably a good thing. It's probably good for any marriage to have a sufficient amount of separation. Then the time you have together is very precious. That's the way it is with us. Who knows? Maybe if we were together all the time we might get on each other's nerves or become less interesting to each other. I don't know if that would happen. At least it's something to contemplate.

Another problem that hasn't been a problem, but we thought we had to deal with it, was establishing some ground rules for this activity. I know one of the things we thought would be important would be to keep it away from our intimate circle of friends and, perhaps, our close colleagues that we worked with just to avoid any awkwardness in those relationships. So I don't get involved with anyone Lou particularly knows and it's the same with her.

The other problem I've had to a degree is that of feelings about myself in relation to the other man. I thought I had it all worked out quite well in my mind, but the first time Lou came back and told me she'd been with somebody, I had some concern about how he might be thinking of the whole thing. What I'm talking about here is the whole cultural thing about masculinity in man-woman relationships. I think this is one of the reasons we decided to put close acquaintances out of bounds. It's the idea, you know, of another man having the feeling of, well, you know, I've laid his wife and attaching whatever significance he might attach to that. The other thing was the sort of derogation that some men engage in when they've gone to bed with a woman. I'm really not putting this very well. I must have some difficulties with it. Do you know what I'm talking about? It's like locker-room conversation or the way a guy will brag, I guess, about getting some woman into bed with the clear connotation that she's been had. You know, it reminds me of my old fraternity days in college when lunch on Monday was taken up with fellows bragging about whom they laid over the weekend. I've dealt with it mostly by trying to put it in some perspective where this is really their problem. I think it's a juvenile, immature kind of behavior and if that's all they get out of going to bed with a woman, then I think perhaps they are more to be pitied than envied.

I think there's a problem, too, of being concerned sometimes about the man thinking that he's put something over on me, or somehow, I don't know how to put it really, won out, you know? The competitive thing. I know there have been a couple of times when I've had this feeling—I really would like to tell the guy that he really hasn't done anything behind my back, that I'm aware of it and that this is our arrangement. But, I don't do that, of course. I think I know what it is—it's the sort of old primitive thing of having a possession stolen or something. That just isn't what's happening, but I think the man might sometimes feel that way. I guess I'm competitive enough that I don't like that, so I'd like him to be aware that he hasn't taken anything from me or put anything over on me. I don't own Lou. She's an independent human being whose freedom I respect, that's all.

Effects

Louise: It's so difficult to evaluate something like this. Our relationship was very good before we started this, so I can't really say it's any better because of it. On the other hand, I know it hasn't hurt. I think it's been a good thing in the sense that it was something that Don wanted to do and I think he would have felt deprived without it. As it's turned to be something that could be done without any harm, there was no good reason to be deprived. I don't mean to sound here like a woman who sees her role as that of the devoted wife concerned with nothing but her husband's happiness. I don't think I'm that type. Still, I am concerned with Don's being happy as well as with my own satisfaction. I think the two are irretrievably intertwined. We both have to be happy as individuals or we can't be happy as a pair. Strictly speaking, for myself, I think what I've had out of it are interesting and enjoyable experiences that I wouldn't have had otherwise. I don't think I would have missed them much if I hadn't had them, but I do think Don would have missed his. I don't mean to depreciate my experiences either. They were fun. As I said earlier, one of the important things to me is that it leaves me quite free in my contacts with men. I don't have to be on my guard.

Don: I think Lou is correct about me. We certainly talked about it. I think I would have felt I was missing something if I couldn't do this. I think it's kept us very much alive sexually also. I don't know if our personal sex life—that is between us—would have dropped off without this, but I know there hasn't been any diminution. I think we're both aware of some additional sexual impetus when one of us has been involved with someone else. I'm quite certain that our sex life picks up some from its regular pace at those times. I know that after I've had an experience with another woman, I go around for weeks in a state of heightened sexuality. So, I frankly feel that it's been a good thing for us. It certainly hasn't done any harm. We've been at it long enough to say that with confidence. I think, though, that each couple has to evaluate it in their own case. The most important thing is to have a very good relationship to start with—one that you both value a great deal. Otherwise, I think it would get to be too threatening, or in fact, it might get out of hand. You know, it might get to where one of the persons was finding more satisfaction outside of the marriage and spending more and more of their time on those activities. I think that would hurt the marriage.

LIFE IS NOT A BOWL OF CHERRIES:
BEN AND NATALIE

Ben and Natalie have a marriage that is built on compatibility but lacks romance or strong emotional interdependence. Ben is forty-nine with a slight paunch and receding hairline. He has a strong personality and some of the glib manner of the successful salesman. Natalie, at forty-seven, still possesses some of the rich dark beauty of Mediterranean women. Her eyes are dark and piercing and hint at the intensity of the emotion that lies within. Ben operates a chain of retail women's clothing stores. Natalie had worked in the business for several years in the early stages but is now a housewife. She is active in PTA and temple affairs. They have four children, aged thirteen, fifteen, nineteen, and twenty-three. It is the first marriage for each and they have been married for twenty-six years. They both had strong religious Jewish backgrounds and both are active in the temple. Natalie was a virgin when she married, although she had gone so far as to get into bed with a young man with whom she was in love; but, at the last minute, she felt she could not go through with it. Ben had very limited sexual experience, mostly with prostitutes, prior to marriage. They have had a co-marital sex agreement for the past seven years, although Ben had engaged in some extramarital activity prior to that time.

Natalie and Ben were interviewed separately. Partly, this was because Ben was reluctant to be interviewed at all and did so only after persuasion by Natalie, who felt that other people might be able to benefit from their experience. Also, they do not discuss their affairs with each other and it was apparent that this would be an impediment in a joint interview.

Motivation

Ben: I don't know how to talk about a thing like this. I'm usually pretty sure of myself but I am feeling quite uncomfortable now. I suppose the main thing is that we never had what you would call a really great love affair. I think we were both just ready to get married. I was never a ladies' man. I started working when I was fifteen and I didn't get around much socially. When I thought I just had to have a piece I would go to a prostitute, but I never liked that, I think I was a little ashamed of it, and I was always worried, you know, about getting something.

So when I got to know Nat, she was a good-looking woman, she came from the same kind of background I did, and I just figured she'd be a good wife for me. I don't think it was a mistake, we've done pretty well together. Those first few years we worked like dogs to get ahead, you know, fourteen to sixteen hours a day. We didn't have much time for fun or social life. We didn't have much time or energy for sex either as far as that goes. Although, we had our moments and they were pretty good. At least, I know for me, it sure beat prostitutes. But it was good, you know, we were building something and we could see it growing. We kept adding new stores and it seemed as though I never really had much time away from the business. As it grew, Natalie wasn't as needed as she was in the beginning and then the children came and she was pretty busy with them so we spent even less time together. We had a very strong family feeling and when I did have free time, I spent a lot of it with the children. I was content. I don't think Nat was, but, she'll probably tell you about that, although, I really didn't know that she wasn't until a few years ago. . . .

When I hit the big money, I started associating with a bunch of successful men—you know, I had made it. I was one of them. I was shocked to find out that most of them, even though they were married, were playing around. It seemed like there would hardly ever be a get-together when they weren't talking about broads. Once in a while, a bunch of us would run down to Vegas for a weekend and they'd all wind up getting laid. I didn't, at first, but then it just seemed like the thing to do. I had learned from watching them operate how to go about it, and I had the desire to try my wings. And then, finally, I did pick up a woman down there and did get laid and I got a bit kick out of it. Part of it, of course, was like part of being a successful man and, you know, one of the boys. But I enjoyed it sexually, too, it was a lot different than sex at home, you know? Getting laid became an important thing, maybe it is some kind of an ego thing, I don't know. Anyway, with all the stores, we employed a lot of women, and, well I'd better explain.

The stores all had managers and assistant managers and some of the women made it clear enough that they wouldn't mind being nice to the boss if it would get them ahead. I took advantage of some of these opportunities. You know, who wouldn't? Finally, it got back to Nat and then we went through the whole *megillah*. She was raving mad and we talked about getting a divorce. Things really looked pretty bad. I felt terrible because, like I said, my family meant a great deal to me and I didn't want anything like that to happen. I didn't know where to turn, the only person I could think of was the rabbi. So I talked to him and he told me to come in with Nat and we did. Well, I can't tell you how much I owe that man, he was pretty modern about it all and didn't give us a lecture on morality but tried to get us to look at where we were and what we had.

Nat didn't commit herself there, but after we got home we stayed up all night talking and that's when a lot of these other things came out. That was the first time Nat ever told me that she wasn't content and she felt something was missing in her life. That really hit me in the gut because I had always thought that she had everything, you know, she had money, nice house, good kids, and I felt that I had been a good husband to her, other than that playing around. And, hell, nobody thinks too much of that these days. She told me that for a couple of years she had been thinking about getting a divorce. She did it very kindly, you know, we were all calmed down then and really leveling with each other and she told me that she appreciated all the things we had and even that she appreciated me, she thought I was a good man, but that she felt something missing from her life as a woman—that she needed love. And she told me about this guy she'd been in love with that she had almost married but she didn't because she knew that he wouldn't make a good husband. And then, she dropped her bombshell, that she thought that we should not get a divorce but that we should continue in the marriage and that she didn't object to my playing around but that she also wanted the privilege to have involvements with other men. Wow! Then I hit the ceiling, I'm a double-standard man, at least I was then, I think I probably still am, pretty much. And I told her that that was ridiculous, you know, it was one thing for a man and just not the same for a woman.

I tried to talk her out of it, but I couldn't. You know, I told her I was very sorry about what I had done and I even agreed that I would never do it again—I don't know if I could have lived up to that—but, anyway, I was ready to promise anything. But I couldn't budge her, so I had a helluva decision to make—I could lose my pride and keep my family or lose my family and keep my pride. I'm saying pride because as I thought it through I think that's what was involved. You know, the idea of some other man laying my wife. I went down to the beach for a couple of days by myself just to be able to think things through and what finally came out of it was that we had a lot together—I don't mean just the money, the home, those things, you know, but, hell, we'd been married almost twenty years then and a lot of things happened in that time. I thought about different things, like there had been a period when I expanded too fast in the business and it looked like the whole thing was going to go down the drain and I remember that it was Nat's suggestion that we sell the house, give up everything and move into a little apartment to save every nickel we could to try to survive and we did that for about six months until the crisis passed and then, of course, things were all right again. But you know, that's a helluva woman in my book, no bitching or complaining.

And then, there was another time our oldest boy had pneumonia and we really thought he was going to die. We sat outside the room of the hospital for two days just holding each other's hand; and, you know, things like that, you don't just throw them away. You know, as I said, maybe we don't have a great love affair, but we've been through a lot together and you got to care something about a person after all that. So I started thinking the other way; you know, hell, if she needed a fur coat, or an expensive operation or anything, I'd give it to her. But what she needed was apparently something I couldn't give her—I couldn't give her love and romance. It's just not in me, you know, I love my kids and I think in a funny way, I guess I love my business, almost like a woman. But, what she wanted, poor 'ol Ben just didn't have it. But while I was down there by myself I seemed able to understand it. I think that is the first time I ever did that in my life — just stop everything and take two days just to think about things, you know. I couldn't get to like the idea . . . I still don't . . . but I had to balance the pros and cons. And, in the end, it seemed to me that I could take that better than losing my family.

So we made the deal, I was free to continue on with my little affairs and Nat was free to do her thing. I did ask her not to get involved with anyone that I knew which was more than agreeable with her and we agreed not to talk about these things with each other. It didn't sound all that bad because she wasn't just looking to get laid, you know, she wasn't planning to go out and hang around bars, or anything like that, she was looking for a romantic affair. And, I figured I'd just have to trust her judgment and hope that it worked out all right.

Dr. Ziskin: Did you then just sort of continue on with the things you were doing, you know, the trips to Las Vegas or women in the stores, things of that kind?

Ben: Yeah, I stayed pretty much in the same pattern.

Dr. Ziskin: How has it worked out? Have you had any problems with it?

Ben: No, no big problems. Nat's a pretty sharp gal. I think she's probably used good judgment, she's certainly been very discreet because I don't think anybody knows about this except me. I know, she doesn't tell me about it, but I know when she's having an affair because she's different—she lights up—she's happier and then I can usually tell when it's over because she gets kind of depressed. I don't think there's been that much of it, to tell the truth, I would guess, if I'm judging it right that within the last seven years there's been maybe two or three affairs. They last for a long time though.

Dr. Ziskin: Do you have any concern that she might fall so much in love with one of these men that she would break up the marriage anyway?

Ben: No, not very much, really; I suppose it could happen but I don't think it will. Certainly it isn't going to happen until the children are all grown up. I know Nat too well for that. And I think she's getting what she wants this way so there isn't that much reason to break things up. It hasn't happened yet and, you know, by the time Artie's grown up, Nat's going to be in her fifties. We both feel pretty much that we're together for life.

Dr. Ziskin: Then you feel you made the right decision.

Ben: Yeah. It's not all that clear-cut, you know. I feel queasy about it sometimes, like I said. I'm not all that happy with the idea. But our family life is as good as it's ever been and that's important to me.

Dr. Ziskin: Has it had any effect on the sexual relationship between the two of you?

Ben: Well, it's a funny thing. Of course, I already told you that hadn't been too great, for a while anyway, but that's another way I know when Nat's having an affair because we have no sexual relationship at all. I think she's a one-man-at-a-time woman. Nothing gets said, and it's funny how you know these things, but it's communicated. And sometimes when it's over she'll put out little hints and we'll have our normal sex relationship. It's not a big hardship on me—I'm getting plenty on the side so—well, maybe it's had a kind of effect—I think that our sex relationship, when we have it, is, well, not so much sexy as it is more loving and affectionate. Not as routine as it used to be. It's still not great, though. I have more of a ball with one of the girls from the stores.

Natalie: I think the most important thing is that marrying Ben was a compromise. Like all compromises you get something but you have to give up something. I wasn't in love with Ben but I knew him pretty well by the time we got married and he met a lot of requirements. He's a good man, considerate, stable, a hard worker; I felt very strongly that he was going to be successful. Of course, he's Jewish, my family approved of him, I think they would have preferred a doctor, you know about that thing, I suppose. The next best thing to a doctor is a stable, promising businessman. Don't misunderstand me, I liked him and I thought we'd make a good team.

Before I met Ben I had been madly in love with a jazz musician. It was an intense, wildly emotional relationship. I had come very close to having a real affair, you know, in a sexual sense, with him. And I even went to bed with him once, but nothing happened because I just couldn't go through with it, you know, in those days things were different—it was a different world. I suppose today most girls wouldn't think too much about it, but not then. I was determined to be a virgin when I got married. I was scared at how close I came, though, to doing it with him. I certainly wanted to. But, of course, the whole thing just had too much against it. My family were terribly opposed to him and they felt, aside from his not being Jewish, that he had no future and that I would have a terrible life as a musician's wife. I felt they were right and I still think so. In fact, a couple of years ago I read his name in the paper where he had been arrested with some other musicians for some drug offense. But I had had these terrific feelings which I had never felt with Ben.

I don't know about other women, I think they must be the same, but I know all through my marriage to Ben there was an emotional emptiness. I didn't feel it so much during the early years. We were so busy with the business, and then with the children, that most of the time the most enjoyable thing in the world was just to drop into bed and go to sleep. Sex, when it happened, was a hurry-up thing, more like a necessity, you know, like brushing your teeth, than a joy. When things got easier for me, I guess that was about nine or ten years ago, you know, we had full-time help, and even with the four children, I had much more free time than I had ever had before. I started wanting something more in the way of a relationship. I heard gossip about other women carrying on affairs, and I wondered about it, I wondered if they were satisfying to them, I wondered if I would be satisfied if I did something like that. But I didn't think I would be. I thought about divorce but that just seemed insane. First of all, there were the children, they were so young and they are very fond of Ben and he is of them, and then, too, Ben just hadn't done anything to deserve it, he had been a good husband and a good father and I just couldn't do it to him. But the idea of being loved and being in love was on my mind a great deal. I couldn't seem to get it resolved.

As I approached forty, I began to feel, well, almost panicky about it because I seemed so stuck, so unable to move and time was running by and I knew that I—well, if I didn't do something soon, the time would be past for me. Then I found out that Ben had been playing around. I was really shocked. I don't know why. I shouldn't have been. I certainly wasn't that naive and I had heard about a lot of other men that we knew, but still it was a shock when it turned out that Ben was doing it. I was angry and I think somewhere in the back of my mind I recognized that this gave me an excuse to get a divorce if I wanted to, and I think that some of my early reaction really involved the idea that, well you know, like I had been wronged and now I had a legitimate excuse to have my freedom.

We talked to the rabbi and we talked a lot between ourselves and, oh I don't know, I wanted something, but I didn't want to disrupt the family. By the time I had calmed down I wasn't all that angry with Ben anymore. It was strange. I found that I just really didn't care that much if he was involved with other women. Then I thought if I felt that way, maybe he would feel the same about me, so I broached the idea of forgetting about the divorce, but for him to allow me the same kind of freedom he had. Of course he reacted like a man—indignant, outraged. I'll have to say this for him, and I respect him for it, that he thought it through on his own and finally agreed. I don't really know what would have happened if he hadn't agreed. I don't know if I would have gone through with a divorce. I think I had some practical thoughts, too, that if I got the divorce, met another man and we fell in love, I wasn't a very marriageable person, you know, I don't think many men would want to take a woman with four children.

So, I thought I might have some love affairs, but I wouldn't have a husband and the children wouldn't have a full-time father. That was not a very appetizing prospect. Well, fortunately, Ben turned out to be more reasonable than I had really expected and we reached this agreement.

Dr. Ziskin: How has it worked out?

Natalie: Pretty good I think. It's not the best of all possible worlds. I mean, if I'm having an affair, you know, I still have to sort of sneak around, not so much because of Ben, but just because it's not something you want to get out, you know . . . I think I'd like it a lot better if I were married to a man I was very much in love with and everything was completely on the up and up. But, as I said in the beginning, life is full of compromises. You get something. You give up something. In a way, I suppose it sounds as though it ought to be very good, you know . . . like I have my cake and eat it too. And I think that's probably true except that the way it really is, the marriage isn't as good as I wish it was and the love affairs aren't as good as I wish they were because well, there's the feeling about them that they are not really permanent and as I say, the need to be discreet . . . Well, like, I've only had three affairs in these seven years. I never allowed a man to call me at home. I always call him at his place of business. We can't always be together when we like to. It's sort of on stolen time, you know. . . . We meet during the day and that means that he's taking time from his business or his occupation and I don't know, what can I say? It's not the same as just being free. Still, on the whole it has given me a chance to, well, to feel more fulfilled as a woman and I think it's been good enough. I can settle for it.

I don't know what will happen in the future, like when the children are all grown up. But, you know I'm forty-seven now and, well, let's face it, I'm maybe still a fairly attractive woman, but, you know, the lines are there. My figure is changing. I don't know how much passion I would be able to inspire in a man in another five or six years. Another thing. I think the affairs I've had have taken some of the edge off my need; you know, I, well, God knows the affairs I've had meant a great deal to me and I just felt so completely alive and turned on, but I don't feel the same pressure for it that I did when we started. I think part of it is the idea that I've had it now. You know, before we got into this, there was the—oh just awful feeling that I would go through my whole life and never experience a complete romantic love affair; and, now that I've done it, I'd like to have more, but I don't think I'd have that terrible feeling of regret if there aren't any more.

So, I think that Ben and I will probably stick it out together; you know, our oldest son is twenty-three and he'll be getting married soon. There'll start to be grandchildren and I guess there'll be enough. Ben doesn't like to think about it, but I've talked to him about getting out of the business, retiring, and I think, well, you know, there are a lot of things that we didn't do when we were younger. We might travel and there are other kinds of things in life that we might enjoy and we are comfortable together. You know what I mean? We're companionable. Who knows? I don't know. Maybe we'll find when we get into, what do they say—the winter of our years—and we have more time together without all the stresses and strains, maybe we'll find we have more than we thought we had.

Dr. Ziskin: Have you had any particular problems?

Natalie: No, not really. Ben had asked me not to get involved with anyone he knew and that was easy enough. I'm on the board of several philanthropic organizations and the men I've had affairs with are men I've met through those activities and that's all pretty remote from our regular life. I suppose there's always a feeling of some risk and, well, the other thing that I've mentioned already is trying to be discreet, not to, you know, be seen by anyone or that sort of thing. I think one thing that's helped is that all my affairs have been with married men and I think, well, we all kind of have the same situation, you know, where we have families and I think even when we start out, we know that neither of us is going to break up our family.

Sometimes, well, because these have really been love affairs, I think there's a sort of wistful regret that we can't turn our backs on everything and just be together all the time, but life isn't like that, I guess.

6.
Separate Vacations

THE THREE-DAY PASS: MEL AND WANDA

Mel and Wanda are both attorneys practicing together in their own law firm. Mel is a thirty-eight-year-old wiry restless man. He has his hair styled and dresses in the latest fashion. Wanda is a smallish thirty-three-year-old woman whose perfect features are accentuated by the simple, severe way she wears her reddish hair pulled back from her face. Her figure is good except for somewhat heavy legs. They have been married ten years and have two boys, aged eight and six. Neither has been married before. They do not have strong religious backgrounds and do not practice or have any involvement with religion at the present time. Their income is in excess of $40,000 a year.

Motivation

Mel: First of all, you have to understand that neither of us was all that eager to get married. I don't mean to each other, but just the idea of marriage as such. We liked living together. I suppose you could say we were in love, but I think we were both wary of getting tied down. After we'd lived together for a couple of years, I think we both felt that we wanted to make it permanent, but the main reason we got married was because I was concerned about Wanda. Neither of us felt any strong desire to have children, at least certainly not at that time, but I was concerned that it was something Wanda would miss, you know, being a woman, if she didn't have children, and that was really the main reason we got married. I think it was the right decision. We both enjoy the boys and I'm pretty sure had we reached our present ages without having children, that we would both be wondering about it, you know, the feeling that maybe we were missing something.

Of course, it has its price; you know, before the boys were born, we were footloose and fancy free. We could pick up and go away whenever we wanted to. We lived in a casual, unorganized way. We didn't have to do much domestic planning, you know, if we felt like cooking something, we did. If we felt like eating out, we did. Of course, all that changed after the boys came. I suppose you have children and you must know what it's like—your life—it's organized around them and around the domestic thing. So we started feeling frustrated and restless, you know, hemmed in. I guess I felt it more than Wanda. We got into a lot of bickering about what to do and how to do it and when to do it and, it seemed as though there was hardly any time for each of us between the practice and the house and the kids and the goddamn housekeeper problem.

Do you have help? If you do, you know what I mean. We had to have full-time help with Wanda working. She didn't want to give up her career and I didn't want her to. I think it's an important thing to her and she's good at it. But this housekeeper bit can really drive you up the wall, you know, either they're no good and you can't depend on them or you get a good one and in a few months her son in Tennessee has an accident and she has to go back and take care of his family. There's always something. Even if you have a good one for a few months, you have the feeling that you're living on the edge of disaster all the time because you learn that it isn't going to last.

Then, also for me, I think sex was a big factor. Before I met Wanda I was well, to put it bluntly, a cocksman. You know, I was never an athlete or a card player or artistically inclined. One thing I was good at and really enjoyed was sex. I wasn't one of those guys who, oh, you know, gets his manhood by counting the number of girls he's gone to bed with. It wasn't that. I just liked the whole sex game, the whole process, you know, from the first meeting till the last goodbye. So I really missed that. I had been faithful to Wanda and in the beginning we had a pretty good sex life, but with all the things I've mentioned already, it had begun to deteriorate—still good sometimes, but less frequent, sometimes more mechanical. So, all in all, I felt the need to be able to break out of the rut once in a while. I don't think people think about this very much, but you know, being a parent, being a husband is like a job and when you're doing it seven days a week, week after week, I think you're bound to get stale, you know. . . . Certainly nobody works that way on their job, you know; we have the weekend, we have vacations from the job, and I don't see where marriage and parenthood is really any different, you know. . . . You need a break from it once in awhile.

So I talked to Wanda about this and she agreed. I think she was feeling the need to be able to get away as much as I was. So we worked out a plan where each of us would be able to take a three-day weekend every few weeks, alone, to see how it would work, and it was good. I'm sure Wanda will agree with that. But then I found, well, you know, we'd go away, there's no use trying to kid yourself that you can be home and say, "Okay, I'm off these three days" because you just . . . everything is there, you know, and you can't ignore it. So our system was to . . . either I would go away or Wanda would go away every few weeks.

Dr. Ziskin: Did this arrangement include sexual activity on these weekend passes?

Mel: No, not at first. It was just the idea of getting out

from under everything and having some time that just belonged
to no one but you. But then I found that I'd go away and I'd
start getting restless wherever I was—Palm Springs, Las Vegas,
Acapulco—I tried them all. I think, like I said, I don't play golf.
I don't do a lot of the things that people do at resorts, and I do
some drinking.

I imagine you know lawyers as a group are a hard-drinking
bunch. So I'd be in bars and I'd see a woman that I felt sure I
could pick up. In fact, I picked some up, but then I would never
let it go to its logical conclusion. Not that I didn't want to. Lord
knows I wanted to, but I'm a responsible guy. I may not sound
that way to you, but I really am and I certainly wasn't going to
violate Wanda's trust in me. I wondered if Wanda had any of the
same kind of feelings. Don't let those big glasses and school-
teacher hairdo fool you. Beneath that Phi Beta Kappa key she
wears on her necklace there beats the heart of a very lascivious
broad. Right?

Wanda: I never heard it put quite that way before. I think
it's probably an overstatement, but not altogether inaccurate.
Could you use a title like "sexually responsive woman" instead?

Mel: Sure, a rose by any other name. . . . So, one night I
just asked her flat out if she ever had any desire to get sexually
involved with another man when she was on a weekend. She got
very cagey and it took a while to get a straight answer.

Wanda: Well, it seemed like a funny thing to have your
husband ask you, you know, I didn't know what he was getting
at. I didn't know what he had on his mind. I wondered if he was
probing to find out if I had been doing anything like that,
which I hadn't. So we had a few moments there where we
weren't very open with each other, you know, we were fencing
and it finally dawned on me that maybe he was asking because
he wanted to fool around. So I just asked him outright if he
wanted to and he said that he had thought about it and then I
was able to tell him that I had too, you know, on my weekends,
being a woman alone and everything, certainly I had been
approached and there were some men that I had thought it

might be fun to have a fling with, but, you know, the same as Mel, I wasn't going to cheat on him. That can be so terribly destructive. You know, we handle a lot of divorce matters and frequently they involve infidelity and there can be so much rage—not so much at the purely sexual thing, you know—what difference does that really make?—but it's the idea of being deceived, being made a fool of that really sets people off.

So, anyway, we finally had the question out in the open. Should we or shouldn't we? And then we went at it in a very rational way, you know, trying to weigh the pros and cons and the more we talked about it, the more difficult it was to find many cons. I'm on the pill so there was no concern about pregnancy and after we got past that, there wasn't an awful lot else. Well, you know, of course it violates the code, but we have both been, I guess you would say, sexually libertarian before we were married—certainly neither of us had any religious scruples about it, but all we could come up with was two unknowns: One was, would it hurt our relationship? and, second was, might one of us, well, you know, find some other person more attractive, more desirable and get more involved? Neither of us felt that would happen. For one thing, I think what we clearly had in mind was just a fling—no heavy emotional thing, you know. I was concerned about how it might affect our relationship and I asked how he would feel if he knew that I had gone to bed with another man and he said that in view of the fact that I had been to bed with some men before we were married, he couldn't really see how that would change me or change us.

Mel: You should understand that I am not a double-standard man. I support Women's Lib, I believe in equal rights for women, and I don't consider sex a great big sacred thing. It's just fun. There was another thing, too; I had been doing some reading on the whole subject and I was impressed when I read about some of these festival times they have, I think in Bavaria, if I remember right, where, you know, once a year for a few days all the normal limits are off and everybody goes to bed with everybody else and, apparently, it works out okay there, so I felt that it certainly might be the same with us. You know, most of the time we were going to be Mel and Wanda, responsible citizens, parents, spouses, whatever and then, every once in awhile, we'd get to take the lid off and step out of those roles for a few days and then go back into them. I think what Wanda said about the divorces we've handled is important here. We've seen so many marriages go down the drain from boredom, from frustration—people get more and more irritated with each other because they're frustrated, that it really seemed as though it might, well, not only not be a bad idea, but it might really be a good idea. So, we decided to try it. We agreed that I would tell Wanda the first time anything happened and she would tell me and then, you know, we could see how we felt and if it looked like we didn't feel right about it, we would stop. Doing it once was certainly not going to be the end of the world. So, there it was.

Activities

Mel: Well, it's been like the finishing touch, you know, like the whipped cream on top of the cake. It really makes these weekends for me. I don't always get laid, but I always try. Usually, I do. You know, some weekends, well, I just don't meet anyone where we click together. Then there've been other weekends—well, there was one wild one a few months ago, where I had four different bed partners. It varies. Sometimes I'll meet someone the first day and we enjoy each other's company and we spend the whole weekend together. I've met some interesting people. There was one woman. . . . I was shocked when she told me she was 52 because she looked younger. I mean, I knew she was older than I was and I really hadn't thought of getting into anything with her. We happened to just start talking in the bar and she was a thoroughly charming woman—a widow. She had taken over her husband's business when he died and built it into a tremendous success and then she sold it and she was retired. She was born in France and we had a marvelous time together. I don't mean just in bed, but really engaged in a lot of personal, philosophical kind of conversation. In fact I told her about Wanda and me and she was very approving. So, I don't know, if you could figure her as a mother figure.

Actually it did feel good to speak to an intelligent woman like this and get someone else's view that agreed with ours. It made me optimistic too, you know, to find a woman that age who was so sexy and passionate and felt that Wanda and I still had a lot of good years left. But, I don't know what else to tell you about it, you know. It's sort of like what you would do if you were single and down at the Springs or in Vegas or wherever for a weekend.

Wanda: I haven't been as active as Mel, I don't think. We don't keep track. We don't necessarily talk about it. If one of us has an interesting experience, we do, otherwise, there may be just nothing said. But I think, well, you know, Mel, I suppose like most men will jump into bed with any halfway attractive girl. For me, I have to feel a pretty strong attraction to the man. I just don't want to go to bed to be going to bed with someone. So, some weekends I meet a man and there is that interest and other weekends I don't and it's no big thing with me either way. I don't feel any pressure about it. I don't feel it's a lost weekend if I haven't had an affair. I think one aspect of it is that we're both talkers. We really enjoy talking to people and it's always interesting to have a conversation with someone new, find out, you know, what they're like, what they think, have some pleasant banter—that sort of thing. I think it's like Mel says, we're not into anything far out, you know, no orgies or anything of that kind. It's pretty much like things we have done and might have done when we were single.

Problems

Mel: None. We just really don't have any. We're not jealous. We're both in favor of what we are doing. You know, we go away together at times also—sometimes with the children, sometimes without—and there's one advantage to this. Like, you know, if just the two of us go away for the weekend, then we're always worried about how things are at home. Are the kids okay? Is the housekeeper looking after things? You know, that sort of thing. This way, there's always one of us at home. I suppose maybe there's a problem in that too, at least for me. If some kind of crisis comes up, I'm not too good at handling it, you know, if one of the kids gets sick or whatever it may be, I get the feeling I wish Wanda were there, but so far, I've managed everything all right. We've been doing this—what?—I guess about four years or so and I just can't say that we've had any real problems. Certainly the thing about emotional involvement hasn't happened. You know, we've had our brief encounter and we've enjoyed it and neither of us has gotten hung up on anybody else at all. Isn't that right?

Wanda: Yes. I think the time is too short for anything like that to develop and you kind of go into it knowing that it's, you know, just for that day or two so you don't have any of that kind of expectation. You're not looking for that kind of thing. So, we really don't have any problems. Fortunately, you know, we can afford this. Money isn't an issue. Once we got past the first time, you know. I don't know about Mel, but I was a little shaky because as we said we didn't know what effect it might have, but once we'd been doing it and found that there was no harm, we felt quite comfortable with it.

Effects

Mel: I think it's been very good for us. I think the main effect it has is to, well, let some of the steam out of the boiler, is about the way I would put it. I know I come back from these weekends with a feeling of being refreshed, you know, recreated, having had my batteries charged and I don't feel so hemmed in, so pressured. We really seem to be much happier all around than we were before we started this. We enjoy each other. We enjoy the children more. I think that's an important thing, you know. I don't see them now as barriers to my enjoying my life, but everything is kind of more in its own place and if I start feeling harried, constrained, I always know that in a week, or two, or three, whatever it is, I'm going to have this weekend again. So, it takes a lot of the edge off of those negative feelings—just the knowledge that it's there to look forward to. It's just like a vacation from marriage, you know. The marriage is okay, but you just need to get away from it once in awhile.

Wanda: I think another aspect that may be more important for me than for Mel is just the sheer luxuriousness of having all this time that's my own. You know, I sleep late. I take my time about getting dressed, I can fool around with makeup, maybe try changing my hair style. There are no demands. I don't have to rush around the way I do at home. There aren't three people, four if you count the housekeeper, clamoring for my attention. I don't have to be wife, mother, nurse, house manager, and lawyer, all rolled into one. I can just be a free woman for those few days. I think that's the most important part of it. I was enjoying that even before we let sex get into the act. I could still enjoy it just for that aspect alone. The sexual part isn't that important to me except that I do enjoy it and, well, if it doesn't do any harm, why not? I think it adds an air of excitement to the weekend which otherwise would just be restful.

Dr. Ziskin: Has this had any effect on your married sex life?

Wanda: I think it has in an indirect way because as a result of these weekends, we both feel, well, happier, I guess is the only way I could put it. We don't seem to be so edgy with each other. I think also that it's restoring and we don't go around so tired all the time. Then, maybe the most important thing is the old "absence makes the heart grow fonder" thing. You know, we've talked about this and we both get the same feeling when the weekend is over—we're very eager to get home and to be together again.

Mel: That's very true. I don't know how to explain it, but I think we both feel an increased desire to make love together after we've been with someone else.

Dr. Ziskin: Does the fact that you or Wanda have just come back from having sex with another person have any particular element of stimulation?

Mel: No. I haven't experienced anything like that. I think it's just being back together again and being, well, just, having more zest for life, I guess.

Wanda: I would say the same thing. I don't think there's any special attraction because Mel has maybe been to bed with another woman. I think those affairs are just something that's separate from us.

Dr. Ziskin: With the door opened as it were to sexual relationships with other people, do you have activities of this kind other than on those special weekends?

Both: No.

Mel: For one thing, we're just too busy. We don't have time for it. I remember an old law professor telling us that the law is a jealous mistress and I can say amen to that. Even when we're home in the evening or on weekends, we spend a good deal of time going over briefs, or researching particular problems and, you know, we do have a normal social life also. So, there really just wouldn't be room for this at, you know, regular times. But, I don't think that's the real reason. I think that the whole concept that's involved here is that of a hiatus—a vacation from marriage. So that when I'm away or Wanda's away—for those few days, I think we already said this—it's as though we were single. When we're at home, we have a very conventional married life—family life. Do you get what I'm saying? Most of the time we simply play by the rules. What these weekends are are just periods when the rules are suspended, that's all.

7.
The Swingers

BALLERS, NOT BOWLERS: DENNIS AND MARTHA

Martha and Dennis are group swingers. Dennis is a thirty-five-year-old insurance adjuster of very average appearance and intelligence. In fact the most descriptive word we could think of for Dennis would be "average." He has completed two years of junior college. He was married once before while quite young for a period of less than two years; there were no children of that marriage. Prior to his marriage he had a moderate amount of sexual experience. Martha is a thirty-one-year-old housewife who, before her marriage to Dennis worked as a typist. She is a moderately attractive, large-boned, somewhat buxom and big-busted woman. She is a high school graduate, was not previously married, and also had a moderate amount of sexual experience prior to her marriage. Their income is in the ten- to twenty-thousand-dollar-a-year category. Both have Protestant backgrounds, but neither one is involved with religion any longer. They have two boys, aged six and four. After the birth of the second child they felt they did not want any more children, so Martha practiced contraception with the pill.

They have been swinging for three years almost entirely in the group mode, although on rare occasions they have had sexual relationships with just one other couple.

Motivation

Dennis: It's a tough question. I guess, you know, it's to enjoy sex. There were a couple of things involved in our case that may be a little different from others. One thing, in my job I go around to people's houses to work out claims and, quite often, because I go during the day there is just the woman of the house at home. I've had some pretty obvious passes made at me and some others that maybe weren't so obvious, but I sure had the feeling that if I pushed it the woman wouldn't object to a little hanky-panky. I'm human, I was tempted, but I didn't want to get into anything like that because—well it may sound stuffy, because I thought it was wrong.

Anyway, like they say, the road to hell is paved with good intentions and I finally wound up in bed with a woman one afternoon right in the middle of trying to settle her claim. Maybe it's a good way to do business, I never thought of this before, but it seemed to be pretty easy to work out the settlement afterwards. Anyway that's not the point. Afterwards, I really felt lousy.

I went around for weeks feeling guilty as hell until finally I told Martha about it. But it's kind of related to the second thing I was going to mention. I don't know exactly how to put it . . . . While I was aware of course, when we got married that Martha wasn't a virgin—and, at one time, I think she started to make a confession but I really didn't want to hear about it; you know, like you see in the movies, the woman starts to reveal her crimson past and the man says, "You don't owe me any explanation," or whatever they say. I'm sort of caught between generations. I guess there's part of me that's pretty hip and I can say to myself, you know, it's okay Martha's gone to bed with other guys; after all, that was before we were married. But there's an old-fashioned part of me that was shook up by it, so I mostly didn't think about it.

Then, one night, Martha invited this old boyfriend and his wife over for a drink; I think she'd run into him someplace. She's a friendly person. I don't think she thought anything about it, but I had never met him before and I didn't know anything about him. I had this uncomfortable feeling while they were there that there had been something between him and Martha, so after they left I asked her about it. She told me she'd gone with him for some period of time and that she'd been to bed with him. Well I blew my stack and I was ranting and raving about how could she have me sitting across the table from a guy that had screwed her. She was trying to explain that she really hadn't thought anything about it, that it was all in the past before she knew me and she really didn't seem to have any idea what I was so upset about. Actually it was after that that I had my love-in-the-afternoon affair. I was probably still angry and I felt sort of justified.

Anyway, the combination of the two things made me do a lot of thinking about the whole sex business. I was shook up by the fact that I had found myself wanting to take advantage of some of these opportunities that came my way. That, in fact, I really had enjoyed going to bed with this woman at the moment. Then, you know, I kind of wondered what it meant as far as Martha and I were concerned. Our sex life was okay, it wasn't what it had been at first, but it was still okay, and I couldn't really say I was a sexual hardship case. I think this all got mixed in together with my trying to work out my feeling about this other guy. I loved Martha, but I was going around angry with her for quite a long time afterward and that was kind of pushing us apart and I didn't want that to happen.

I had to try and work it all out in my mind as to what I was reacting to, I wasn't able to avoid thinking about it as I had before, so I finally decided to hit it head-on and I would, like say to myself, "Okay, here's this guy that had laid Martha and there I was sitting across from him, so what?" and sometimes I would kind of force myself to imagine them in bed together and I kept coming back to the same question, "Okay, so what?" It finally dawned on me that the answer was so nothing, it didn't really make any difference. Martha was the person she was and what we had together, we had, and it really didn't make a damned bit of difference that she'd been to bed with other men.

I don't mean this happened all at once, I think it was three or four months before I got to where I felt more or less okay about it; and that's when it got all mixed in with my own desires to have experiences with other women. Because the next step, it seemed to me, was, if it really doesn't make any difference, why not? I really didn't like the idea of cheating. I had felt too guilty after that other time and I didn't want to get into anything where I was going to worry about getting caught or coming home with lipstick on my collar or something. So that's when I decided to talk to Martha about it. I had heard people talk about the swinging groups and the idea appealed to me.

Martha: When Dennis suggested this I was shocked and scared; I was shocked because it was just not anything I would ever have thought about. I had the usual ideas about marriage: when you got married you don't go to bed with somebody else. And I was scared because I felt that Dennis was still angry with me for having invited Phil over that time. I thought it was some way he was using to get even with me. I was also scared about some of the feelings I had after I got over the first shock. I know I had some feeling of like, okay if that's what he wants, I'll just go ahead and do it and show him. I was afraid that I was still angry about his having gone to bed with this woman whose claim he was trying to settle. I had appreciated his telling me about it and I understood or thought I understood what had been going on, and I thought I'd gotten over any feeling I had about it, but I think I still had some anger anyway.

Still, there were my feelings of a woman and mother that I wanted to protect my home and family and I just felt we might blow everything if we got into this kind of thing. So at first I just said no and got pretty angry about the whole idea, but we talked about it some more. Dennis was pretty insistent and, as we talked, I was more impressed with the idea that our marriage was in something of a rut. I don't mean by that it was bad; it was a comfortable kind of rut. I think we both felt that our life together was okay, but by then we'd been married about six years and it wasn't very exciting anymore.

I must say when I had seen Phil that time it did remind me of my younger days that were more fun, not that I had any interest anymore, but it was kind of like remembering some of the fun and excitement of dates and being interested in a man, and things like that. I didn't have any big moral thing about sex when I was younger. I wasn't promiscuous, but if I was out with a guy and I felt like going to bed with him I did. I think I was feeling some confinement too. Since we got married I hadn't worked, and just the idea of meeting new people, the flirtations, passes that guys make at you, and just the generally more exciting kind of life when you're working, compared to being a housewife. . . . I mean I love my kids, and I enjoy taking care of them, but it does get monotonous and I think with our kind of life neither of us is very important, and we don't do big interesting things, and we don't have a lot of money, so our social life became kind of a set pattern between two couples that we know and maybe we would get together and play cards once in awhile or go to a movie or, once in awhile, go out to dinner, things like that.

Dennis and I didn't have a great deal to talk about, just the domestic things and things like making plans for vacations and that sort of thing. Still, I think I was sort of content; but once Dennis had talked to some people about the swinging thing and I could see how eager he was I got the idea that it was probably something we ought to try. He was so intent on it that I didn't want to be the one to frustrate him about it and I have to admit that it did sound like it might be an exciting thing to do.

Getting Started

Dennis: After we had talked it over several times, I called one of the clubs that advertises in the *Free Press* and it was amazingly simple. They just asked me some questions about us, as they put it, to try and put us in a group that would be compatible. They had an initiation fee of $50.00. I didn't know whether we were really going to stay with it and I talked the guy into giving us, letting us pay $25.00 for membership with the agreement that I would pay the rest if we continued. Then he gave me a telephone number to call to give me the location of the next party and explained we would be charged $5.00 for refreshments and mixers and that we should bring our own liquor if we planned to drink. Another thing that was very important was, he said there is absolutely no pressure to participate, and the whole thing was built around the idea of freedom, sexual freedom which he said is freedom not to engage as well as freedom to engage—whatever you want.

Martha: Yes, I think that was pretty important to me because I was really worried about the whole thing. I felt better knowing that I wouldn't have to do anything if I didn't want to. In fact I had made up my mind that I would go along with Dennis, but that I really wasn't going to get involved with anybody there, sexually I mean.

When we arrived, a little bit late, at this party we were introduced to the people; everybody was just sitting around the living room talking, having drinks, there was music, some people were dancing. I think there were only five or six couples at that party. After we were there awhile I began to feel fairly comfortable, I don't know what wild ideas I had gotten into my head about what the people would be like but they turned out to be very average, ordinary people like ourselves. The conversation was just the sort of usual thing you would find at any party, at least at first. Later on there seemed to be one couple that we were fairly compatible with and they began to ask questions about whether or not we had ever swung before and we go into kind of a whole conversation about that, about how they got started. I felt better when the woman described the same kind of feelings that I'd been having, about being scared and concerned about how it might turn out.

After awhile couples began to drift off into the various bedrooms. I think there were three bedrooms in the house. This couple we were with didn't seem especially interested in getting started in the sexual activity, for which I was thankful because we could continue just talking with them. I kept watching Dennis with that kind of heart-in-my-throat feeling, waiting for him to make some move but he didn't seem all that interested either.

Dennis: Well I think I was pretty scared myself, I had been pretty confident when I was talking about it, but once you're right up against it, that's a different story. So I was pretty content to sit and talk.

Martha: Then some people came back from the bedrooms and I guess it was sort of strange, I knew what they had been doing—but everybody being so easy, comfortable, that I really didn't think that much about it. In fact, a little later there was a funny thing; I guess at that time there were two other couples beside us sitting in the living room talking, and this woman came down the hallway naked, she just kind of stood there with her hands on her hips and, in a kind of kidding complaining tone stated that she needed another man right away; and, of course, one of the men in the living room with us quickly obliged. I think they went into the nearest bedroom because in a few minutes we could hear her sighing and moaning while the rest of us were carrying on an ordinary conversation. It was kind of weird, but at the same time it was a very comfortable kind of situation and I think that was fortunate for us. It gave us time to kind of get into the mood of the whole thing; but later on, I guess it must have been about eleven o'clock, I was dancing with one of the men and I noticed that Dennis had disappeared. When this man asked me if I'd like to go into one of the bedrooms I just thought why not? I can't say that I was terribly excited but I began to feel some of the sexiness of the party and it was just easy, that's about the only way I can describe it.

Dennis: I was worried when I went off with this other woman, but I felt that we really had to make the plunge, and I had the feeling that if we didn't go ahead with it that night we would probably back off and never do it. It's like if you're scared of something and you just back away from it, then you just get more scared. I hadn't felt awfully excited about this woman, but when we got into the bedroom I found myself getting very, very excited, and I really got a big charge out of it.

Martha: I had the same kind of feeling. I was not very much aroused by this man, but then, when we got into the bedroom he was very patient and as things kept going I found myself getting quite excited. It was really just so different and when I finally got going I was really ready I guess, because I had several orgasms in a row which I don't usually do; but what was really important was that there wasn't any pressure. I think that if someone had tried to get me into the bedroom right after we arrived there I would have just frozen up.

Dennis: Then after we got home we were still very excited. We had sex together and it was much more exciting than anything we had had in many years.

Martha: Yes, that's right, I think the only bad moment that I had was when I came out of the bedroom and saw that Dennis was back in the living room and our eyes met and for a moment I couldn't look at him, but then I looked again and I could see that everything was all right. Then when we got home we were really hilarious . . . laughing and giggling and both just feeling real excited so that when we had sex together it was just wonderful. It was more like it had been in the beginning when we were so terribly excited about each other.

The activities

Martha: Well after that the floodgates were open; I mean it's kind of like losing your virginity, once it's gone, you're suddenly kind of free. There isn't anything that has to be protected anymore. So over a year we were like most of the other couples we talked to. Really into it. It was like every weekend, sometimes two parties on a weekend, we were like children with a new toy. We just had a wild, wonderful time. We stayed pretty much with the group thing. We did meet one couple and had relationships with them on the side, but it really wasn't as much fun, and it seemed to be getting somewhat involved, so we cooled it. Then after about a year or so we began to taper off because it was just getting to be too much of a good thing, I guess, and we found we weren't as interested as we had been.

We haven't given it up and we still enjoy it, but we're going a lot slower now. We go to a party every month or two and that seems to be enough. Also, if you go all the time, you keep running into just the same people over and over again, where if you space it out, by the time you return to the group, there are always some new people and that makes it more interesting.

Dennis: We stuck pretty much to man-woman normal intercourse kind of thing. We experimented a little with three-somes and with several couples in a room, but our style seems to be more just the one to one kind of thing.

Problems

Dennis: I can't think of anything in the way of problems that we've run into. We mentioned our anxieties the first time. We haven't had that since then. There are some minor things, just like, you have to be careful who you talk to about it and, at first, there was a little concern about maybe being raided by the police, but we soon found out it just doesn't seem to happen. Martha's on the pill—so no worries about her getting pregnant or anything. Sometimes we run into some kinky people who make an evening sort of unpleasant, but you don't have to get involved with them and that doesn't happen much in the groups we go with. We've seen some jealousies crop up in some other couples, but we haven't had any problems with it.

Dr. Ziskin: Can you tell me about some of the jealousies you've observed?

Dennis: I think it happens mostly if somebody seems to be getting too much involved with one other person. Like, there was this man who seemed to have a big thing going for Martha, whenever they were at a party that we were at, he would always head for Martha right away, and after a few times, his wife blew up and made a big scene, and we never saw them at another party did we? I don't know if they gave it up, or just found another crowd. I think maybe I did have a little feeling about it too. It's kind of, well, you know, with these group things, it's just kind of spread around. And when you see two people, well, it was mostly him, Martha wasn't doing anything. When you see somebody getting too interested in your wife, I guess you get a little worried or angry, I don't know.

Martha: The only other problem that I can think of is that after awhile there may be times when Dennis would want to go and I wouldn't, or the other way around, and we worked that out by agreeing that if one of us wanted to go we would both go to the party, and, like, if I didn't want to do anything sexually I just wouldn't. As we said, the way these groups were that was okay. I could just sit and talk. Or, if it was the other way around, if I wanted to go with somebody, we would just do that. I'm sure they wouldn't let us do that all the time, but they knew we weren't holding out and that if one of us didn't want to swing it was just because we didn't feel like it that night, and that was okay. We noticed some other couples seemed to have the same kind of arrangement and the funny thing is that sometimes we'd both go to a party and not swing. We'd just go and neither of us really felt that we wanted sex with anyone else then, so we'd just sit around and talk and have an enjoyable evening. I think there's a certain bond that develops between swingers.

Effects

Martha: I think it's been good for us, it's put life into our marriage. It certainly picked things up sexually, I mean between us as well as the other. I think also it's something we could share. Like, I know there are a lot of couples where they both play golf or bridge or whatever and we don't have anything like that, I guess we're ballers. So it's something that we share and it gives us an interest in common that we have and I think it's been good for our relationship all around, don't you think so?

Dennis: Yes, I agree with that. I think we're closer than we ever were and I think that we're, well, closer, and more comfortable with each other. And I know for myself there's this other effect. Like I said, before I used to be bothered by the temptations that came my way and I'm not anymore because I know I can satisfy any desire for variety that I have without having to do it behind Martha's back; so I think that's helped me to be more relaxed.

Martha: One thing I guess I should mention. You probably have heard this from other people, but I've had the experience that they talked about, where it was the man who talked the woman into it, but then the women really go wild about it. I've been through that myself. I have to say that I was sort of shocked to find out how strong my sexual desires were, but it's true women really go for it. Not all of them, but most of them. I think some of them continue swinging more or less to please their husbands, but I think the majority are like me. They really get to like it.

TWO BY TWO: GUS AND JANE

Gus and Jane practice swinging in the two-couple mode. Gus is fifty-two years old, he is tall, trim, tanned, with iron gray hair, a handsome distinguished-looking man. He is an advertising executive who was married once before for ten years. There were two children of that marriage who resided with the mother but who are now adults. He has a bachelor's degree in business administration. He has had considerable sex experience.

Jane is thirty-eight, somewhat tall, with a figure that would grace a movie star. She is not pretty but has an attractive intelligent face. She has a master's degree in English and was on the staff of an advertising agency before her marriage to Gus. She is not employed now, but is active in civic and cultural organizations. She also devotes a good deal of her time to entertaining, giving dinner parties, for example, in connection with her husband's business. This is her first marriage and she was a virgin when she married Gus. Neither came from strongly religious backgrounds and are now "practicing agnostics." They have been married thirteen years and have two children, a boy of nine and a girl of six. Their income is in the $20,000-to-$40,000-a-year bracket. They have been swinging for about five years.

Motivation and Getting Started

Gus: We didn't plan it or really work it out; in fact, we hadn't really talked about it except in a joking way. From time to time Jane had been kidding me about the fact that I was the only man she had ever been to bed with, and wondered what it would be like with someone else. I kidded back by saying we ought to look into wife-swapping, but neither of us took any of it seriously. Later on, when we could look back and talk about it, it became clear that Jane was speaking the truth in a joking way and she really was curious about having an experience with another man, and that I really was interested in having more sexual variety. We had done just about everything together that there is. In my first marriage, which wasn't a very good one, I had cheated a good deal, but I hadn't done any of that with Jane. So I think I was just ready for some variety and, as I said, Jane really did have a desire to find out what it would be like with other men.

Anyway, one night these friends of ours, very good friends of ours, were over and we all had a lot to drink and were feeling pretty high and I got the bright idea that the two girls should do a striptease. Everybody seemed to think that was a great idea, so they did. Ralph and I just sat back and made ribald jokes like you hear at the burlesque house, and it was a ball. Then, when they were naked they thought it would be funny as hell if Ralph and I did a striptease so we went through a kind of satire on it and suddenly there we all were with no clothes on. Well, Ralph just grabbed Jane and started making love to her and I was feeling pretty horny myself by then so I grabbed Lucille and that was it. It just happened.

Jane: I think it's terribly important that it happened that way. I don't think I could have gone through with it if it were something we had planned ahead. I would have been sick with worry about how we would feel afterward and everything like that. This way it just happened and, later, we were all sitting around drinking coffee and we just felt very warm and close and merry. I had always been sort of straightlaced, almost prudish. When I was a younger woman I was sort of skinny and spindly and I didn't think I was at all attractive and I think I developed a kind of looking-down-my-nose attitude towards sex. It was only after Cathy was born that I put on a little weight and my figure filled out. Most women worry about getting the weight off after they have a baby but it just happens to look good on me. Anyway, I think this is the first time in my life I was totally able to let go sexually. I felt utterly and deliciously wicked and wanton. Then, after that, it was easy to continue, once it's done it's done and when you find out that everything's okay you just don't worry about it anymore.

Activities

Gus: We went on with this couple for about six months, and there was an all-around great relationship; we were enjoying it, they were enjoying it. We'd get together once or twice a month and, then, one time, we went down to Las Vegas for a weekend together and that was a ball. Then Ralph was transferred back East and that kind of put us out of business. But after awhile we began to miss the activity and we started talking about trying to find another couple although we had some doubts as to whether we could really be as comfortable with a different couple. Finally we started answering some couples' ads in the *Free Press* and, eventually, met another couple that was compatible.

Jane: We're very discriminating; neither of us wants to do it with just anybody for just the sake of doing it. We have to find that the people are attractive and that we are simpatico with them. We had a rule that we just wouldn't swing with a couple the first time we met them. Usually, what we would do would be to invite the couple to our house for cocktails and that way we could sit around and talk for a couple of hours and get acquainted and, then, after they left, Gus and I could discuss it and see if they were a couple we wanted to go further with. We had a lot of difficulty finding couples right for us, but we did find them. I don't think we had as long a relationship with any other couple as we had with Ralph and his wife. Some of them went on for two or three months, and other times there would be couples we would swing with just once. Sometimes it was our choice and sometimes this was apparently their style— just one-time things.

From some of these couples we learned more about the swinging game and we learned about clubs and different ways of meeting couples. We went to one commercial-type party and got very turned off by the people there; they just weren't our type. Then we heard about one of the swinging bars in the Valley, and we went there and got to know the owner and his wife pretty well. They introduced us to some people, and that actually turned out to a good source of couples for awhile because the owner knew what we were like and he would make an effort to introduce us to couples he thought would be compatible for us. I think, also, we found it a somewhat more relaxed way of getting acquainted with people. After all it's a crowded place and there's the music and dancing and so on, so there's a little less tension than there is when you invite a strange couple to your home.

We haven't done any of the more exotic things swingers do, like threesomes or mass orgies. I don't think we'd care for anything like that. Oh, we have another rule, which is that we will only swing together, that is in the same room. I think Gus could go either way but I feel more secure when he's there and I think it makes more of a sharing kind of thing out of it.

Gus: Well, yes, that's true. I think I could enjoy it either way. I think I understand what Jane is saying and I feel quite satisfied to do it that way. There are some advantages and some disadvantages of course, in being together. The advantages, aside from Jane's feelings of security I guess, is like sort of the voyeuristic thing and, maybe, some exhibitionism, but at the same time that gets to be distracting. I think what we found was that the first three or four couples we swung with we were pretty much involved with paying attention to what was going on on the other side of the bed. After you've seen it a few times, it becomes less important, and at least I'm finding I'm concentrating more on myself and the partner I'm with. Of course, every once in awhile somebody comes up with something new and different; a different move, different approach, different technique, and then this is interesting to pay attention to. As I said, I've been around a good deal, and thought I knew everything there was about lovemaking, but I must admit that through swinging I've learned some things I didn't know about.

Jane: I think that there's another aspect to being together, it makes it a kind of fun thing, sort of a lark, where I think if people go off into separate bedrooms and there are just the two of them, somehow, at least for me, that has a more personal and a more serious kind of connotation. I think two people alone is just more intimate you know. I reserve that kind of lovemaking for just Gus and myself.

Problems

Jane: I don't think we've had any particular problems between us in regards to swinging. Occasionally, we've disagreed about a particular couple. For example, I might like the man and Gus wouldn't like the woman, or more commonly I guess, Gus might be interested in the woman and I wouldn't want to swing with the man. So there have been occasional disappointments or frustrations of that kind. I really think the biggest problem we've had is finding compatible couples. It really takes an amazing amount of time and effort reading the ads, answering them, or placing them, or trying to sort out the responses and then setting up meetings with the other couples. I would guess if you find one couple out of thirty or forty that is compatible, you're really doing pretty well, which means you spend an awful lot of time with people you really don't care for, although sometimes you meet a couple and you know very quickly they are not right and you break it up pretty early. But even then, usually you have to be sort of polite, so it's hard to break off in less than an hour. Then, there have been some cases where the people have been pleasant enough to be with. It's just that we didn't want to swing with them.

I suppose there's the other side of it, though, that we've had some pretty hilarious encounters too, at least we thought they were hilarious. Well, like for example, this couple that sent us pictures of themselves and they really looked quite attractive and, then when they showed up, well to say the least, they were obese and they mumbled some apology about the picture having been taken a couple of years ago or something like that. Of course, we got rid of them in a hurry and after they left, we just cracked up—the idea they thought they really might get away with something like that. But I suppose, as they say, hope springs eternal. Then there was another couple where our correspondence had been very dignified on a high intellectual plane, and they sounded as though they would be very charming people and, then, when they came over, the guy was barely inside the door before he had his hand up my skirt. I suppose he thought that women really liked to be handled that way, maybe some do, but I don't. We got rid of them.

Gus: Then there was the Orange County couple—that was really an experience. This couple came up from Orange County, which, as I guess you know, is a generally pretty conservative area, and they were pretty ultra-right-wing, dyed-in-the-wool conservatives. Well, when you meet a couple this way, you usually spend at least the first hour talking just general conversation. You don't talk about swinging right away, and so we got onto politics and the state of the nation, and so on. Well, we're politically and socially liberal, I guess you could call it, and this couple was just carrying on about keeping the blacks in their place and all the sins of welfare and the lack of morals today, and they were up here with the idea of jumping into bed with us, so it just seemed to strike us funny.

Jane: Yes, then other funny things happened to us. Like one couple we met and they seemed okay, and we made arrangements to meet them again. Of course, everybody understands that you expect to swing on that occasion. I think they were new at it, weren't they, Gus? Yes, and I think they felt awkward; so this fellow had some stag films and he thought that maybe that would be a good way to work into the situation. He got his films and his projector and we had a couple of drinks and we were sitting around talking. Finally, he suggested showing the films, and we weren't really interested in that, but, we figured fine, if he's going to be more comfortable then let's do that. He started to set the thing up, and he couldn't get the projector to work, so he started fussing with it and I guess an hour went by. I think the problem was he couldn't get the bulb to work, and he started calling to see if there was a drug store open where he could get a bulb. Finally, his wife just walked up and smacked it with her hand and the thing started to work. I guess the light bulb had been loose. Anyway, by that time nobody was in much of a sexual mood so we kind of unanimously decided to pass on the whole thing.

There is one other problem I was going to mention. It's just my problem, but I get terribly tense when we're going to meet a new couple. I don't know what it means or why I do it, but once we set things up to have a meeting I get very tightly wound up, literally sick with tension, all during that day. And then, if we arrange to meet again, I have the same thing the day of that meeting. Once we've swung with a couple it goes away, but before then I just have never been able to control that tension.

Gus: I think it's the same kind of thing that athletes get, pregame tension and then, I think, like athletes, once you get into the game, the tension goes away.

Jane: You may be right, but I suppose it's got something to do with how I'm going to be evaluated and how I will come across, so I suppose there is a performance aspect to it. It doesn't stop me—I enjoy what we do and I wouldn't give it up—but I wish I could do something about the tension.

Dr. Ziskin: You haven't mentioned anything about the feelings you might have about it, like jealousy or, you know, Gus, how you feel about another man having sex with your wife, or how Jane feels about you having sex with another woman.

Gus: No, there isn't anything like that. You just can't go into this if you're into that bag, it could never work. I think we're very secure with each other, we know our marriage is good, and if I were jealous or if Jane were jealous, or if I worried about the other guy being better in bed than I am, if he had a bigger thing or whatever, you just can't. I think what really has to get across is, it's not that Jane is being unfaithful to me with another man, there isn't any unfaithfulness involved. We're doing it together and we're both doing it.

Like, in relation to the other man, okay he's screwing Jane but I'm screwing his wife, so where's the competition? I think another thing is, and it's our experience and we've talked to other couples about it, that really doing it with somebody else is not quite as good as doing it with your own wife. It's a different kind of thing, enjoyable for what it is. It certainly provides fun and variety, which we like, but oh, I don't know, we've swung with maybe thirty couples and if I had to pick one woman to have sex with I'd pick Jane. But that doesn't mean that I don't enjoy it with these other women; I do.

Jane: I would say the same thing. It's a different kind of excitement and a different kind of experience with somebody else. I'd say the same thing as Gus—that for the best sex I'd pick him. There is so much more to it when it's just the two of us.

Effects

Gus: Well, obviously we think it's a good thing for us or we wouldn't be doing it. I think a time comes in a marriage when you need some sort of pick-up, and this had done it for us. After a certain number of years, you do get into a rut, and you're just used to each other, and I think we were about at that point. I don't mean that there was anything wrong with our marriage. I've had two experiences now, and I know that this is a good marriage. We like what we have, but I think if we hadn't gotten into swinging I might have started cheating again, sooner or later. For one thing, I have been used to a certain amount of sexual variety, and I think when you've once had that, it's hard to be satisfied limiting yourself to just one person.

Then, I was getting older and beginning to have thoughts about how many good years do I have left, and knowing that there's more out there and I suppose, well, I was going to say selfish, but I don't really think it is, the feeling of wanting to have all that I can. So I think this is really much better—it beats cheating—and when I did it before, I was never really comfortable about it. It's something you do, and you justify it one way or another, and you give explanations to yourself, but cheating is still cheating, and I think—well, I know for myself—and I think most people probably would rather be honest if they could, and this just allows us to be honest.

Then, another thing, I'm sure you've heard this from other people you have talked to, I know we've talked to other couples about it, it does juice up your own sex life. There's no question about it. I don't know that I can really explain it, except I think you have a much more sexual orientation, and it kind of breaks you away from the domestic routine. We had the kids and we were pretty involved with them and with the usual domestic stuff. It loosens the bonds of matrimony without untying them. Maybe that's a good way to put it. It sounds like a slogan.

Jane: I agree with what Gus has said—that it made for an improvement in our marriage—and I certainly agree it has sparked our sex life, which I think had begun to lag a little. It's hard to describe without giving the wrong impression. Our marriage was really alright, and I think we could have easily stayed with it the way it was, but I think it's better now than it would have been. One thing, maybe it's different for me than for Gus, is that I really feel more secure about our relationship since we've been swinging. I knew about Gus's former marriage, and while I didn't think he would cheat on me, you can't help having a little concern about it when you know someone has done it before. I think there is also some security in just the sheer survival of us. I guess, I mean, here I've seen Gus with another woman many times, and he's seen me with another man many times, and after all this we're still together, and we feel happier than we ever have been. You just get a very secure feeling out of it, like you really feel like you're okay. I guess there's a funny paradox between Gus and me. He says he was used to variety and he felt he needed to have more of it. On the other hand, here I had no other experiences, and I felt the need for that, I really think if we hadn't gone into this, I don't think I would have cheated on Gus, I don't think I would have had the nerve—but I think I would have grown more and more frustrated about it. Feeling that I had led a very limited life, not knowing anything about sex with other people. That's another thing. I think swinging has helped me to develop sexually—I mean Gus mentioned it earlier. Different people make love in different ways and you're bound to learn things, not only about technique, but about yourself.

EVERYTHING BUT THE KITCHEN SINK:
AL AND MAGGIE

Al and Maggie swing in all ways, shapes, and forms. Al is a forty-seven-year-old administrator employed in a government agency. He is a large man with a slight tendency towards corpulence. He was born and raised in Europe and was sexually sophisticated by midadolescence. He had been married before, divorced, and the children of that marriage are adults. He holds a bachelor's degree in business administration. He had been involved in swinging prior to the end of his former marriage. In that instance, swinging was an unsuccessful, last-ditch effort to save the marriage. He has a great deal of sexual experience.

Maggie is forty-four years old, and is a legal secretary. She is a petite, charming, although not pretty woman. She's had two years of college education, and is a very bright, articulate person. She was also married before and had two children, both of whom are now adults. She was a virgin prior to her former marriage at age eighteen, but between the divorce and her remarriage, she had considerable sexual experience. Both had religious upbringings, but neither have any involvement at all with their religions. Their income is in the $20,000 to $40,000 a year category. They have been married for six years and have been swinging from the beginning.

Motivation

Al: If you ask why, I would just say, why not? We like sex. We like swinging so we do it, that's about all there is to it. We don't have any sexual hang-ups. We're not religious, and we think life is to be enjoyed, so we just go ahead and enjoy it. I mentioned before that I had gotten into swinging before my divorce, so I had a taste of it and found that I liked it.

Dr. Ziskin: I meant to ask you, did swinging have anything to do with the divorce?

Al: Not really. Well, maybe, in a way. I think we would have been divorced anyway, but I guess swinging put the last nail in. We didn't have a very good marriage, I think. I don't mean to knock marriage, but I think most marriages aren't very satisfying; but we had the children, we had the house and the usual paraphernalia, and so, you know, you just kind of stay in it. I know that I wasn't very satisfied. Then, about a year before we got the divorce, I just told Shirley that I couldn't see spending the rest of my life like that and I wanted to have more action sexually.

Of course, she went through the whole scene—anger, tears, martyrdom, but I had pretty well had it by then and I have to say I didn't care too much. Anyway, we talked about the various possibilities and I guess maybe I cared a little more than I thought, because I thought maybe swinging was the thing. There might be something in it for her too, so I pretty much twisted her arm. I think she went into it with the feeling that it was probably the only way to save the marriage if it could be saved.

So we got into it and we went to a few parties and I enjoyed the hell out of it. Shirley, on the other hand, never liked it. It was really a chore for her, like doing the dishes; it had to be done so she did it and got it over with. Like, we'd go to parties and she'd get with one guy and get her clothes off and do it, put her clothes back on and go sit out in the living room the rest of the evening. It was just a token sort of thing with her, and after about a year of it she just couldn't take it anymore, and by then I think she was blaming me for getting her into it so there just wasn't anything we could go on with; so if you want to say swinging caused the divorce, okay.

After that I was probably lucky that I was able to continue swinging with some of the people I had known before. They don't usually like single men around, but I'd already been in it and they knew me and as they say in the trade I'm well endowed, and I have the stamina to go four or five times a night. So with all of that I was still acceptable at swinging parties and I did it for years after my divorce. I told Maggie before we were married that I was a swinger and that I would like to continue with it, so it was no big shock to her.

Maggie: I wouldn't say it was no shock to me, it's just that it wasn't something he popped on me after we got married. In fact, we talked about it quite a bit before we were married until I was clear in my mind that it was something I was willing to try, but I think, knowing what I know now, that Al's "why not" would go for me too. I was a virgin when I got married the first time and spent six unhappy years with the man until he finally left me, and then I spent another twelve years raising the two boys by myself, supporting all of us and just living a very constricted life. When the younger one went off to college, that was about two years before I met Al, I was fairly young and I made up my mind that I was really going to live it up and make up for all the years of deprivation. I began to date in earnest and I think I wound up in bed with almost every man I dated, I would guess it comes to somewhere in the neighborhood of fifty in those two years. I was in no hurry to get married again. I was pretty self-sufficient. I'm good at my work and it pays well so I didn't have to have a man to take care of me financially. In fact, I hadn't had one to take care of me for a long time. Anyway, the point I'm making is that I didn't have any great chastity to preserve, color me crimson. Also, I should mention I had a hysterectomy, so there was absolutely no concern about pregnancy. That makes a big difference. I think I was coming off it a little when I met Al and I don't think either of us was particularly looking to get married. We certainly didn't need to get married for sex, but we started going together and it was a very comfortable kind of relationship. Al is a very easygoing, comfortable guy to be with. He's not very demanding and he respects people's individuality. We just seemed to enjoy being together and, after a while, it seemed very natural to get married. When we made that decision, that's when Al told me about swinging and I think I was shocked, but the more we talked about it the more reasonable it sounded to me. We were really quite free, we had no obligations except to each other and if it were something that we both could enjoy, there it is again, why not?

Activities

Maggie: What do we do? Just about everything. We've swung in groups, we've swung with just another couple, we've had a couple of long-term relationships with just one other couple, we don't have any particular pattern. I think the only rule we have is that it should be mutual. I don't know how much detail you want, sometimes we do it in the same room, sometimes we do it in separate rooms, sometimes we'll go off into separate rooms the first time and then we'll all come back to the same room for a second round. This weekend we are going out on a boat, one of the couples we know has a pretty good-sized boat, and there are five couples and we'll take the boat and go over to Catalina and it will be a swinging party for a couple of days. We've done threesomes and foursomes.

Dr. Ziskin: What's a foursome?

Maggie: God, I'd have to draw you a diagram, diagrams in fact, because there's more than one way. Okay, do you know what a daisy chain is? For example, I might french the other guy while he frenches his wife who's frenching Al who's frenching me. Then you can reverse the pattern so that everybody gets a little of everybody else. You lie on the bed at right angles to each other, you sort of form a square, I don't know if it would be fair to describe it as a "square" activity. (*Laughs.*) Yes, then there's making love with another woman, there's quite a bit of that in swinging groups. The first time it happened I was absolutely shook up, I wondered if I was a Lesbian, but it was very clear to me that I'm not. I enjoy sex much more with a man than with a woman but that doesn't mean that I don't also enjoy it with a woman. The lovemaking has a different quality to it, a different kind of sensual quality.

Al: I started to try it once, too, another man, just to see what it would be like, but it only took about ten seconds for me to find out that I didn't like it, so I stopped.

Problems

Maggie: We don't have any psychological problems about it, no guilt or shame or anything like that, no concern about whether we're psychologically alright. One of the things that happens is that after you've had a number of experiences with other couples who are really quite respectable, decent sort of people, it becomes clear that there just isn't anything to be disturbed about. I know that some people think people who do this must be sick, but it just isn't so. I think the biggest problem, I'm sure other swingers have told you this, is making new contacts. Not that we don't enjoy swinging with the same people—we swing with the same people we have been swinging with for three or four years. I guess, the aim of the game is variety, so part of the fun is doing it with new people, and part of the fun in that is making the contacts, going through a courtship period until you find out whether these are people you want to swing with. So that takes time and effort, writing letters, telephone conversations, meetings.

We like to meet a couple outside of the home, on neutral ground like a cocktail bar. We've tried inviting couples over to our house for the first meeting but then if you don't want to go with them, it gets to be awkward and sometimes it drags on for hours and you can't get rid of them. So if we meet in a bar and we don't think we're interested, we can make an excuse after a polite period and leave. You may find this amusing, but most couples have worked out a system of signals between themselves, so that they can let each other know if they're interested in swinging with a couple or not. For example, Al and I have a system where after a little while—usually in a half hour or so—you can really tell if you're interested. I'll take off one of my rings and put it down on the table and that tells Al that I'm interested. If I'm not interested, I take off both rings and then he knows that I'm not interested. It's a sort of "one if by land, two if by sea" system. If I give him the go ahead signal then he starts twisting his watch if he wants to go ahead, if he doesn't want to he just folds his hands together and we don't go any further with them.

Al: Even then problems develop. Sometimes you may misjudge people or they may have misjudged you. Our rule is once we've made a decision say to go back to our house, it's pretty much every man for himself. It may still turn out that Maggie will make it with the guy and I won't with the woman, or the other way around and you have to be prepared to accept that, and we always are.

Maggie: That tends to happen mostly with couples that are very new at it. Couples that have never done it before, it's a big step for them and they usually have talked about it but they don't really have their heads on straight about it. So, sometimes, when they get right down to the action they want to back out. I think there have been one or two times, haven't there Al, when the woman panicked at the last minute, or the next to last minute and just couldn't go through with it. I've had a few experiences with men, not so much that they wanted to back out as that they just couldn't. They were confused or felt guilty or whatever, but they just couldn't get it up. Of course, that's a disappointment once we've decided to go ahead. I don't have to hold back if Al is having a problem with the woman and he doesn't have to hold back if the man and I aren't making it. If the guy tries and can't, I don't have any hard feelings about it and we just sit around and talk while Al and the woman are doing their thing. Then it's kind of friendly, and I enjoy talking to people. In fact, sometimes we relax that way until the guy gets himself together and we're able to do it later.

There was one time I really got furious though. We had answered an ad and a man called; we talked on the telephone. We have two phones so we can both talk to the people at the same time, and he had indicated that his wife was interested but quite ambivalent about it. They had tried once before and what happened was they sat around talking, and there was so much talk that they just finally talked the whole thing to death. His wife said the longer she sat there the colder her feet got, so he suggested on the telephone that if we were going to get together on it he thought things ought to move very swiftly, that Al should pretty much just sweep her off her feet; he felt that once she had done it she'd be okay. So that was sort of in the background. Then we arranged to meet in a bar and have some drinks. They were an extremely attractive couple and it was just "click," and in about five minutes I turned on to the guy. He was very masculine, intelligent-looking and my motor was running. So we invited them back to the house.

When we got there Al and I had agreed that it would be a good idea if we tried to separate them. With new couples that usually is a good idea because if you're in the same room, they are sometimes so hung up on each other that it spoils everything. So I suggested to this fellow that he help me make some drinks and we went into the kitchen to do that, and my plan was that that would leave Al free to make out with the woman in the living room. I would try to get the guy from the kitchen into the bedroom. It seemed to be working. We went into the kitchen and he immediately grabbed me and we did some pretty passionate stand-up necking, and, as I say, the guy was very attractive and I was ready right then. I mean I would have been glad if he had just picked me up and carried me to the bedroom and gone right on with it. We did this for about ten minutes or so and then I said maybe we ought to go into the bedroom, and he said okay, and he started to just look into the living room and see that everything was okay there. By that time Al had her skirt up and was trying to get her panties off and she was going through this sort of feeble, feminine resistance that women do when they really want it but they don't want to appear willing. So she wasn't helping him any and she was trying to push his hands away, but of course, she wasn't making any real effort to get away. This guy took a look, gasped and just stood there, literally transfixed. I touched his arm and whispered that maybe we ought to let them have a little privacy, and he didn't even reply. I swear I think the man was in a trance. It became clear that all he wanted to do was to watch, which left me feeling like a bump on a log—the proverbial fifth wheel. I didn't know what to do with myself. I'm not much of a voyeur and I wasn't interested in watching, but there just wasn't anything for me to do. I tried to catch Al's eye to signal him to call the whole thing off, because I could feel myself getting angry. But of course, like a skillful waitress, he scrupulously avoided looking my way. I went and sat down in a corner, grabbed a magazine and pretended to read. I kept glancing over, not because I was interested in what they were doing, but because I was just hoping that Al would get it over with in a hurry. He finally exerted himself a little more, got her panties off, and thank God for zippers, didn't bother with anymore undressing himself, and just started to screw her. I was praying, please Al, get it over with quickly. He is so practiced at prolonging it that it just dragged out. I suppose he was enjoying it and not in any hurry. As I say, he managed to make himself quite oblivious to me. Besides, by then she had given up her fine-lady act and was responding quite vigorously.

Meanwhile, my friend, the statue, didn't move a muscle. Finally Al came and got off. She grabbed her panties and went into the bathroom and the statue went kind of limp, staggered over to a chair and just fell into it. I sat there glaring at Al, who gave me a sort of sheepish look and shrugged. Then to add insult to injury, the guy sort of recovered his poise and realized that he had behaved badly and started to apologize to me which just made me angrier. So I just told him that I really just didn't give a damn and that I would appreciate it if he would just shut up. His wife came back and they took a hasty departure, and then I really let Al have it. Although later on I realized that he really hadn't done anything particularly wrong, I was just furious with frustration and anger. I think that was probably the worst experience we had, or I had, I guess I should say. Al seemed to enjoy it enough. Well, that was sort of one of a kind.

We've had some other odd experiences like a couple of times we've been involved with people with sado-masochistic tendencies. In fact, there was this one couple that had come back to

the house and the guy worked the conversation around to
bondage and whips and finally said that he had some fascinating
whips in the trunk of his car. At which point Al and I made eye
contact and made haste to get rid of them. I think I used the
old feminine thing about getting a very sudden bad headache;
but it was just a mild disappointment, it wasn't like the other
thing.

Al: You have to expect the bad experience once in awhile,
if you're into this kind of thing. I would say that in the six
years we've been swinging that we've had four or five poor
experiences.

Effects

Maggie: Well I'll say for sure that neither of us goes around
sexually frustrated. It's hard to evaluate the effect on our
marriage because it's been part of it right from the beginning,
not like most people who get into it sometime later in the
marriage. We have a good relationship, I think. Perhaps at the
time we got married we were a little past the age for being
wildly in love but we do love each other. Awhile back I was
sick, Al was very kind, considerate, devoted himself to taking
care of me. I would do the same for him. We have interests in
common. I don't want you to think all we do is swing, we both
enjoy music and we go to many concerts, we like to travel and,
being as free as we are, we were able to indulge in that together.

Al: I think what Maggie said about the sexual thing is
pretty important. I don't feel sexually constrained. I don't go
around looking for strange pieces. I know that I'm having an
abundance of sex life. I'm saying this because I know from
talking to other men that there is a lot of desire for variety, but
for most people, they are too tied up with the traditional thing
to do it, or if they do it they feel sneaky and they have to make
some excuses that their wife is cold or something like that. So I
think that part of it is being, well, the way Maggie puts it,
pretty comfortable together, and I think part of the reason
we're comfortable is that we're not frustrating each other, or
standing in each other's way.

Dr. Ziskin: Are all of your sexual activities limited to swinging?

Maggie: (Laughing.) No, a lot of our sexual activities are just with each other.

Dr. Ziksin: I mean you don't have any extramarital activity outside the swinging context.

Al: No.

Dr. Ziskin: Do you find the sexual activity just between the two of you is diminished because of the swinging?

Maggie: No; maybe we're both very highly sexed people, or maybe we're just free enough to be as sexual as we are, but we lead a very active sex life together, in addition to swinging.

Dr. Ziskin: Do you think that swinging has improved your own sex life?

Maggie: It would be hard to evaluate that because they have both been going on together all the time.

Al: I think that it probably has an influence because we've been married six years now and there hasn't been any decrease in our sexual interest in each other. I can't say that swinging has improved our sex relationship, I know that other swingers say it has. I think maybe it wouldn't be as good as it is if we weren't swinging.

Three Is Not a Crowd

Many writers include couples that practice the sexual threesome under the category of swingers, and this may be quite appropriate as many swingers, particularly the group swingers, do engage in three-way sexual activity. A study in *Psychology Today* of July 1970, reveals that 15 percent of the men and 9 percent of the women who responded to the questionnaire, had experienced sex with more than one person at a time. This substantial number takes the activity out of the realm of the bizarre and the freakish. However, some of the couples in our sample do not properly fall into the category of swingers, as they practice the threesome exclusively and are never involved in the two or more couples kind of activity. Their motives, satisfactions and practices seem sufficiently different from swinging to justify treatment as a separate category.

THE ART OF LOVE: FRED AND JENNY

Fred and Jenny practice three-way sex as a loving art form. Fred is twenty-six, Jenny twenty-four. They have been married three years, and neither had been married previously. They have no children and do not plan to have any. Fred is an architectural draftsman who is continuing his education with the goal of becoming an architect. Jenny is a teacher of mentally retarded children. They are very much of the younger generation and were quite ambivalent about going through the legal marriage ceremony because of their feelings that it was a ritual that meant nothing and that their real marriage was in the love they have for each other. However, because of Jenny's occupation they felt it would avoid problems to go through the ceremony. They both have bachelor's degrees and are artistically inclined. Both came from Protestant backgrounds, but neither practices his religion. Their income is in the $10,000 to $20,000 bracket. Both had experimented with drugs and various forms of sexual behavior while attending a well-known northern California university. Neither is a hard-drug user, but they occasionally smoke marijuana, and both have been active in the peace movement and women's liberation.

Motivation

Fred: The two of us making love with another person is a special kind of turn on. It's an expanded kind of sexual experience. It's a very warm, loving, sharing thing between the three of us. It's quite different from two people making love because, well I don't know how to put it, there's just more of it.

Jenny: I think that's the essence of it. That if you abandon yourself to the purely sensual feeling there is more outlet for expression. If you think of it as expressive behavior, as we do, an additional person adds another dimension or another color, or another medium to work with.

Getting Started

Fred: It wasn't anything we had planned, it just happened spontaneously. Grace, a girl we had both known in college, was spending the week with us, I think it was about a year after we were married, wasn't it? We had had a good deal of wine with dinner and we were sitting in front of the fireplace, I think with a kind of feeling of lassitude, and we were all sitting very close together and feeling very close. It was raining that night, and we live up in the canyon, and what with the wine and the rain and being up in the canyon that way, I think we had a feeling of being separated for a time from the rest of the world. I had my arms around each of the girls and they were kind of leaning against me with their heads on my shoulders while we talked, and then we were sort of stroking each other and caressing and very gradually it became sexual. We were touching each other more intimately and kissing.

Jenny: Everything just seemed very natural and very right. Nobody said anything, we didn't have to. Grace and I started undressing Fred and then we undressed and then we started making love to him and he was stroking us and then somehow we're all down on the floor and just all making love to each other, moving around and taking turns stroking, touching, and it was just beautiful. A beautiful experience and we were all terribly turned on, and we finally went into the bedroom and Fred had sex with both of us.

We all went to sleep together after that and woke up the next morning with this marvelous, close, warm feeling. Then we were able to talk about it and there was no embarrassment or anything, it just made us all feel close again. So that night, we just took it for granted that we would go to bed together and we did. Then we invited Grace to stay on with us, which she did for about a month. She was kind of at loose ends with her life at that time, but after a month or so we all knew that it was necessary for her to move on, and start putting her own life together.

Fred: After she left, we returned to our normal way of living, but I think the experience had created an appetite for us. We talked about finding somebody else and we talked about trying it with another man, instead of another girl and we thought of answering some of the ads in the *Free Press*; but the idea of that really turned us both off. It is so cold and calculating, and we finally agreed that we wouldn't particularly try to set up this kind of situation, but that we would be open to it if another opportunity presented itself, which it did eventually.

Activities

Fred: Well, I think without consciously planning anything sexual, we were pretty constantly inviting friends up for dinner and most of the people we know are pretty liberated. So eventually we had some other experiences, but it always happens spontaneously, at least without any deliberate planning.

Jenny: Most of our experiences have been with another girl, but we did have one experience with a fellow and you would probably like to know about that. We had invited this fellow we knew from the peace movement up for dinner. We were working on some posters with him and again it all just began to happen spontaneously. It's quite different with two men than it is with two girls because they don't really get involved with each other, and all the attention gets focused on me. It was a marvelous experience for me and I don't know how to describe it exactly, but I think it was, well four hands can do more than two hands, and two mouths can do more than one mouth, and all this loving sexual affection was being lavished on me and I really turned on to it. I think it also helped me to understand what Fred must feel when another girl and I are making love to him, so this heightens my enjoyment of that kind of experience also. I'd like to have this kind of experience again, but it's pretty hard to find men who can get involved with it. I think they have this funny kind of thing though, because I'm Fred's wife, that they sort of back away when it seems to be happening. Girls are really much freer about it.

Dr. Ziskin: How did you feel about that experience, Fred?

Fred: I enjoyed it very much. I think you're asking about my feelings about another man making love with Jenny. I really didn't have anything like that. I think I enjoyed it more when it is two girls, but I enjoyed this because I could see how it turned Jenny on, and I knew how much she was enjoying it, and it was a different kind of experience with both of us getting her excited. I think she described it very well, the difference with another girl is it's all three of us together. With a man it's the two men and Jenny, and that's not quite the same.

Problems

Fred: No problems. When it happens we just enjoy it, we're not hung up on it or obsessed by it and as we said already it's not a dirty thing at all, it's a very warm loving kind of thing. I suppose I should make it clear that neither of us has had any kind of sexual hang-ups since long before we were married, so it's just an enjoyable kind of thing and no harm done and we don't worry about it. I suppose we might be concerned about Jenny's job if anybody found out about it, but it just isn't going to happen. The people we're with are not going to run and tell somebody.

Dr. Ziskin: Well, Jenny, what about any feelings of jealousy toward the other girl?

Jenny: I'm having a marvelous time, why should I feel jealous? We're all doing it together.

Effects

Jenny: I don't think it's had any particular effect other than what we said already about adding another dimension to sex for us. Our marriage is good, it always has been and this just hasn't changed anything very much, except that it's another form of enjoyment for us. Another way of relating to people we like.

WIVES AND HARLOTS: TONY AND LIL

Tony and Lil practice threesomes and moresomes, involving additional men making love to Lil. Occasionally, Tony participates in the lovemaking, but more commonly he watches, and then, afterward, he and Lil make love. Together they run a small theatrical booking agency and dramatic school. They have been married for three years. Tony is forty-six and had been married before. He was born and raised in Europe with a strict religious background, and his first marriage was one that was arranged by the two families. He and his wife were scarcely acquainted when they were married. Neither had had any prior sexual experience and Tony describes himself as having been nervous and inept, and his wife as sexually cold.

Tony became impotent a few years after their wedding, although the marriage continued for some years after that. When Tony came to the United States his wife became quite unhappy and left him to return to the old country. Tony went into analysis in an attempt to restore his potency and it was successful to the extent that he was able to have sexual relationships with prostitutes and women he considered "cheap." He is a tall, dark, thin man, not handsome, but not unattractive, with a gentle manner, but not much sparkle to his personality. Lil, in contrast presents a dramatic, flamboyant appearance and personality. She is forty-four years old, blonde, with a good figure and is almost, but not quite, pretty. She comes from a strict Jewish background, was also married before to a man ten years her senior, and after a period of being, as she put it, "a typical devoted Jewish wife and mother" began to engage in extramarital affairs. She had two children in that marriage, both of whom are now adults. After her divorce and prior to her marriage to Tony she returned to college to complete a bachelor's degree, majoring in drama. She loves show business, has worked occasionally as an extra in films or doing bit parts in stage productions, and is very active with Tony in their business. Their income is in the $10,000 to $20,000 category. Neither is actively religious at the present time, although Lil still observes the Jewish High Holy Days.

Motivation

Tony: I think our settling on the threesome bit goes back to my problem. I told you that I had been impotent. When I was in analysis what emerged was a hang-up about sex with "nice women." I was raised to be very respectful to respectable women and then my first wife had also been raised to be very modest and, I don't know how to put it, to put up with intercourse with her husband, while remaining psychologically a virgin. It was very hard for me to let go with a nice woman, I felt it was wrong, nice women don't like to screw and you're bad if you try. The analyst called it the madonna-whore complex; that's why I was able to do it with prostitutes, or with women I didn't consider respectable. Funny thing, that's actually how I met Lil. I asked a friend if he knew of any broads that were good lays and, among others, he gave me Lil's phone number. When I met her, she kind of threw me for a loop, because she didn't seem to be a hot broad or anything like that. She wasn't what I expected. I think if this guy hadn't told me about her I would probably have gone out with her a couple times, and I would have been very respectful, I wouldn't have tried to touch her.

Lil: Yeah, and I would have thought that I didn't appeal to him, so I probably wouldn't have gone out with him anymore.

Tony: So we finally made it in bed. You know, it was a completely new kind of experience for me. By then I liked Lil quite a bit and I thought she was a very nice person, but she liked to screw and I had no problem functioning with her. I would say that the first time with Lil was probably the greatest sexual experience of my whole life. Then later we knew we were right for each other and we decided to get married, and Lil told me about the affairs she had had before. I was shocked, I don't know why because this guy had told me about her, but it also turned me on sexually. It really opened up communication between us, it got to where we were very comfortable talking about sex. I was able to tell her about the problems I had had and I was even able to tell her that hearing about her sexual activities excited me, and neither of us felt any shame about it. I think it helped to get us very comfortable about sex.

Dr. **Ziskin:**   So you went into this pretty much as a resolution of the kinds of sexual problems you were having, Tony?

Lil: No, you haven't heard my story yet. I was raised as a very nice Jewish girl, a Shirley, like in *Marjorie Morningstar*. Like, when I went out on dates my mother would always warn me not to let a boy touch me. I remember once a boy put his hand on my breast and I thought I was pregnant. She caught me masturbating once and I thought she would die; I thought we both would die, there was such a scene. You know what she was concerned about, that I might rupture the hymen and then I would be a ruined woman. They sent me to college, making it clear that my objective there was to find a husband. After I had been in college a couple of years, when they saw that I wasn't even engaged they became quite alarmed and that's when they introduced me to Irv.

He was a nice Jewish man who went to services every Friday night, was well established in business already, and they thought he would be a good catch. I was inclined to agree with them. I wasn't going anywhere particularly with college, and I really felt that getting married would give me a chance to get out from under my parents' domination. I should give the devil his due and say that I found Irv attractive. He wasn't a handsome man but he had a virile quality. So we planned to get married and I was really looking forward to it, even sexually. I had some fantasies about how it would be and I was pretty excited about it. Unfortunately reality never came close to fantasy. Irv's idea of sex was to roll over on top of me—wham, bam, thank you ma'am—and roll off and go to sleep.

I was frustrated and disappointed, but I kept thinking that there must be something wrong with me, that I was wicked for having the desires that I had. After all Irv was a good husband, good father, good provider, and it wasn't nice for me to feel the sort of lust that I felt. This went on for several years; meanwhile we grew richer, we had a bigger house and I had a maid and a lot more time on my hands. I started going to the races in the afternoon for something to do and I found it exciting. I got dressed to the hilt for it and the inevitable happened. Eventually, a man I had seen there several times started talking to me. One thing led to another and we had an affair. It was quite a different experience for me. He had to woo me sexually, get me turned on, which probably wasn't too hard at that stage—I was going around horny all the time anyway—but, you know, he went to the trouble to court me, get me excited, and for the first time in my life I enjoyed sex. Then, of course, I was overwhelmed with guilt and I resolved never to do it again and, for a while, I didn't. I had tried to get up enough courage to talk to Irv about our sex life, hoping that maybe we could improve it, but I just couldn't bring myself to do it. We just didn't have that kind of communication. I stopped going to the track so I wouldn't get involved with that temptation again, but, as several months went by I began to get restless again. I started dropping into a neighborhood cocktail bar for a drink in the afternoon and, mostly I think, for some companionship. I've never cared for Mah-Jongg or hen parties or things of that kind, and I really needed to do something. And I needed someone just to talk to. I think you'd be surprised to know how many men there are who spend a good part of their afternoons in bars. Anyway, wouldn't you know, the first one I got acquainted with was a bookie, which meant I could start betting on the races again without going to the track. The next step was beddie-bye with him, and then with another man, and I was off and running. I became quite popular—the belle of the bar. I enjoyed it a great deal. I became quite well known there and I was the center of attention. I continued to feel guilty about it, but I was so much in need of attention and some sexual satisfaction that it kept me going. Strangely, most of the time I wasn't getting any real sexual satisfaction out of it. Maybe the guilt I felt interfered with it. Or maybe it was the lack of any kind of real relationship. I don't know. This went on for a few years until I finally realized there just wasn't any sense in my staying married to Irv and we broke up. After that, I felt much freer and became quite promiscuous. I was enjoying sex for the first time in my life and, while I think I continued to be somewhat discriminating, it seemed as though I couldn't get enough of it. I really had not given a lot of thought to getting married again. I went back to school and finished my degree and was trying to get into the theatrical field, and then I met Tony and we just clicked, and I realized that I did have the desire to have someone to be close to. I think an important thing there was the way Tony and I could talk to each other. When we decided to get married, one of the things we talked about and agreed on was that we wanted to be very open to our sexuality. I suppose we were both overreacting to the sexual constriction we had learned, but we both felt that it was very important to be able to have freedom of sexual expression. This may sound strange to you, but we had really come to love each other a great deal and we trusted each other. I think what I mean is we trusted the relationship we had. So we agreed that we would each be free to have any kind of sexual experiences we wanted, either together or apart. For both of us the most important thing involved was the freedom.

Getting Started

Tony: After we were married we decided that we would make a whole new start and we moved to California. Of course we wanted to take advantage of our declaration of sexual independence and started looking for outlets. The first thing that caught our interest was swinging, so we went through all of the preliminary steps; got acquainted with a group and swung a few times. We enjoyed that. I, in particular, was really riding high and I just felt that I—well, as though I had just been let out of a prison, and was just overjoyed to find that I could function and enjoy sex in a free and wide-open manner. Then, as I said, we had been able to be completely open with each other. Lil told me about this fantasy she had of having several men make love to her at once.

Lil: Yes, I had often had fantasies of being the object of love-making by several men. You know, I would get wildly turned on at the thought of having every orifice filled.

Tony: So I felt, you know, if that's something she really wanted, what the hell . . . let's try it. So then the problem was how to work it out. You know, how to get it all together. And this turned out to be more difficult than we had thought. We tried answering some ads in the *Free Press* from men who indicated they were interested in sex with a couple. But they mostly turned us off. Quite a few of them were bisexual, you know, they wanted to play with me as well as with Lil. Some others were just not appealing. Anyway, fate finally provided an opportunity. A rock group that had just come out to the Coast came to us to represent them for booking.

Lil: There were four of them. They were a very sweet bunch of guys and they really seemed lost in the Big City. So, we sort of looked after them and they were broke, so we told them we would put them up at our house until they got on their feet. Of course, there they were living in the house, and one night we were all pretty high and Tony just blurted out that I was interested in this kind of experience. They were a pretty hang-loose group and they thought it was great—let's do it. So we did, and it was just a fantastic experience. There I was and there were men, you know, kissing my hands, kissing my feet and just all over me. And I felt like a queen—a love goddess—and I got unbelievably turned on and, well, I realized my fantasy. Three of them had sex with me at one time and it was enormously exciting and, through it all, Tony was there. He held my hand and I can't tell you how much that meant to me. His hand was telling me that he was with me. That it was okay and that I should just enjoy it.

Tony: That's the way I felt. That it was really just good. That there was something Lil wanted and I wanted her to have it. I didn't feel any kind of jealousy or embarrassment, and I found that I got a big charge out of it also, just watching. I think the fact that we had swung together in the same room and that I had seen her with another man before probably helped there.

Lil: And then, afterward, you would think that I would have been satiated, exhausted, but I was just flying so high that when Tony and I went to bed I was so turned on that I wanted more. And Tony was certainly more than ready, so we had more sex together and it was wild and exciting, wasn't it?

Tony: That's the truth. We felt closer than we ever had before. It was as though sharing this experience had created another bond between us. We didn't repeat that exact experience because, just the way things turned out, I booked the group in a spot up north and their career was launched.

Lil: We talked about the experience afterward and discovered that we both liked this type of activity better than swinging. I think mostly it was the feeling closer and, well, being more together in it than you are in swinging, that was the big thing. So, after that, we looked for similar experiences. We never had the group thing again, but we've had a number of experiences with one other man besides Tony. Sometimes they both make love to me and sometimes the other man makes love to me while Tony watches. I understand this gives him quite a turn-on and I think that adds to my enjoyment. For me, I think maybe the biggest part is the feeling of being the center of attention—having so much attention lavished on me. It really turns me on. Maybe it's the ham in me.

Tony: I find that I liked it both ways. Sometimes I like the idea of both of us making love to Lil, and other times, I think maybe more often, I just get very turned on watching. I don't know what it is. Just the idea of the whole thing. And then, afterward, when Lil and I are alone together, we're both very turned on and I think we feel freer, wilder, more abandoned, than we normally do. We don't do it very often anymore. I think, in a sense, we're freer now because we don't have this compulsion to do it anymore. But I guess we get into it—oh, maybe once every four or five months. Or sometimes it'll be a longer period, and sometimes it may be a couple times in the space of a month. It's just whatever we feel like. We feel free.

Problems

Lil: We just don't have any. I know you probably expect that we must have some, but so far we don't, except there's always the problem meeting the right person.

Tony: I think part of it is that the joy we feel in being free is so powerful that we wouldn't even notice any problems if we have them.

Effects

Lil: I don't know if it's all because of this, but I know that we feel very much in love. We're happy. We feel alive. We're excited about life. You know, we're little fish in a pretty tough business. We don't make much money, but we bounce out of bed in the morning filled with joie de vivre.

Tony: It's a feeling of freedom and togetherness and the fast, exciting, active sex life.

Dr. Ziskin: Earlier you had mentioned that your agreement included separate sexual experience.

Tony: Yes, that's true, but neither of us seems to want it.

Lil: It's really amazing. A few months ago I was rehearsing for a bit part in a show and, you know, you're thrown in with a lot of people, and this man was interested in me and we went out after the rehearsal and I was kind of turned on by him. So, we wound up going to his apartment and, as soon as we got to the door I knew I wasn't going to go through with it—that I didn't want to go through with it. I knew that if Tony had been there I would have enjoyed having this man make love to me, but I just didn't want to do it without Tony being there. So, I don't know what that means, but it's true. Neither of us seems to really have any desire to get involved, you know, apart from the other. I don't think we've ruled it out, and I certainly don't think it's, well, because of any scruples, and maybe at sometime in the future it will happen. But so far we just don't seem to want it. I don't think we feel that it would be as good if we're not together. Being together is a big part of it.

Part III: Origins of Prohibitions

8.
Reasons
and Realities

In the midst of a great social revolution, and in the light of great advances in technology and in sociological and psychological knowledge, it is appropriate to pause and examine the assumptions and concerns that initiated, fostered, and maintained the prohibition against extramarital sexual activity. In this chapter, we shall undertake such an examination of the bases for the rules that have evolved governing the sexual behavior of married couples. In each case, we shall raise the questions: Were the rules ever valid? Are they valid now? What would be the effect of changing the rules?

THE ORIGINS OF PROHIBITIONS AGAINST
EXTRAMARITAL SEX

Nearly all societies place some constraints on the sexual behavior of their individual members. Some of these constraints consist of regulations, codes, and customs concerning the sexual behavior of married and unmarried people. These constraints may range from the very minimal types found in some relatively primitive societies to the absolute prohibitions that represent the stated, if not practiced, American position. The degree of observance of the regulations also varies from society to society, as do the penalties imposed for infractions which can range from a verbal wrist slap or a small fine up to the ultimate— torture and execution. While religion has been most commonly viewed as the source of sexual constraints, many other forces have contributed to current mores and rules in Western society. What, then, are the bases for the development and continued existence of such constraints?

The Needs of Society

Many of the customs and regulations of a society stem from the survival needs of the society itself, as well as those of its individual members. As an example, we may cite the dietary laws of the Jews concerning the prohibition against eating pork and shellfish which, it is popularly believed, had their origin in the danger involved in consuming these foods at a time when refrigeration was nonexistent and when the medical means of controlling trichinosis was not yet available. Yet, there are many Jews who still adhere to these rules as a religious duty in spite of the fact that, today, the dangers are minimal.

Rules that protect the family are also based on survival needs. The survival of the family unit as one of mankind's oldest known institutions, may be traced to the need to protect the young who are the guarantors of the survival of the species. The human infant is helpless and dependent longer than any other animal, and the family makes it possible for him to receive the loving attention that is essential to his survival. It provides for the care of the sick and the aged, and appears to have been the best vehicle for the satisfaction of the human needs for a secure congenial relationship, intimacy, and dependency, and for the ongoing sexual needs of both men and women. Thus, its functions have been biological, social, and psychological. It seems, therefore, most reasonable that society should have created rules of custom, religion, and legislation to protect the family and its expression in the institution of marriage.

In the past, extramarital sex relations have been regarded as threats to the family unit and, therefore, in need of regulation. An awareness of such human emotions as possessiveness, jealousy, and insecurity contributed to this attitude. If we recognize that the earliest societies generally consisted of small nomadic groups, it is not difficult to imagine a high demand and limited supply with regard to mates. Granting that sexual attraction is one component of mating, it seems most likely that sex relations with someone other than the mate would be perceived by the mate as a threat to the union. Those who had mates would fear attempts by those who did not to steal them. At a time when brute force was a principal tool for securing what one needed, the potential for violent interaction between competitors was very real. Violence was a threat to the existence of the society, not only intrinsically, but because rivalries impaired the cooperation that was so essential to the group's survival. Extramarital sex threatened the family unit in two ways: If one spouse took up residence in the tent of a new partner felt to be more attractive than the old, obviously, the unit was destroyed. Secondly, with violence a means of resolving competition, the chances for destruction of the spouse and, along with the spouse, the union, were high. Furthermore, with lack of contraception the chances of "interlopers" entering the family unit were also high, a matter of intense concern to the early Jews from whom much of our moral code is derived.

Another concern of society with the preservation of the family unit relates to the needs of children and the needs of society regarding children. During the periods just before and after giving birth and during the woman's involvement with a new child, both the children and the woman needed someone to protect them and provide for them. This dependency continued during the child's infancy and childhood where its requirements limited the woman's ability to fend for herself. In these early times, when physical strength was important to survival, obviously the services of the male, in the areas of protection and providing food, were superior to those of the female. As societies developed, it was apparent that much of their welfare depended upon the successful training of the young to fill the necessary male and female roles. The training of about-to-mature young men was viewed as an appropriate task for the men and seems to have been the practice in nearly all primitive societies.

Even today, in child-custody matters, the courts are more prone to award custody to the father when the child, especially a boy, is considered to be of an age where "preparation for entering into the adult world" should take place. Thus, extramarital sexual activities of the father could be viewed not only as a threat to the union in terms of its dissolution, but also as a threat to the society should the father find extramarital sex so delightful as to partially or totally neglect to fulfill his assigned role adequately. Similarly, during the child's early years, when the mother is so important both to his physical welfare and normal development, the mother's involvement with others might carry the threat of neglect of the child's needs and of the requirements of the society for the child's development.

There is yet another facet to society's interest in restraining sexual activity, including extramarital sex. As societies become more civilized they require more and more of the time, talents, and energies of their citizens to be devoted to its needs. Numerous authorities have pointed to a relationship between the rise of various civilizations and the existence of sexual constraints. Unwin *(Sex And Culture)* has pointed out that societies on the rise tend to be sexually repressive, apparently on the basis that bottled-up sexual energy will be channeled into productive output. However, when societies have arrived at their "predestined position," a swing toward hedonism and sexual freedom occurs which is frequently accompanied by the decline of the civilization. The rise and fall of the Roman Empire seem to have followed such a pattern. A modern example can be seen in Communist China where extremely strict regulation of sexual activity, even between spouses, is occurring as that nation strives to rise to a position of strength and prestige. During the development of the United States, the atmosphere was generally sexually repressive. The current cries of ultra-conservatives to return to the "old morality" or face the destruction of our society are not entirely without historical foundation.

Of course, the relationship between sexual repression or freedom and the rise or fall of a civilization may represent nothing more than the coincidental occurrence of the two events, without proving anything as to causality. It is, at least, conceivable that there is an inherent boundary to the ascent of any particular civilization. When one has reached the top, become "number one," there may be no place else to go, and the people turn their attention to reaping some of the pleasurable harvest of the attainments of their society. It may be that the momentum required for the sheer survival of a "new" society initially carries it to the top, but once the top is reached the compelling reasons for repression and denial are gone, and hedonistic motivations replace them. Whatever the case may be, in the past it seemed reasonable to argue that because sex consumes the energy of the population, its free expression may deprive the society of some of its resources. Similarly, the devotion of time and talent to the pursuit of sex were thought to detract from the productivity of the society. Thus, many societies have perceived sexual repression as being in their best interests.

If we accept the premise that the family unit is desirable, and ask only whether the extramarital prohibition is essential to its survival, the answer would appear to be a clear "no." The family has survived as the basic unit under a variety of arrangements, both in societies where a multiple number of wives (polygamy) and in those where a multiple number of husbands (polyandry) have been the standard practice. Of course, the multiple sexual relationships in a polygamous marriage do not, strictly speaking, constitute extramarital sex, occurring, as they do, within a marital relationship (although in some of these societies the wife is sexually available to the husband's brothers, to whom she is not technically married). In any event, the point is that multiple sexual relationships do not in and of themselves imperil the family unit. This does not mean that all families are happy ones under such arrangements, or that such arrangements are necessarily the best and are without problems. It does mean that where the wife is having sexual relations with several men, or the husband with several women, under a socially accepted and agreed-upon arrangement, family unity and cohesiveness can be maintained. The degree of unity may vary according to the people involved much as it does in monogamous arrangements.

Of more direct relevance to the effects of extramarital sex on the family unit are those societies which provide structured periods of complete sexual license usually in connection with religious, harvest, or other traditional types of festivals. These are annual periods in which adulterous sexual relationships are not only condoned but expected. No increased detriment to the family unit has been observed in relation to these socially approved extramarital sexual activities.

In addition to evidence which comes from anthropological and cross-cultural studies, some common observations of our own society along with some rather sophisticated research bear more directly on the point. Infidelity, discovered or undiscovered, does not lead to destruction of the family unit in all or even in most cases. Statistical data does not appear to be available, but most of us are familiar with couples where known infidelity has been tolerated. The relationship may suffer because of it, but the family is maintained. J.C. Ibert and J. Charles *(Love the French Way)* received almost 200,000 responses to a survey put to the population of France selected from various regions of that country. They found that approximately 40 to 50 percent of the men and 50 to 60 percent of the women would be prepared to forgive an act of infidelity, although they found the usual differences based on social class and education. In the United States, Julian Roebuck and S. Lee Spray (1967) performed a sociological study of men frequenting a particular cocktail lounge ("The Cocktail Lounge: A Study of Heterosexual Relations in a Public Organization") and found the extramarital sex activities of the men in the study had no disruptive effect on the marriages, although it should be pointed out that the men kept their activities secret, and there was no evidence the infidelity was known to the wife. Cuber and Harroff *(Sex and the Significant Americans)* cite cases of extramarital sex by agreement without destruction of the family unit. Similarly, Bartell *(Group Sex)* found that the incidence of family breakups was no greater among swingers than among nonswingers. In those societies where adultery is either openly accepted or only mildly disapproved of, the family unit is not destroyed unless a pregnancy occurs and only sometimes even then.

Thus, the general picture suggests that the concern that extramarital sex will destroy the basic family unit is not valid. Where such disruption occurs, it seems to be related to severe opposition to the behavior by the society and to the deception—the "victimization" of the spouse—that occurs. It is the element of cheating—the violation of the marital agreement or of the relationship—that seems to be critical. Of course, if one spouse wrongs the other in any respect, not only sexually, the relationship may be threatened. But, if a couple agrees to this kind of activity, where is the cheating? Who is wronged when agreed-to extramarital sex takes place? It would seem, on the contrary, and particularly in view of the amount of infidelity that takes place without agreement, that such arrangements would go a long way towards reducing the disruption of the family as a result of extramarital sex. This result, of course, would be further enhanced when fairly wide social acceptance of such agreements prevails.

If we accept as true that the welfare of children depends on preservation of the family unit, then the discussion in the preceding section should, hopefully, calm fears in this regard. If the family unit is not threatened by agreed-to extramarital sex, then the welfare of children is likewise unthreatened. This does not mean that the possibility of such a threat is nonexistent, but only that extramarital sex, in and of itself, does not solely pose such a threat. Family units will continue to be broken for a variety of reasons.

The possibility that the welfare of children will be affected through their neglect as the result of extramarital sexual activities is another fear often mentioned. However, there is no reason to believe that this is a necessary, or even frequent, consequence of this activity. No doubt there have been and will be cases where neglect occurs as a result of a parent's over-involvement with "affairs." Neglect can also occur as a result of any excessive preoccupation by a parent with any activity—golf, drinking, Mah-Jong, business, painting, or whatever. The parent who is adequately concerned about the child will manage his activities so as to avoid neglect of the child's welfare. The parent who is not concerned, may very well be neglectful. However, the problem then is the parent, not any particular activity.

It should be noted that the historical evidence of a relationship between sexual restriction and the advance of a society maintains as its criteria for "advancement" such categories as conquest, industrial development, and material wealth—criteria which themselves are often related to each other. In the face of a growing tendency for people to search for other values and other meanings of life, the appropriateness of these criteria as measures of the success of a society can certainly be questioned. Military conquest is certainly not a conscious goal of most Americans. Many, especially among the young, are questioning material wealth as a goal of society.

Disregarding these questions of values, and taking a position that the productivity and creativity of its citizens are important to the well-being of the society, the issue is reduced to whether or not a restrictive sexual code is necessary for adequate productivity.

Obviously, time and energy spent in the pursuit of sex reduce the total time and energy available for production. This is particularly true if the pursuit takes place during what would normally be "producing" hours. However, considerable change in working hours has occurred which distinguish the present from the historical precedents. For most of the past, agricultural and early industrial workers worked from dawn to dusk, six or seven days a week in contrast to the fairly typical current eight-hour day, five-day week, with the four-day week looming on the horizon. Similarly, the amount of energy required for a steady diet of twelve- to fourteen-hour work days made the conservation of such energy a matter of considerable concern. It seems likely that only the prodigious could combine such a workload with any appreciable amount of boudoir activity. Perhaps, that is why holidays were invented.

Another line of evidence suggesting that sexual constraint is not essential to productivity comes from modern personnel theory and practice. The professionals and executives involved with the output of employees have generally found that employees who are, in the main, fairly happy or content are the most productive. While some people are able to direct their frustration and attendant angers into productive channels, most people are likely to sulk, withdraw, or channel these feelings into overtly or covertly destructive behavior. A person who is discontented, in general, rarely feels like putting himself enthusiastically into tasks. If reduction of frustration, including sexual frustrations in personal life means happier workers, increased productivity should result.

Further, there are numerous instances of people who have been both highly creative and productive and (at least by their own declarations or those of their biographers) highly active sexually. Even highly successful politicians have managed to carry on in their personal lives activities which they would publicly decry as "immoral"; this category does not even exclude some former presidents of the United States. The point is an important one because we often tend to equate a libertarian sexual approach with a lack of discipline. Yet we know that to achieve success in literature or the arts requires a high degree of discipline. There is strong support from the lives of such people that it is possible to be disciplined, indeed, obsessively hard-working, and quite active sexually, although not always at the same time. It seems quite possible that greater productivity may result from alternating periods of disciplined productive effort with free and unrestricted periods of enjoyment. Even such a minimal gesture in this direction as the coffee break has demonstrated that relaxation and diversion increase productivity. An approach to life that is filled with zest becomes a life-style which carries over into work. The advice of many successful people to work hard and play hard seems sound.

Finally, it seems clear that rules based on conditions existent in small nomadic tribes, perpetuated through periods when survival was a hard proposition, may have little or no relevance in a technologically sophisticated society where the raw material for survival, and even comfort, are relatively easy to come by. What is the basis of pressure for productivity in a society that pays its farmers not to produce? in a society that produces more than it can consume? in a society where at least 5% of the potential work force is unemployed, and an unknown number, such as women, underemployed?

As psychologists, we have generally seen people expand in most or all areas of their lives as a result of the growth and release that takes place in psychotherapy. Increased sexuality and increased productivity and success frequently go hand in hand.

Thus, it appears, generally, that concerns over the effects of reasonable sexual liberality on the material well-being and status of our society are not well-founded.

Religion

Most organized religions participate in the regulation of sexual behavior. This is natural since religions take positions with regard to most important aspects of human behavior and have long been among the main sources and guardians of morality. Religion has been particularly powerful in the regulation of sexual behavior because of its status as a monitor of the spiritual welfare of the people. The mandates of religion have held added force by virtue of the promise of entry into heaven as the reward for obedience or hell for disobedience. For those who are believers, this force must be far greater than could be brought to bear by any other social institution, even the law. In many instances, religion has operated in the interest of and in alliance with the economic and political power groups of a given society, adding the force of civil authority to its own.

Most modern religions have their roots in antiquity. This, of course, is true of the Judeo-Christian religions of which Christianity is dominant in America. It is important to note a particular effect of these roots in antiquity. Most of the "moralities" of the different religions were promulgated thousands of years ago. They may well have been appropriate in the conditions that existed at the time and place of their origin. However, religious precepts are highly resistant to modification as times and conditions change because they are generally presented as "natural laws" given by God. If they are intrinsically "right" and God-given, they are immutable forever and ever. This must be so or religions would have to acknowledge that God, or his earthly representatives, are fallible and faith would be diminshed. Thus, what may have been merely socially necessary or desirable at a certain time has become incorporated into natural law and the Word of God and must be followed no matter how ludicrous or inappropriate in the light of new knowledge and changed conditions. The dietary laws of the Jews may again serve as an example. They were promulgated with good reason at the time of their origin. In terms of serving any objectively useful purpose in a modern society, with all its hygienic sophistication, they are simply ridiculous in the Western world. There is no reason for anyone to avoid properly processed pork. Yet for the Orthodox Jew, the consumption of pork is a sin because, although the bases for the rule have long-since vanished in countries that are medically advanced, the rule is not to be evaluated but obeyed, because it is a moral and religious issue. Bacon with one's eggs may add to the enjoyment of life, but surely is not worth the price of one's soul!

The principal impact of religion on sexual morality, especially in America, stems from the early Christian ethic of emphasis on the spiritual over the corporeal, the virtue of self-denial, and the concept of sex as sin. It does not appear that Jesus concerned himself greatly about sex, but that Paul was the progenitor of the Christian sexual ethic. Paul, personally, apparently took a dim view of sex, viewing abstinence as the key to the ideal life. However, he was sufficiently realistic to recognize that most people could not give up sex totally, and that at least a minimal amount was necessary for purposes of reproduction, so he issued his famous declaration that it is better to marry than to burn in hell, thus setting the stage for the development of the monolithic code which proscribes sex outside of marriage. Later leaders of Christian thought adopted Paul's position so that, for two thousand years, the development of Western civilization, under the domination of Christianity, incorporated these precepts. With heaven or hell as the stakes, and with the vast majority of the people ignorant, uneducated, and trained to obey rather than to think independently, a sexual morality based on these religious principles was inevitable. Purity and chastity became the hallmark of the good person, although these criteria were applied more rigorously to women than to men.

We believe that man needs religion and strongly suspect the time is not far away when a new religion will arise, a religion more capable of accepting man as he is rather than attempting to impose the values of individual religious leaders on him. Such a religion will of course have ideals, but they will be ideals based on a more realistic view of man, God, and the world than those of the ancient religions. But that is for the future. At the present, it is clear that religion has lost much of its influence on human behavior in America, not only among the young, but among an increasingly sophisticated and increasingly disillusioned older population as well.

The old notions of heaven as a reward for being "good" according to the principles laid down by the high priest of a particular religion, and its converse, hell and eternal damnation a punishment for disobedience, are finding less and less acceptance. This is true, even of people who ostensibly remain members of a religious group. The removal of the threat of loss of heaven as payment for a little romp in bed, of course lowers the price for such an activity making for a greater traffic in that particular commodity.

It is evident that a shift away from the antipleasure, suffering-is-good approach is taking place, at least for a substantial portion of the population. The notion of "sex as sin" has all but vanished. Instead, a new set of values is developing. More and more people are finding that pleasure-seeking is good—not as replacement for everything else in life, but as one of many life-goals and activities. This is made possible by the fact that after securing life's necessities, time and resources remain for enjoyment and recreation. More people are finding spiritual development in terms of involvement with social issues and self-actualization rather than in religious virtue and self-denial. More emphasis is given to the enrichment of life through the full development of one's "earthly" self—the search for and experiencing of the multiple aspects of one's self and of others. Since Freud made it possible for respectable people to talk about sex, more and more people have been discovering that sexuality is one very important part of the self.

Along with this shift, there has also been a widespread rejection of authority. Particularly in the area of sex, many people, especially the young, have found the pronouncements of political and religious authorities simply absurd. Helped along by the general views and findings of mental-health and behavioral-science professionals that acceptance of one's sexuality is "good," these people are exploring their sexuality and sexual aspects of life that would have been considered unthinkable for the multitude a hundred years ago.

The validity of the concepts of purity and chastity as promulgated by some religions can also be questioned, particularly with regard to married women. Some authorities have reasoned that the notion of impurity is based on the secretions resulting from sexual activity. If that is the basis, then obviously no married woman could be pure after her wedding night —assuming of course that the usual activities took place on that occasion. If purity and chastity meant sex only with the husband, one wonders about the fairly widespread practice of the jus primae noctis—the right of the lord of the manor to spend the wedding night, or part of it, with the bride, presumably doing something other than discussing current events. This practice was at least condoned by the church. What possible meaning could the concept of purity and chastity have in the light of such practices? Whatever validity such concepts may have had in the past would seem to disappear in the face of the facts of modern life. Modern rejection of the notion that sex or sexual secretions are dirty, renders notions of purity or impurity on that basis meaningless. Further, the increasing prevalence and acceptance of premarital sex, and the devaluation of virginity as a criterion of marriageability have diluted concerns with purity. If sexual intercourse with someone other than a husband makes a person impure or unchaste, then a large number of young women are doomed to such a status before they even have a husband. If purity and chastity mean that a woman (it is women to whom these concepts are nearly always applied, although Christian men were also supposed to come to the marriage bed as virgins) must have only pure nonsexual thoughts, then these notions are simply psychologically unsound. Normal women do have sexual thoughts, fantasies, and desires. To be pure in this sense, would mean to be so repressed, rigid, and inhibited as, probably, to constitute psychopathology.

Finally, there are indications that even the church may be changing its position with regard to extramarital sex. According to *Time* magazine (December 13, 1971) some of the major churches are loosening the absolute prohibition against extramarital sex, and there are indications they are moving in a direction of defining circumstances under which adultery might be justified: for example, where a spouse has suffered permanent mental incapacity. According to the *Time* article, some theologians are challenging the ecclesiastical natural-law doctrine that lies behind the church's moral standards. Such theologians are indicating skepticism that the church can be certain about what "natural" actually is. Of course, once the church moves to a position that there are some conditions under which adultery is permissible, it has entered into the realm of situation ethics. Acceptance by the church of the concept of situation ethics would reduce all questions to the issue of whether people then should decide for themselves what is right in a situation or have it decided for them by the church.

Of course, we cannot say that any given religious principle or teaching is not valid or correct; to the devoutly religious, the teachings are right because they are promulgated by their religion. To the less devout, or the nonreligious, they may be questionable in terms of earthly knowledge or practice. The point which is most relevant to the consideration of a change in married-sex mores is that the influence of religion is diminishing so rapidly that it does not constitute a deterrent to change for large numbers of people.

A Woman's Place: The Concept of Women as Property, Inferior, and Evil

With few exceptions, the rules of societies have been made by men. Very likely this practice had its origins in the early stages of mankind when the possession of the brute strength to enforce his will against women was sufficient to allow man to be the rulemaker. It is also likely that man, as the hunter and protector, could, by force and by threat of withdrawal of his services, dictate the rules. From such bases, social and familial roles of men and women were defined, becoming more firmly entrenched with each generation of practice, even though the conditions from which they stemmed had disappeared. In this manner, most societies became patriarchal with the man as the head of the family unit and with men as the leaders of the social unit. There have been some societies where women held the power and positions of leadership, but these were rare. Taken as a whole, men made the rules. It follows then that, in part, the rules he made governing relationships between the sexes would be determined by his view of women at a given time and place.

One of the most significant perceptions of woman was that she was property. Webster defines property as "something subject to the possession, use, and disposal of another." In the mainstream of history, the definition fits woman. She has been subject to sale, for the purpose of marriage or otherwise, and has even been required to obey the husband to the point of joining her living to his dead body on the funeral pyre. Another male attitude was that of viewing woman as an inferior being, lacking in the capacity for thought and decision. Such beings, like children and animals, were thought to require a firm albeit in some cases loving, hand to regulate their behavior. A third perception of women defined them as the embodiment of evil. This percept is perhaps related to religious and societal considerations. In Christian theology, woman was seen as the temptress, luring man away from spirituality into sensuality, and diverting his energies from activities valuable to society. Given the notion of sex as sin, and the fact that it is a common human tendency to blame others for our own wrongdoing, it is quite understandable that in the bibles which were produced by men, the blame for mankind's downfall should be placed on Eve rather than on Adam.

Because of these various perceptions of woman, operating independently at some times and cumulatively at other times, more constraints were placed on the sexual behavior of women than men, and quite often the penalties for violation were more severe for women than for men. No one ever got rich making chastity belts for men.

However, the place of women in modern Western society and in marriage has changed markedly from its historical past, and the end of change is not yet in sight. It seems quite likely that change will continue until women stand on an equal footing with men socially, occupationally, politically, and sexually. It is true that at present, political and moralistic leadership rests in the hands of men, but women have been acquiring increasing power in these areas, and an accompanying change in the double standard is already in progress. The right to vote, to hold public office, to own property in her own name, to share ownership of family property, and to have equal employment opportunities are evidence of the changing status of women.

The notion of women as property, to be managed and controlled, is a vanishing phenomenon. Fewer men wish to sustain the role of "lord and master" and fewer women will submit to it. Those anachronistic husbands who wish to cling to this irrational, inequitable, unrewarding position that detracts from the mutuality of a marriage relationship, are finding it increasingly difficult to do so. With increasing education and worldliness, women tend to reject such relationships, and men tend to find such women more fulfilling as marriage partners. Women's liberation, both as a social and political force and as a concept will further these changes.

Likewise, the notion of women as "inferior" has been largely exposed for the myth that it is. Women in all aspects of life have demonstrated that they are quite capable of handling themselves as independent human beings without the benevolent paternalism of a man. They have demonstrated their capabilities vocationally, socially, financially, parentally, and sexually. (Of course in the latter case, some sort of cooperative relationship with men is usually necessary.) Of course many women still wish to be cared for and looked after by a man, but, if they do, they must be prepared to accept the inferior status that such dependency always carries with it. For that growing body of women who do not wish such status but prefer to be independent and full partners in the relationship, there is little to prevent them from doing so.

Finally, especially with the waning influence of old religious ideas, the notion of woman as the embodiment of evil finds diminishing acceptance. If woman is indeed the temptress, man is becoming more willing, perhaps even eager, to be her victim. If woman is evil, one need only spend some time in cocktail lounges to conclude that never have men pursued such destruction more avidly. If anything, far from feeling a need to restrict women, men are viewing women's freedom as a blessing from which they can derive much pleasure. This view is not necessarily shared by all men. There are still many who maintain, not only the double standard as between men and women, but also a double standard among women. There is a group of men who divide women into two categories—in one category are those women whose open and free sexuality these men enjoy and encourage. And in the other category, are wives. They like sexually liberated women with whom to have sexual adventures, but cling to the notion of purity and chastity in their wives. Not infrequently this leads to a rather sterile and unsatisfying marital sex life for both husband and wife. And, of course, there are still those men (and women, too) who view sex as evil and dirty and feel that if women, with their greater sexual capability, are restrained, this nasty business will be curtailed if not eliminated. For a growing number of men, however, the liberated sexuality of women is pure joy.

Thus, the changes in the roles and perceptions of women in modern society foreshadow changes in sexual mores. The change is already under way in the realm of sexual freedom for unmarried women. Can similar changes for married women be far behind?

The Law

Quite often the law follows the current mores, lending its force to an effort to make people "be good" by imposing institutionalized penalties for deviations from the moral code. For example, early in this century many states had laws that forced businesses to be closed on Sunday to encourage participation in the religious activities associated with that day. Similarly, laws regulating certain sexual behavior have their origin in the sexual morality promulgated by various religions; for example, the legal prohibition against oral-genital sex between husband and wife, an otherwise harmless activity. Partially on the basis of then current mores, the law also came to regulate extramarital sexual behavior. Criminal sanctions against such behavior are long-standing.

It is important to note that the relationship between morality and law is not a one-way street. Just as the law tends to follow morality, so does morality tend to follow the law. Generally the populace views that which is illegal as bad. To commit a crime is to do that which society has defined as wrong. Thus, a reciprocal relationship develops—that which is "bad" becomes illegal, and that which is illegal is "bad." Laws, once established, are difficult to overturn, partially because of inertia and partially because there always seems to be a hard core of dedicated and effective fanatics who defend the moral basis for the laws even though such basis may be outdated.

Particularly in regard to sexual laws, it should also be noted that, most commonly, laws are enacted and maintained by older men in the society who have a generally conservative tendency to maintain the status quo or "return to the good old days," and who frequently are less motivated towards freedom of sexual expression than younger people. Fear of the younger men as sexual rivals may also be a factor in the reticence of older men to loosen the laws regarding extramarital sexual behavior. Thus, sexually repressive laws tend to persist. Change occurs only when a major shift in public sentiment becomes sufficiently established to exert a strong influence on legislators.

Yet, lawyers and judges are fond of describing the law as a "living thing." By this they mean that the law is capable of changing and adapting itself to social change. Thus, as the law is basically a set of codified mores, it may be expected that it will change in conformance with changes in public mores. The enactment and repeal of the Prohibition law provides an example. The Eighteenth Amendment was an attempt to change the drinking habits of Americans by law. After a brief period, the law had to be repealed because it was unenforceable: The people were determined to drink—law or no. Similarly, in the case of laws against adultery, such laws remain on the books, but enforcement is virtually nil. Public figures, some with and some without divorces pending, live in open and notorious adulterous relationships without prosecution. At one time, in the state of New York, with some 30,000 divorces granted on grounds of adultery, there were less than 300 criminal prosecutions for this "crime." The public at large had little interest in the vigorous prosecution of this offense, and without such public interest law enforcement is likely to be lax. It is doubtful that any great hue and cry would be raised if the adultery laws were to be repealed, although some opposition might come from religious groups and self-styled guardians of public morals.

A movement in the law toward greater permissiveness in sexual matters is already apparent. The Model Penal Code, drafted by the highly respectable American Law Institute, recommends that sexual acts between consenting adults should not be subjected to the constraints of criminal prosecution. While this position has not yet been widely adopted through legislation, its existence indicates that legal thinking is beginning to incorporate social realities as well as the thinking of many behavioral scientists in the area of sexual behavior. Typically, the law is slow to change but such signs as the Model Penal Code, liberalizing of abortion laws, and liberalizing of obscenity laws indicate the course on which the law is embarked no matter how long it may take to reach the destination.

PSYCHOLOGICAL BASES FOR EXTRAMARITAL SEX CONSTRAINTS

The four historical bases of current sexual morality for married people previously discussed—society's needs, religion, status of women, and the law—exert an influence on and become part of the psychological makeup of individuals, and thus, in part, determine their feelings, attitudes, and behavior in regard to extramarital sex. Psychologically, people are an amalgam of biological, personal, and socially determined needs, urges, drives, appetites, fears, and concerns. Social and environmental factors are a major, if not the major, influence on people's attitudes and behavior. Except in those rare times of great social upheaval, such as the current so-called social revolution, people generally tend to be conformists. They grow up in a certain social milieu and typically incorporate the values, attitudes, rules and practices of that milieu.

Americans, for example, in the process of growing up, learn to hold the fork in the left hand while cutting meat, shifting it to the right hand to raise the meat to the mouth. Australians grow up learning to cut and deliver the meat with the fork in the left hand. It would be difficult to find a clear-cut superiority of one method over the other. Each culture continues the practice because it is "the thing to do." It feels right to them. Similarly, with sexual behavior, people tend to follow the practices of the society as given, because it is "the thing to do." Violation of the mores, as with violations of manners, subject the person to the possibility of ridicule, shame, ostracism, and feelings of guilt. Violation of established mores is looked upon by society as a rejection of the society, and elicits a rejection of the violator by society in turn. Even where a particular behavior is clearly seen as nothing more than a tradition, without any other useful purpose, deviation, while it may be tolerated, is disapproved and discouraged.

Generally, people are most comfortable when surrounded by others who are like them or appear to be like them. Perhaps this represents some deep residual archetypal process left over from primitive times when a stranger encountered was a potential enemy. Further, if an individual deviates sexually from the norm, it creates a temptation for others to do so, another reason for society to discourage deviations. In addition, people generally believe that if rules or practices have existed for a long time, have "withstood the test of time," as it is often expressed, these rules must be good. It matters not whether such a principle is valid. As long as people believe it, it is a determining factor in their behavior. For over two hundred years, physicians believed that they were curing a variety of diseases by bleeding their patients, and pointed to the longevity of the practice as proof of its efficacy. The practice was abandoned only when the longevity principle had to yield to an accumulation of contrary evidence. In sum, because of the needs of people to conform to established rules and mores, their very conformity tends to perpetuate the rules.

The need to conform and have acceptance in the social unit not only affects the behavior of the individual, but may also affect his reaction to the infidelity of his spouse. For example, a particular wife may have no deep personal objection to her husband's occasional philandering, but she might be extremely concerned about what the neighbors will think if the activity is discovered, and oppose it on that ground, or perhaps feel obliged to take drastic action to maintain her status in the group. That is, the expectations of the group may compel her to take some destructive action although her own personal feeling would be to ignore the whole matter.

Conformity is not only an important element in the psychology of marital sex rules as they have been developed and maintained, but it also interacts with several other psychological factors yet to be described.

However, as we have pointed out, extramarital sex mores which have become part of us, rest upon a number of grounds which are either invalid or tenuous or matters of faith. We would assert here, that there is nothing inherently repugnant or evil in extramarital sex so far as human beings are concerned. The fact that it exists as part of the social fabric in some societies gives evidence that opposition to extramarital sex is not a "given" of human nature. It is reasonable to assume that people who might grow up in a society where extramarital sex is an openly accepted form of behavior, would have no different feelings towards it than to any other normal part of their daily lives. For example, if Americans had grown up learning to use the knife and fork as the Australians do, they would find that to be a natural and comfortable practice. We already see this process in operation with regard to the sexual behavior of unmarried women in America. While the process is still going on, and the transition is incomplete, the opprobrium which attached to sexual relations for unmarried women a hundred years ago is rapidly diminishing. This is a case where the increasing commonality of the practice has led to its acceptance. Single women who have affairs are no longer objects of scorn or social outcasts, nor are their lives ruined. They are engaging in sex without guilt or moral conflict. They have, to a large degree, simply become part of the "scene" except in the view of rigid moralists. This is not to say that at present everyone could suddenly discard imprinted moral codes. Some could and do. Others might need to work these conflicts through in order to come to a rational decision as to what they want in sexual matters. Some probably could not overcome this early training, and some might not want to. But for those who are willing and able, acceptance of extramarital sex could be accomplished easily given the appropriate change in the psychological and social environment. In such an environment, one would not have to be concerned with what the neighbors might think concerning one's own spouse's extramarital affairs.

Security Needs

The needs of people for security are too well known to require any elaboration. Traditionally, when a person married it was expected that the act would provide assurance of the gratification of economic, interpersonal, affectional, and status needs. Extramarital activities of the spouse have been viewed as threatening that assurance. One aspect of this threat is the concern that if a spouse does not conform to the mores in this regard, other obligations of the marriage may also be violated thus lowering the security that is felt; but the major security threat lies in the possibility that the spouse may find another partner more gratifying, and decide to change one marriage partner for another.

While people vary a great deal in their self-concept, there are very few who feel completely confident that there is no one else who might be a more satisfying mate for their spouse. Given the inevitable limitations, real or imagined, on what any one person can do or be, one is haunted, however greatly or slightly, by the fantasy of some ideal person, out there, to whom one's mate could be lost. It is always difficult to compete with such ghosts. This concern could be heightened by an awareness that sexual relations with an extramarital person are less likely to suffer from some of the impairments of sex that are concomitants of marriage, as described earlier. The security of the marital relationship has been thought to benefit in two ways from the prohibition against extramarital sex. First, the prohibition prevents the extramarital relationship from achieving the intensity of gratification which accompanies most sexual activities while at the same time maintaining a high reward value for the marriage relationship by virtue of its being the sole source of sexual gratification. Secondly, there is no opportunity to test the potentially superior sexual delights of the other person.

Extramarital sex also poses some other threats to security. Economic loss can be envisioned as a result of money spent on another or spent to make oneself attractive to the other. There may be loss or diminution of income or inattention to duties because of time spent in pursuit of and with the other, in some cases—especially in those affairs which take place during working hours. Dissipation of both physical and mental energy in such affairs can also be seen as threatening to maximum income production. Similarly, this expenditure of physical and mental energy can be seen as potentially detracting from the supply available to fill the sexual, affectional, and interpersonal needs of the spouse.

A spouse could also be concerned about possible loss of the status which comes with being a member of a respectable marriage. Further, where one spouse has fully accepted the romantic idealized version of marriage—the one and only forever and ever—the possibility or actuality of extramarital sex obviously could be threatening, and the destruction of this ideal be experienced as a great loss.

In one sense, then, it is the fact of deviation from the code itself that is the source of concern. While this concern may seem valid under the present code, it seems obvious that under a code where extramarital sex does not constitute a breach of obligation, this concern would lose any basis for its existence. If extramarital sex were not a deviation, it would cease to operate as a signal for other potential deviations. Further, as shown in the cocktail-lounge study, this deviation from the code does not in fact seem to signal other deviations from marital obligations.

For those who accept the romantic ideal of marriage—the one and only—extramarital sex is viewed as a threat to that ideal. This may or may not be valid depending on what is meant by "one and only" and on whether the person feels that sex and love are separable or inseparable. If by "one and only" one means that husband or wife should have no interest of any kind in another member of the opposite sex, the concerns may be well-founded. In most cases, they would also be quite unrealistic. Husbands and wives are likely to develop relations with men and women other than their spouses. These relationships may have varying degrees of intensity and intimacy short of sexual relations. A man may develop, for example, a very close personal relationship with his secretary in which a sharing of problems and feelings occurs and, in which mutual dependency and importance develops. The term "office wife" is most descriptive. Wives in business or the professions or civic activities may develop similar relationships with colleagues. Sometimes these relationships, which are nonsexual in the strict sense of that term, develop in other settings. In any event, it seems likely that many people do not invest all of themselves personally and emotionally in just one other person—the spouse. If "one and only" means the only romantic love in the spouse's life, then it is not necessarily violated by extramarital sex; whether or not one feels the marriage vow violated depends on whether one can separate sex and love. It is quite possible for John to have and enjoy a sexual experience with another woman, while Mrs. John remains his one and only true love. This can happen if the social milieu permits it, or if Mr. and Mrs. John recognize that love is love and a romp in bed is a romp in bed, and that they may be, but do not always have to be, combined. The men in the cocktail-lounge study previously referred to, generally indicated that they loved their wives no less, despite their extracurricular excursions. Most of the men with whom we have discussed this matter agree with that conclusion and feel no guilt, although they do try to avoid being caught. Some feel guilty, but only because of the deception of the wife that must occur in the absence of a mutual agreement concerning this matter. Somewhat like the income tax, the present code makes "cheaters" of many people.

Threat to the family's well-being, either through money expended in relation to the affair or through loss of income due to neglect of duties, seems to have a basis in reality. Dating, clothing, grooming, gifts, hotel rooms—all the paraphernalia of amour—cost money. On the other hand, one could argue that as a hobby, sex might be no more expensive than golf, for example, with its green fees, cart fees, equipment costs, special clothing, caddies, and tips, and might even be less time-consuming. As with all things, the good judgment of the spouse is the vital key in this area. A man or woman who spends more than the family can afford on any activities is depriving the spouse and children. On the other hand, the person who keeps spending on his own recreational activites within appropriate limits will not be depriving his family. Quite clearly the costs of playing the sex game are no greater than such activities as golf, or attending the races. Thus, while there does seem to be some real risk in this area, it seems to be a small risk—one which should be weighed against the potential advantages of extramarital sex agreements.

Emotional investment in extramarital sex could deprive a spouse of some fulfillment of his or her sexual, emotional, or other personal needs. However, it is equally true that the happier, toned-up, more energized and vital spouse that may result from extramarital sexual activities would be able and *willing* to contribute more to the happiness of his or her mate than might occur under the more repressive and frustrating present marital situation.

Fears of loss of the status of respectability which may have been valid under prior and present codes would seem to become groundless if the code were to change to permit extramarital sex. The "unrespectable" would simply become respectable by common practice.

The most potent threat to security comes from the possibility of a deep involvement with the extramarital partner, such that the termination of the marriage, either legally or psychologically, becomes highly probable. We refer here to those "genuine" affairs where there is much more than sex involved, those that become true love affairs and where the participants come to feel that they wish to be married to each other, or at least to have that modern equivalent of marriage, "living together." There can be no doubt of the reality and importance of such a threat. But we can question whether extramarital sex is the culprit in such cases. Of course, it can be and likely it is, in some cases. What starts out as a casual adventure can ripen into something much deeper. Yet, the question we must ask is whether this is more likely to occur when extramarital sex is practiced than when it is not.

We know that married people meet and fall in love with others and break up the marriage without any sexual activity with the new love. A comparison of the number of instances of this type against the type where there is a prior sexual relationship is not possible because data is lacking. Some arguments can be made on rational grounds, however. To begin with, it does not seem likely that a man or woman, in love with the spouse and enjoying a relatively good marital relationship, is going to get that much involved with someone else. In such cases, it would be unlikely for the new relationship to be sufficiently strong to overcome all the forces in favor of retaining the marriage. Surely, this is true where there are children to consider. Beyond this, there is the wrench of breaking up an established relationship, particularly if it has been one where there has been an accumulation of shared experiences and cooperation (see case of Ben and Natalie). Sheer inertia favors the reasonably good marriage. If the marriage is a poor one, it is likely to break up anyway and little would be lost, although an innocent spouse may not think so at the time. Perhaps it is the mediocre marriage that is most threatened. However, mediocre marriages may also benefit from the extramarital sex agreement, which may serve to make life within the marriage sufficiently enjoyable that there is no substantial reason to change (see Dennis and Martha). It is also, at least possible, that intimacy with a new love, as it progresses and endures, may run into some of the same problems as married sex—habituation, routineness, diminished interest, more frequent frustrations, acting out other conflicts sexually, and so on. Before Mr. Smith and Mrs. Jones sleep with each other, they may have expectations of a marvelous sexuality. After they have been to bed fifteen or twenty times, the thrill may be diminished. This, combined with the increased sexual enjoyment of the spouse that often accompanies extramarital sex, may very well keep the balance tilted in favor of the marriage. Referring once again to the "Cocktail Lounge Study," none of the men (only the men were married) became sufficiently emotionally involved with the woman to break up his marriage. In fact, the participants in that study made it clear that all concerned were seeking to avoid emotional involvement and worked at keeping it that way. The risks might be further diminished in a permissive marriage which would enable people to gratify their extramarital sexual desires without guilt and without the concomitant need to denigrate the spouse or the marriage in order to justify their behavior. None of the foregoing is meant to deny the fact that the problem of excessive involvement exists, and that some marriages might be broken up as a result of extramarital sex, with or without agreements. What is suggested is the possibility that more marriages might be helped than destroyed by extramarital sex agreements, and those that are destroyed may not be worth saving.

The Cuckold Catastrophe

Historically, when the extramarital activities of one's spouse have become known, the other spouse has been cast in the role of a victim. Where the husband has been the victim, he has commonly been the object of ridicule, as exemplified by the term "cuckold." He has had to endure the (real or imagined) contempt and ridicule of his peers as one who has been unable to function effectively as a male in terms of satisfying his wife sexually and maintaining effective domination and control over his supposed-to-be subservient wife and property. He has been cheated, deceived, and had, by both his wife and the other man. He has, according to the existing standards, failed in that most critical psychological matter, his masculinity. Often, he has suffered the humiliation of exposure of his failure and, in many cases, he has been caused intense inner concern that he might not be a real man. Public knowledge of this failure has a spillover effect in which he is viewed as weak and ineffectual, depriving him of the respect of his peers and, perhaps, even casting him in the role of one who can be preyed upon easily in other respects. Thus, while revenge may be one of the motives that have led men to violence in regard to infidelity, in many cases, injuring or slaying either the offending wife or the other man or both, has involved an attempt by the husband to restore his image of masculinity both publicly and to himself.

The wife whose husband strays has also been considered a victim, but usually more a tragic figure to be pitied rather than ridiculed. Women were not expected to be able to control their husbands. With wives generally perceived in a passive role sexually, there was less expectation of sexual talent, this being more in the province of the courtesan than the wife. For this reason, their feminine identity was less threatened. They were pitied for having a husband who shamefully disregarded his marital obligations, perhaps with the additional connotation that the wife was a person of little value to be treated in this manner. However, to be the object of pity is little improvement over being the object of scorn. Further, it seems likely that the wife would also have had some degree of concern as to her own sexual attractiveness. So, that while this may have been less intense than in the case of the male, she would still feel threatened in this area. Of course, some women have also been violent in the circumstance, as the expression, "Hell has no fury like a woman scorned" suggests.

Thus, the fears of both men and women that they might suffer loss of public respect or self-esteem through the extramarital sexual activity of the spouse, have lent force to the maintenance of strictures against it. They have attempted, not altogether successfully, to ward off such narcissistic blows by throwing up a shield of legal and social proscription.

In the traditional roles assigned to husbands and wives the pain felt upon the dereliction of a spouse seems clearly to have been genuine and justified. The faithless wife diminished her husband's masculinity. The faithless husband derogated his wife's femininity. Public humiliation and private anguish were difficult to avoid. Only the insensitive could attribute the infidelity entirely to the wickedness of the spouse and feel no twinge of self-doubt. But were these consequences not sometimes based upon misconstructions of the nature of people and of marriage? In the light of a more open view of human sexuality, it seems clear that these so-called sexual delinquencies could occur without fault or deficiency attributed to the innocent spouse. They could occur as a result of the erosions that inevitably occur in marriage. They could result from a rage to live that could not be satisfied even with a married life that was quite good. They could, in essence, be expressions of perfectly natural desires, unrelated to adequacies of the spouse. Yet, because in at least some cases, the infidelity did, in fact, arise out of some deficiency of the spouse, the concept of cuckoldry has had a long life.

Under a new system where this behavior would be understood to occur as a result of agreements between spouses, it seems clear that it would no longer provide any basis for derogation of qualities of the spouse. It is possible, as we have seen, that it might even speak well for the spouse, for one of the elements of love previously discussed is concern for the happiness of the other.

Feelings of Inadequacy

Deep down inside, most men and women have some doubts about their sexual attractiveness and capabilities. Most men are aware that they are not Adonises or Casanovas or Clark Gables, and most women are aware that they are not Cleopatras or Madame Du Barrys or Elizabeth Taylors. Granted that sexual attractiveness is a relative thing, and frequently more in the eye of the beholder than in the individual beheld, still, on a statistical basis alone, probably one-fourth to one-third of the population would be rated relatively low in sexual attractiveness. Many more, who would be considered at least adequately attractive sexually, tend to compare themselves with the very attractive rather than the unattractive and, thus, are prone to have a somewhat low opinion of themselves in this regard. They may be satisfied that they are attractive enough to a spouse, but do not feel themselves sexually attractive in general. In regard to sexual capability, the ideals of virginity and chastity are highly relevant. A person who is not too secure in regard to his ability to deliver sexual satisfaction can take considerable comfort from the knowledge that the virgin and chaste spouse has no basis for making a potentially unflattering comparison.

For this rather large population of people having some doubts about their sexual adequacy, the constraints on sexual behavior, and particularly the constraint after marriage, have been a godsend. The sexual codes have relieved them from pressure to expose their inadequacies by competing in the sexual arena and would have been welcomed for that reason alone. The codes, however, have not only provided this relief, but have made a positive virtue of the monogamous practice, thus providing a source of pride for these people in their virtue. For this population, and indeed, for many who felt more secure about their ability to compete sexually, living according to the code gave them the opportunity to achieve a certain amount of social status by being respectable or good. Many people have been able to achieve some feeling of self-worth by being able to say, "I have been married forty years and never looked at another man (woman)." To be rewarded for refraining from acts that we doubt we could perform well anyway is, indeed, delicious. It is small wonder that the considerable portion of the population to whom this occurred, contributed to the perpetuation of the monogomous code.

Prohibitions against extramarital sex may have served as a source of psychological reassurance against possible exposure of sexual inadequacy in the past. Coupled with adherence to the principles of chastity and purity, in practice as well as in words, it meant that if total sexual experience was limited to a spouse, no one would ever have a basis for comparison. Lacking such knowledge, it was reasonable to feel that spouses would be inclined to accept the sex they were having as the ultimate. In view of the long history of the double standard, it is likely that this may have worked more to the benefit of men than women. With men more free to have premarital sex, many wives must have wondered how they compared to other women with whom their husbands had had sexual experiences. Husbands—men, the rulemakers—were also able to gain an additional advantage by blaming their wives for sexual inadequacies of the marriage. The wives, in ignorance of their own sexual possibilities, would have no basis for disputing such a claim. The psychological security offered by the thin shield of a moral code hardly seems capable of offering more than minimal assurance in this area. Of course, with the trend towards premarital sex, much of this security fails, anyway. Both men and women can be expected to have sufficient knowledge of sex to know when it is good and to know what their own capabilities are.

Yet, for those who have doubts about themselves as sex partners, the rule has value. It offers them an acceptable way out of competing in an area in which they do not feel capable of competing. For such noncompetitors, the rule would continue to be valuable, by justifying their avoidance of the sexual arena. However, for that substantial group that places the full experiencing of life above security needs, and for those who are ready and willing to compete in the sexual area, the rule is a burden rather than a benefit. Further, in view of the common knowledge of the extent of adultery in this country, the rule seems to be violated so often that it fails to offer the full protection hoped for in this area. That is, in view of the extent of adultery in this country, those who are not engaged in it may have cause to question themselves anyway. Since the discovery that women are capable of orgasm and sexual enjoyment, many will refuse to accept married sex that is not as satisfying as all they can hope for, and will not be content with a lifetime of no more than doing their duty sexually.

THE SICKNESS SYNDROME

With the arrival of the age of psychiatry, behavior formerly designated as bad began to be considered in terms of mental illness. Several late-nineteenth-century and early-twentieth-century psychiatric and psychological theorists as well as marriage authorities of the same period, tended to label extramarital sexual behavior as "sick" or "deviant." In the swift growth of psychiatry, many practitioners went overboard in categorizing behaviors which did not conform to their social values and concepts as symptoms of some underlying mental illness, thus adding the force of medical stigma to the social stigmata already existing. Disregarding a still woeful ignorance regarding human nature, in general, and sexuality, in particular, many of these self-styled pundits confidently asserted that adultery was the product of the sick psyche of the adulterer. Later, with the rise of the profession of marriage counseling, emphasis was shifted from the deficiencies of the individual to the deficiencies of the marriage, and adultery was then viewed as a symptom of a sick marriage. As sickness is no more desirable than wickedness, these pseudo-scientific pronouncements lent themselves to the perpetuation of the restrictive codes.

In light of increased information, the tendency of psychiatrists, psychologists, and marriage counselors to label extramarital sex as sick is disappearing. As the noted psychologist and sexologist, Dr. Albert Ellis, has pointed out (in Neubeck, *Extramarital Relations*), adultery can be based on either perfectly healthy motives or can arise from some psychological disturbance in the individual or in the marriage. Which of these it is must be evaluated in individual cases with no blanket pronouncement any longer tenable. Some psychotherapists and marriage counselors today are even recommending extramarital sex to ameliorate some marital or inner personal problems. Finally, recent research (*Group Sex, Sex and the Significant Americans*, "The Cocktail Lounge Study") demonstrating that by and large psychopathology is no more prevalent among adulterers than in the rest of the population, would seem to completely debunk the myth of sickness.

Fear of Disease

Mankind's realization of the relationship between sexual activity and venereal disease provided further support for constraints on sexual behavior. Gratification had to be viewed in relation to the possibility of the medical consequences. In the case of extramarital sex, the picture was further complicated by the risk to the innocent spouse of suffering the disease without the gratification. The spouse who did not dance would be most unhappy to find himself or herself paying the piper's fee. A fringe disadvantage of venereal disease was the exposure of the extramarital misconduct when the symptoms of the disease appeared. It would be rather difficult to deny one's adultery to the spouse whose virtuous behavior made certain that the source of the disease was outside the marriage.

Finally, society also had a stake in this regard, as the number of possible transmitters of the disease would obviously be held down if spouses confined their sexual activities to each other; thus the restrictive code appeared to aid in the socially desirable control of such diseases.

There is little doubt that fears concerning venereal disease were well-founded in the past, and continue to be valid in the present. Venereal disease is reported to have reached epidemic proportions in the United States. However, such fears are somewhat reduced under modern conditions. Advances in medical treatment and diagnosis reduce the seriousness of the consequences of these diseases when they are detected and treated in time. A report in the *Los Angeles Times,* December 13, 1971, discussed medical research in the field of preventive drugs for venereal disease. While no conclusions can be drawn at this time, the initial testing has produced encouraging results. Similarly, Fosebury (Rosebury, Theodor, *Microbes and Morals. The Strange Story of Venereal Disease,* The Viking Press, New York: 1971) points out that while the goal is yet distant, some progress is being made in the development of a blood test for gonorrhea. Success in these areas might have almost as much impact on sexual behavior as the pill. It also seems likely that increased education concerning these diseases will contribute to a lessening of the problem. Elimination of shame or fear of disclosure, as would be the case with the co-marital sex contract, would remove one of the deterrents to seeking medical help when appropriate.

However, as with some other aspects of the co-marital sex contract, the central issue is that of weighing the gains against the risks. Automobiles are dangerous, but because of their utility no one seriously proposes abolishing them. Cigarettes are harmful to health and have much less utility than automobiles, but their sale and use is not prohibited either by law or social sanction. The amount of nonmarital sex (pre- and extra-) that occurs suggests that large numbers of people feel the gains outweigh the risks.

While we would not make light of the present serious situation regarding venereal disease, some facts need to be noted. Despite the epidemic of such diseases, the reported statistics indicate that less than one person in a hundred has the disease. Rosebury cites the data indicating that a relatively small percentage of those having sexual relations with such a person contract the disease. Thus, on a statistical basis alone, the chances of infection are small. Further, as Rosebury points out, the prevalence of the disease is highest among the poor, the young, and the ignorant. It should be hastily added that Rosebury makes it quite clear that being rich, educated, and middle-aged gives no guarantee of immunity. However, these data may explain the fact that among our sample there were no cases of venereal diseases.

In sum, the threat of venereal disease, while still a factor to be reckoned with, has lost much of its force.

PREGNANCY

The possibility of unwanted pregnancy has always ranked very high as a major contributor to constraints on sexual behavior. Fear of pregnancy has been an effective brake on premarital sex, both in terms of the disgrace of the unwed mother when the pregnancy makes her unchaste behavior public and the undesirable social and familial status imposed on the illegitimate child. The possibility of exposure of misbehavior is also a factor in extramarital pregnancy. The Crusader who was greeted by an infant when he returned home after five years' absence did not have to be a genius to discern some hanky-panky. Similarly, if a child bears a too striking resemblance to a neighbor or friend, only the literally or psychologically blind will fail to draw the obvious conclusion. Even for such oblivious ones, there would usually be some kind soul who would call attention to the resemblance. A further disadvantage of those pregnancies where the husband is obviously not the father, lies in the ensuing public knowledge of the wife's infidelity and cuckolding of the husband, matters which both might prefer to keep private.

However, the major concern seems to have been with the more usual case where a child might be conceived extramaritally but such a fact would not be detectable or known (except for such suspicions as the wife might have which she might prefer to keep to herself). Even in those cultures which have a liberal attitude toward extramarital sexual activities, it is, characteristically, expected that if a pregnancy occurs that is obviously the result of extramarital sexual activity, the wife shall divorce the husband and marry the lover. The possibility of undetected illegitimate pregnancies generated much concern over consequences that were thought to be highly undesirable. Possibly one of the most important of these was the matter of inheritance. Lacking evidence to the contrary, a child born in wedlock would be assumed to be the husband's child and entitled to whatever heirship that status conferred. With the male as the gatherer, conserver, and disposer of property, one can readily understand the repugnance he might feel at the thought of the product of his labor (or that of his ancestors) going to the child of another man—especially a man who had violated his rights and his manhood.

While these concerns were those of husbands in relation to the products of a wife's infidelity, wives had concerns of a similar nature regarding a husband's extramarital progeny. These children posed a threat to the children of the marriage, the legitimate children to whom the wife was mother, and in whose interests she could be expected to be fierce. The wife could also foresee a threat to herself from the bastard child. The responsibility or affection felt by the husband for such a child, could result in deprivation for the wife as well, providing a continuing link to the illegitimate child's mother. In most families, the wife also probably contributed to the family's wealth by her dowry or by her services, and would feel the same repugnance in sharing the product of her labor with the child of a rival as the husband felt in the reverse situation.

No one can doubt the past validity of concerns over pregnancies resulting from extramarital sex. It is not necessary to make a point by point analysis of the future validity of these concerns under a new extramarital sex code. The problem of an unwanted pregnancy is minimal now, and likely to vanish altogether in the reasonably near future. The liberalization of anti-abortion laws is becoming adequate to take care of such accidents as may occur, and it may be expected that such laws will be eliminated by enlightened legislators in the future. This concern, which has been one of the most powerful underwriters of the present code, is simply no longer a great threat, statistically. Even with the present, slightly less than perfect, preventive and curative procedures, the risk is small enough that the advantages of extramarital sex can be weighed against it.

THE NEW SEX PHILOSOPHY

Aside from all of the foregoing considerations, the new philosophy and new view of sex must be taken into account. The overvaluation of sex that existed in the past is diminishing, and sex is being seen in a more reasonable perspective. Currently, sex is being viewed as a form of play, or as a normal expression of affection between people who are not necessarily in love or otherwise bound to each other.

SUMMARY AND CONCLUSIONS

There are strong indications that some of the cornerstones of the proscription of extramarital sex were never really valid, some were valid only for some people, some were valid but are so no longer, and some are still valid but would not be in a society that accepted extramarital sex openly and honestly.

Whatever success the "code" may have had in the past, it seems clear that it is not working well now. The prevalence of divorce and adultery, negative attitudes towards marriage, destruction of relationships within marriage, guilts, fears, anxieties, frustrations, denigrations of the spouse in order to justify infidelity, all of these attest to the failure of the code. If the institution of marriage is to survive, something must be changed. Some way must be found to make marriage the most desirable and satisfying way to live, to make marriage the warm, glowing, exciting, secure relationship that it can and ought to be. We believe the extramarital sex agreement can help to accomplish this.

ALTERNATIVES

Of course, many couples have found alternative methods to add spice to marital sex without co-marital sex contracts. While adding excitement and stimulation, these alternatives present little risk, or none at all. They involve activities of a sexual nature with other couples, short of the point of actual sexual intercourse with the others; some are activities exclusively between the spouses, generally in the nature of a variation from the more usual sexual activities; some can be carried on by one partner of the marriage by using his imagination; and, finally, some may practice alternative forms of marriage, such as the "term" marriages which have been suggested as solutions for the dilemmas of a lifelong marriage when life itself is so much longer. Each of these alternatives seem worthy of description in a book such as this dealing with issues of sex in marriage. By and large, these alternatives do not provide the same degree of excitement and satisfaction as the co-marital sex arrangements. However, as with most things in life, the risks are proportional to the potential gains.

Look, Ma! I'm ——

Engaging in voyeuristic and exhibitionistic activities involving two or more couples provides all but one of the elements of an orgy. This practice resembles swinging in that the activity is shared by the spouses and is usually preceded by a period of social activity. It may occur between couples who are old friends or it may result from a process of trying to locate another couple who have similar interests, much in the manner employed by swingers; for example, by placing ads in an underground newspaper seeking couples interested in exhibitionism and voyeurism. The basic ingredients in this alternative to co-marital sex are that each couple engages in a period of petting, disrobing, sexual foreplay, and, finally, sexual intercourse in the presence of the other couple. Some couples perform this drama simultaneously; that is, each couple proceeds through the various stages at approximately the same pace. This is generally not rigidly adhered to due to somewhat different needs in terms of arousal time, but in a rather general way they do keep pace with each other so that about the time that husband "A" initiates sexual intercourse with his wife, husband "B" initiates sexual intercourse with wife "B." While this has the advantage of being equitable in terms of equal opportunity to observe and be observed, it has the disadvantage of being somewhat distracting, and some couples have indicated that they are in some conflict over whether to pay attention to what is going on within their couple unit or to watch the other couple. A variation is to perform in sequence; that is, couple "A" watches couple "B" and then couple "B" watches couple "A" with the observing couples sometimes engaging in precoital activities while watching. This avoids the problem of too much distraction, but carries with it the problem of who goes first. Most couples who practice this form of activity indicate that they find it highly stimulating to observe another couple in sexual activity and that the fact of being observed heightens their own excitement while they are engaging in it themselves. However, nearly all couples agree that the sexual excitement value is much greater before reaching climax than afterwards. Therefore, in this situation, it seems to be more desirable to be the last couple to perform rather than the first except for a few couples who find they get their kicks much more out of being watched than watching. However, despite the disadvantages of either method, many couples report that they do find this a stimulating and exciting addition to their married sex life and, much like the co-marital sex people, find that it tones up the marriage and generally has a carryover effect in that there is a period of heightened sexuality within the marriage both before and after such encounters.

Some of the more daring voyeur exhibitionists practice a form that comes closer to actual swinging without actually doing it. This form involves "switching" partners for stimulation—for the sexual preliminaries and foreplay—but returning to the married partners for final consummation of sexual intercourse. In this situation, the foreplay generally consists of a certain amount of necking, petting, fondling of genitals through the clothing and finally mutual disrobing. Most couples return to their own partners at this point, although some go a little further in terms of genital fondling in the nude and some even to brief oral genital contact.

A related practice is that of sharing pornography among two or more couples. Sometimes the pornography is in the form of books, pictures, or magazines, but more commonly it involves viewing 8 mm. stag-type films together that depict lascivious and sexually arousing scenes. These films are quite easily available, at least in most major cities. Generally, no sexual activity takes place until each couple is alone in the privacy of their own home, although some voyeur-exhibitionists use such materials as an added stimulating element.

As described to us, these activities appear to be carried on in an atmosphere that is somewhat fun-filled and tongue-in-cheek with mild feelings of wickedness and a considerable amount of bawdy, ribald conversation.

Flirtation

Flirtation is a generally harmless type of behavior that adds a dash of spice to the sex lives of many married people. It appears to be most prevalent among young people not too newly married, as the sacrosanct feelings about marriage begin to wear off and desires for added stimulation begin to arise. While, at times, there may be an explicit agreement concerning this type of behavior, most commonly, it seems to develop naturally as a result of common social activities and is more or less implicitly accepted by the spouses. Often, it starts with the usual type of bantering, provocative, man-woman conversation that is found at cocktail parties. In a number of social groups, flirting may progress to the point of very mild necking, which, despite its mildness, in a small way, seems to provide some of the benefits available in the all-the-way co-marital sex arrangements. Flirtation provides some incentive to maintain one's appearance and heterosexual attractiveness. It also serves as a stimulus to be as charming, attractive and sexy as one can be as well as providing a degree of reassurance that one is, in fact, still able to be attractive to members of the opposite sex. Further, as some couples report, there is a degree of sexual turn-on or toning-up resulting in increased sexual interest, which may then find expression back home with the spouse.

Of course, there is some risk that a man and woman might get carried away in the flirtation process and go further than they intended, but this appears to occur extremely rarely. Almost always, the people engaged in flirtations are aware that it is just that, a flirtation, and that they neither wish nor would allow the opportunity to go beyond those bounds.

Office Wives and Other
Tangential Relationships

Aside from flirtation, many men and women, because of activities outside the home such as their occupations, civic activities, or other endeavors, develop intensive nonsexual relationships with members of the opposite sex. The classical example of this, of course, is the so-called "office wife," the secretary who becomes an important part of a man's life and with whom rather deep emotional attachments frequently develop. Often, the two spend more waking hours together than the man spends with his wife. They are united in the pursuit of common goals involving the welfare of the enterprise, whatever it may be, and, in many cases, where the relationship is one of long standing, it transcends the purely business aspects. The capable and empathic secretary, providing a sympathetic ear for her employer's troubles of a personal as well as a business nature, has been immortalized in literature. It is a less publicized fact that in many such situations, the boss reciprocates, and many a secretary has found a warmth and concern in her employer that may exceed that obtainable from her husband.

While the misgivings of a wife concerning her husband's employment of a shapely young woman to be his secretary have been the object of much humor, the fact is that such a secretary generally poses little threat to the marriage because she is likely to be romantically involved with younger men, and, in all probability, is taking the job as a way station on her road to marriage. It is the more mature woman, either unmarried or desiring a career of her own, who poses the threat because it is this type who is much more likely to remain over a long period of years, thus allowing an emotional relationship to develop. But it is not the threat aspect of such relationships that is of concern here, but rather their potential for supplementing or complementing the emotional supplies provided by the spouse. Quite often, they allow a man to relate to a woman who has characteristics which are different from those of his wife. Not uncommonly, the secretary is more capable, more competent, more independent than the wife, which makes for a somewhat different kind of relationship. Sometimes, because the ties are looser, the relationship is an easier and more comfortable one. Of course, such relationships are not confined to the employer-secretary relationship but may exist in other contexts, such as with occupational colleagues of the opposite sex or outside of the occupational area in terms of long-enduring relationships in connection with other activities. For example, a woman who is involved in political or civic activities may develop a similar type of relationship with a man who is also involved in such activities, a relationship in which sex, as such, plays no part, but in which an emotional attachment occurs that may help to fulfill personal, interpersonal, and emotional needs that cannot always be met in the marriage. While such relationships may very well add an enrichment to the life of a particular married individual, because of their nature as defined here, they are unlikely to contribute anything toward greater sexual satisfaction in marriage except as they may reduce dissatisfactions generated by the failure of the marriage to meet some of the needs of a spouse.

Tea for Two
And Me for You

Aside from those activities involving other people, there are a number of practices involving only the husband and wife which serve to increase or maintain sexual interest within the marriage at a relatively high level. Some of these have been well-publicized in marriage books, but others are little known outside the confines of the counselor's office.

Probably the best known of these behaviors is the practice of continuing courtship-type dates with the spouse after marriage. All too often, couples find that after marriage, their social and recreational patterns involve activities with other people almost exclusively. In the early years, this may include going out with other couples or going to parties; later, as children come along, it may involve primarily activities of a similar nature plus those in which the children are involved. It becomes rare for the couple to go out for an evening alone, just the two of them. In contrast, some other couples make a point, some almost to a fanatical degree, of continuing their dating practices into marriage. Howard and Annette are a couple who have developed this practice to a fine art. Both had been previously married at early ages and could well be models for the thought expressed in the song about love being better the second time around. While they had engaged in many of the usual social activities during their courtship period, what each had found the most satisfying was an evening spent going out to dinner, usually at a "better" restaurant where they would have a cocktail or two, enjoy a leisurely dinner and, of utmost importance to each of them, devote themselves entirely to conversation that was stimulating, interesting, and, usually, of a personal nature. They continued this practice after marriage and even after the children came. Of course, they have a social life with friends and engage in some other activities just between themselves, but they have religiously set aside one evening a week for dining out together and break this pattern only when strong reasons so dictate.

Over the years, experience has taught them that on these dates it is highly desirable to avoid domestic talk. As Howard puts it:

> The best way to destroy an evening of this kind is to get involved with conversation about domestic needs or problems of the children or anything of that kind. It is not that all problems have to be avoided, but these seem to particularly depress the kind of feelings you want to have on those occasions. For one thing, these evenings are meant for fun and enjoyment and I can't imagine anyone who enjoys confronting domestic problems. Of course, it has to be done, but there should be another time and place for it. We have established Friday night as "our night" and I know that by noon on Friday, I'm beginning to glow with anticipation of the evening to be spent with Annette. My thoughts are running to soft lights, sweet music, pleasant atmosphere, good food, and the close intimacy of our conversation. These evenings are not all the same. Sometimes we get sexy. Sometimes we just feel very loving and romantic. Sometimes we are just hilarious and lighthearted, but whatever it is, it's something that is exclusively ours. We found, years ago, that it was almost impossible to have this kind of mood if early in the evening or any time in the evening, one of us would bring up some domestic problem. I think you get too intellectual then and turn off emotion so that you can try to deal rationally with the problem. Of course, you can't be completely rigid about it. If it's Friday night and there is some kind of pressing problem or one of us has had a great disappointment with one of the children or something like that, it's no use kidding yourself. If you're bothered by it, you might as well talk about it and clear the air, but outside of that kind of situation, we do avoid domestic talk. It has been a very important thing for us. I think maybe it's one of the cornerstones of what we feel is a

very successful marriage. I don't know how it would work for other people. I'm sure many of them love each other, but I think in addition to that, it has helped us to maintain the feeling of "being in love."

Annette adds:

I think there are some other important aspects of it. For example, I never just put something on to go out and eat. On these Friday evenings, I take a long time to dress and I dress with all the care that I did when I was younger in anticipation of a very important date, and you know, it has a remarkable effect. I think I get the same feeling that I had when I was dating—that feeling of anticipation that I'm going out with someone I like—the desire to look my best and be at my best. Howard almost always notices what I'm wearing, compliments me on my appearance and, frankly, it just makes me feel like a girl. Also, we're both busy, professional people and handling that along with all of the problems of home and family sometimes a whole week will go by without much real opportunity to talk to each other. So each of us saves up different experiences or incidents for Friday evening and I think this also adds to the anticipation—this expectance of sharing things in our lives. I think it all has a sexual effect also. I think what goes into it is my feeling that Howard is noticing me and finding me attractive and then, I think just the sheer intimacy and the intense conversation stimulates me. I am a very verbal person and conversation stimulates me. So, I think with all of these things, there's no question but that before the evening is over I often find myself aware of an interest in sex. It makes this night different. You know, usually, we go to bed and then we may feel affectionate and finally feel sexual desire, but on these nights, the sexual interest begins to develop long before we go to bed.

As Howard and Annette indicate, this practice allows them to keep romance and sexual excitement alive in their marriage.

Anytime—Anyplace

Recognizing some of the ways, particularly habituation and routine in which marriage depresses sexual interest and excitement, recommendations concerning sexual experimentation and variation are in current vogue with marriage counselors and writers of marriage manuals. They suggest that couples practice variations of position and of both precoital and coital practices. In view of the multitude of reference works covering variations of position and technique, those topics will not be dealt with here. The values of varying times and places of sexual activity are less well-known and are well worth some mention. Such variations offer the opportunity to avoid the sex-in-the-bed-room-after-retiring rut that many couples fall into. Where there is sufficient privacy—that is absence of children or other adults in the house—many couples have found a heightening of sexual excitement by extending their opportunities for sexual activity; that is, within the home some couples take advantage of their freedom to have sex in the living room, on the sofa or floor or standing up in the kitchen or wherever, whenever, the mood happens to strike them. This provides for a greater variety as well as spontaneity. Saturday afternoons and Sunday mornings are commonly times for such activities, and some couples have found enjoyment in sex before dinner during the week.

Even in the absence of such privacy, this kind of variety is still attainable. Howard and Annette may again serve as models. From time to time, at the conclusion of one of their dates, particularly if both are in a sexy mood, rather than return home they register in a nice hotel or motel and have some of the added spice of feeling just a little bit illicit as well as the added stimulation that comes from being in pleasing and different surroundings. By doing this, they avoid such mood breakers as putting out the milk bottles or looking in on the children. At times they will drive up to the local lovers' lane, park the car, neck, much in the manner of younger lovers, and wind up having intercourse in the back seat of the car. They indicate that the loss in comfort is more than compensated for by the added stimulation of the circumstances. They also point out that, at least in their case, this type of sex with their clothes (at least most of them) on, also adds an element of variety that they find stimulating. Perhaps the value of their activities is attested by the fact that their fairly high rate of sexual activity remained undiminished over the term of their fifteen years of marriage.

Walter Mitty Had a Point

As so perfectly illustrated by James Thurber in his famous Walter Mitty story, a great many people have fantasies about being different from the person they are and doing things that are different from those that occur as part of their normal life. It should be no surprise, then, that many people have fantasies of behaving in a sexual manner or of having sex with partners that vary considerably from what they actually do or have in reality. Some couples manage to achieve their fantasies to a degree by engaging in role-playing; that is, by enacting some of their fantasies with each other. For example, one rather staid housewife will, from time to time, play the role of a harlot with her husband to the delight of both, as this meets a mutual fantasy. With another couple, the wife has fantasies of being "ravished" and her husband is happy to oblige her. Of course, he does nothing to injure her, but he is much rougher and more aggressive than he normally is in their sexual activity. This sort of role-playing does appear to provide at least partial satisfaction of the desire in a manner compatible with the individual's personality makeup as he sees it, and without any of the risks that might accompany such behavior outside the safety of the marital relationship. It goes without saying that success in this type of endeavor requires a reasonable amount of mutuality between the spouses. It must be something they both desire or, at least are willing to engage in. A little acting ability does not hurt, either.

The pure use of fantasy is a common practice. One of the greatest assets human beings have is their capacity to use their imagination. Through this process, they can, in their fantasies, engage in all manner of behavior which they might scrupulously avoid in real life. Thus, the man who wouldn't dream of cheating on his wife, but who is quite taken with the new secretary in the next office, can, if he wishes, imagine himself having sexual relations with her during intercourse with his wife. A completely loyal wife stimulated by the muscular, half-naked torso of a workman during the day, can imagine herself in his arms while actually in the arms of her husband.

Recent research (Abelson, et al., *Public Attitudes Toward and Experience with Erotic Materials*, 1970) indicates that approximately 20 percent of men and 15 percent of women at times engage in such fantasies while having sexual relations with a spouse, suggesting that the practice may be far more common than one might imagine. Therapists, of course, for many years, have been aware of such practices. As with role-playing, the practice may fall short of what the experience might be in real life; on the other hand, it may be better, since things can go exactly as you wish in fantasies, and it provides at least partial gratification of the desire without any attendant risks or detriment. As innocuous as it may be, some individuals perceive a disloyalty to the spouse even in this type of fantasy if it occurs during sexual relations with the spouse. Some of these people will simply not allow themselves to have such fantasies at all. Others find their form of expression in masturbation to the accompaniment of such fantasies. It seems to work for a number of people and it is harmless.

Absence Makes the Heart Grow Fonder

Some couples find that cycling patterns of closeness and separation adds stimulation to their marital relationship, both sexual and otherwise. In its most extreme form, this is practiced by one couple, both in the creative arts, who have no children. They maintain separate apartments in which each resides during the week so they can work, and they are together on weekends and during vacation periods. Other couples practice occasional separate weekends or vacations of longer duration without sexual activity. These practices allow the marriage partners an opportunity to live and enjoy themselves as individuals, as well as reversing some of the processes of irritation and habituation that occur when there is constant contact. Anyone who has ever enjoyed a good relationship knows the great joy of being reunited after a period of separation. Rather than leave such joys to change or the exigencies of a particular situation, these people plan ahead for the enjoyment of such reuniting. Some couples who do not practice actual physical separation derive similar benefits from varying the patterns of closeness psychologically. That is, they have periods in which they may be very much involved with each other alternating with periods in which each is more concerned with his individual life goals and activities. Several couples practicing this form of separation indicate that they, also, experience much of the joy of coming together after periods of being apart psychologically in this manner.

To Have and to Hold
for the Next Five Years

Another alternative to marriage as currently practiced is the so-called "term" marriage as suggested by Margaret Mead and other social scientists. Term marriages are those in which the parties do not marry for a period lasting "until death do us part," but for a specific term of years, ordinarily with the option of renewing the contract for an additional term if both parties so desire. One of the suggestions advanced is for a five-year renewable contract under which the parties would understand at the outset that their marriage contract was limited to five years, and that it would be dissolved at the end of that period. If both parties wished, they could then opt to renew the contract for another five years and continue exercising this option for as long as they both desire. Others have suggested a twenty- or twenty-five-year contract designed to correspond to the period of family raising, recognizing that one mate for a lifetime may not be the best pattern, but, nevertheless, displaying concern for the maintenance of the family unit in the interests of the children. It may be noted that this period of time corresponds to the twenty-year syndrome described earlier in this text. As it is the more popular version, we will focus here on the five-year renewable contract.

This type of arrangement has certain obvious advantages over the conventional marriage. It avoids the feelings of being chained, confined, or trapped, that are negatively experienced by a number of married people. It may avoid some of the rancor that occurs when the conventional marriage breaks up as, when the parties fulfill their term, they have met their expectations. The avoidance of trapped feelings and the existence of time limitations on the relationship can have spillover effects. That is, faults and characteristics of a partner, which might be viewed as intolerable if extending over a period of a lifetime, may be easily bearable for a period of five years, particularly when weighed against certain virtues of the relationship. Thus, by reducing some of the strain and negative·expectation it may be possible for the partners to relate to each other more comfortably than they might if they felt they were bound together for life. It also provides recognition of the fact that people do change over time and that a couple who were suitable for each other when they got married may, as each grows in his own way, become unsuitable for each other after a period of time. Of course it has the additional benefit of recognizing that at the end of the term the parties may find they are quite happy together and wish to continue the relationship and, of course, can do so. On the negative side, the principle disadvantage appears to be the potential for frequent breakup of the family unit to the possible detriment of children, although there is certainly no conclusive proof that this is an inevitable result. It also seems likely that at least for a good many young couples whose marriage is based on "being in love," it may be jarring to their feelings about each other and the relationship to acknowledge that it may not be permanent, and many would prefer to enter matrimony with the belief, however illusory it may be, that this is a fine union, destined to last forever.

On a sexual basis, the five-year period also seems to make sense as it is often the time when interest in marital sex begins to taper off and desires for sexual relations with others may surface.

All These Loving People

Finally, some mention should be made of communal or multiple marriages. Under these practices, several people are, in effect, married to each other. It may be as small a number as one extra husband or one extra wife, or it may extend to the genuine commune, in which several men and women live together as one family, sharing duties, responsibilities, and care of children, as well as sex life. At this stage of their development, such communal arrangements do not appear to be markedly successful. Many of the same problems and strains develop among the several partners as among just two partners and may be further complicated by the addition of the strains and frictions that may occur as the result of simply having more people involved in the relationship. Problems such as habituation and the desire for variation in sexual experience probably are met to some degree by this type of relationship, but some of their feelings of being confined may nevertheless remain. While there may be more sexual variety in the multiple marriage, it is still limited and bounded by the marriage partners. It is, however, too soon to draw firm conclusions about the effectiveness of this type of arrangements. As with any social experiment, too little time has elapsed to give it a full opportunity to succeed. Additionally, up to this time, it has been practiced largely, although not in all cases, by relatively young people who are, in effect, seeing it as a way of dropping out of the main society. A better test would come with attempts by solid, stable, middle-class types to achieve marital and family happiness in the multiple marriage.

If It Was Good Enough for My Father . . .

With all of the variations upon the theme of marriage described so far, it may still be that the conventional, traditional form of marriage is best for many people. If it is true, as stated, that conventional American marriage has failed for a large number of people, it is equally true that it has been reasonably successful for a large number of people. While it is true that marriages may fail because they were poorly thought out to begin with, or because of circumstances that may not have been anticipated, for the most part when marriages fail (or fail to provide sufficient satisfaction), they do so because of the characters of the person involved. Some people need or desire more variety, more excitement, more adventure in their lives than can be provided by the conventional marriage. On the other hand, there are many people whose needs and desire for stability and security are great, and whose needs for change and excitement are smaller, who find that they much prefer the safe, enduring, traditional forms of marriage, to the chancier alternatives. As one man's needs may be another man's poison, it seems best that each should sup at the table at which he may find the most appropriate nourishment. If a pluralistic society can survive at all, can it not survive, tolerating many different styles of man-woman relationships?

9.
Summing Up

At this point it is possible to advance some answers to questions that were raised at the beginning of the book. Of course, the answers must be viewed in the light of several considerations stemming from the nature of the study. The number of couples participating in the study is quite small and they come from limited geographical, economic, and social areas. Further, although they must exist, data is lacking of couples who have attempted the co-marital sex arrangement with negative or even disastrous results.

Beyond these obvious limitations, however, the degree to which the participating couples may be considered representative of the larger population is very much open to question. They are overwhelmingly from the middle and the upper-middle class. On the whole their incomes and educational level are above that of the national average. Relative to the nation as a whole, only a small percentage are actively involved with religion or committed to religious principles. Their practice of the co-marital sex arrangement, of itself, sets them apart from the general population. They must be considered sexually libertarian, although it may be fairly stated that, at least in some of the cases, this libertarianism followed rather than preceded the arrangement. Perhaps the most distinguishing attribute, however, lies in the nature of their personality makeup. They seem to possess a more than average amount of that quality psychologists often refer to as "ego strength." This quality represents the capacity to function effectively, to handle one's life independently, and to exercise independence in decision making. As Marty put it, they are not "timid people." They seem to be more aware of themselves as people than the average and more open to experience. Such people are also very adaptable in new situations which they therefore often seek out. Their relationships within the marriage appear to be characterized by a high degree of emotional involvement with each other and openness of communication. A high degree of consideration for each other (not approaching martyrdom, however) characterizes their relationships. Perhaps it is to people of similar characteristics that any conclusions to be drawn here may be most applicable.

With these precautionary considerations in mind, some conclusions may be ventured.

EFFECTS ON THE INDIVIDUAL

To determine, accurately, cause-and-effect relationships requires evaluation before and after the fact. That, of course, was not possible in this study as there was no opportunity to observe these people before the introduction of their arrangement. The most that can be done is to make some inferences based on their own declarations and our observations of them in the present.

On the whole, these people appear to be relatively happy. They have considerable zest for living and confidence in what

they are doing. Some are happier as indicated by the extrav-
agant delight of Marty and Alice than others, such as Ben and
Natalie, where the arrangement represents more "making do"
than ecstasy. Most of the people felt they had grown and
expanded as individuals as a result of the arrangement. They
seemed to suffer less from the common plagues of our time—
guilt, anxiety, depression, and boredom—than the average person. Most of the group appeared to function, at least adequately, in their various life roles.

It is not contended here that all of these people were or are
at all times free of worry and anxiety concerning their activities.
Several have indicated considerable concern during preliminary
discussions and the early stages of implementing the arrangement. Many of these concerns dissolved when feared effects
failed to materialize. A number of the participants, particularly
those whose activities are the independent type, have not
entirely eliminated concern over the possibility of a deep
emotional involvement which might terminate the marriage.
However, with the accumulation of experience, this type of
concern, while it may still be present, is considerably diminished.

EFFECTS ON THE MARRIAGE

The study indicated quite clearly that, in this group of
couples, the arrangement has had beneficial effects on their
marital relationships. In some cases, improvements in one or
more aspects of their relationship were noted, while in others, it
was the feeling of the couple that the arrangement enabled
them to preserve the relationship at a previously high quality.
Many couples reported increased warmth and closeness,
strengthening of the bond between them, and generally
increased enjoyment of their life together. Of course, some of
this may be attributable to the fact that they were enjoying life
as individuals and were therefore more able to enjoy the
benefits of their marriage than is a person who generally finds
life providing insufficient satisfactions or who relies almost

entirely on the marriage to provide satisfactions, often with consequent frustration. Many indicated that the arrangement diminished the feeling of confinement that is so often found in marriage.

The beneficial effects of the arrangement on the sexual relationship of the married partners is of particular significance. In contrast to the diminished sexual relationship either in quantity or quality found in conventional marriages, the co-marital sex couples almost uniformly report either increased frequency and enjoyment of marital sex or maintenance of marital sex at a previously high level. There appear to be several possible explanations for this phenomena. It may be that the overall feelings of well-being and zest for living that appeared to accompany the co-marital sex arrangement, simply provide a climate in which there is more interest and enjoyment of many things, including sex, and in which there seems likely to be a more affectionate and enjoyment-oriented relationship between the spouses. A second reason, as indicated by statements of many couples, is the heightening of sexual awareness and sensuality that seems to occur along with the arrangement. There seems to be a background of constant potential sexual stimulation which carries over into the marital relationship. A third possible explanation may be found in the totally unexpected finding that a considerable number of the men experienced a different kind of sexual excitement with their wives on those occasions when their wives had recently had sexual relations with another man. While this did not occur universally among the men participating in the study, or even the majority, it did occur with sufficient frequency to suggest that it may, by no means, be an exceptionally rare occurrence.

A finding such as this, which runs so contrary to traditional beliefs and expectations, surely warrants an independent investigation in its own right. However, some speculations may be offered as to its basis. The madonna-harlot conflict as suggested by the case of Tony and Lil may offer one explanation. It is at least possible that many men who have this particular sexual orientation experience a greater release of inhibition in relation to a wife who can be perceived as possessing some kind of harlotlike quality based on the fact of her sexual relations with other men. As an alternative explanation, it may be that the husband is responding to the state of heightened sexuality in which his wife returns to him from her previous lover, as described so graphically by Marty and several other men in the study.

Whatever the underlying reasons may be, the finding of an improved sexual relationship between the spouses as a result of co-marital sexual activity is consistent with the findings of other researchers. The fact that several investigators have reached the same conclusion clearly justifies the acceptance of this phenomenon as a reality. This fact alone represents a powerful argument in favor of the co-marital sex arrangement.

The minimal amount of jealousy demonstrated by these couples represents another unexpected finding. Prior to the study it had been anticipated that jealousy, in the sense of rivalry or competition with a rival, would be a very difficult problem in arrangements of this type. The data, however, indicates that for some of the couples it simply doesn't seem to exist, and that for those couples where jealousy is present it is of a minor nature and accepted by the participants as a price they are willing to pay for the benefits of the co-marital sex arrangement. This minimal operation of jealousy seems best explained by the attitudes of the participants towards each other and towards sex. On the whole, the participants are simply not possessive and, while they attach great importance to their shared life, they recognize that each is an individual with the need and right to a portion of life outside the relationship. They also are able to accept the realization that some desire for sexual relations with others is natural and do not attach inappropriate significance to such relationships. Along with these attitudes towards sex and towards each other, the strong sense of security regarding their relationship expressed by most of these couples, makes the lack of jealousy appear more reasonable. There is a poster hung in the counseling center of California State University at Los Angeles, author unknown, showing a flower and bearing the inscription, "Love Means Giving a Person Room to Grow." This quotation seems to express the willingness of these participants to give their spouses room to grow, to expand, to experience.

EFFECTS ON SOCIETY

Accepting the validity of the premise that the family unit is the essential basic building block of a society and that such units are best found in a formalized structure such as marriage, it follows from the data of this study, that society would benefit from the co-marital sex arrangement. Anything that aids in sustaining marriage works to the best interest of the society. The findings of this study along with others, strongly indicate that the co-marital sex arrangement can, indeed, strengthen a good marriage.

Critics of this position may well cry with alarm that acceptance of the co-marital sex practice will lead to the often predicted moral breakdown in America. It is difficult to know what the term "moral breakdown" means. If it means that there will be changes in the traditional and outmoded moral code, then, of course, the charge appears to be true. However, this does not necessarily have negative connotations, although it may sound that way to many people. The fact is that it may be desirable to have a breakdown of a moral code that diminishes rather than enhances the well-being of mankind. Of course, this statement does not apply to a conception of morality as being given by God or by nature and, therefore, immutable. To those who view morality in terms of their religious beliefs, no argument can be made and none will be attempted, except to state that there seems to be considerable uncertainty and division of opinion as to just what the laws of God and nature are. This, at least, leaves the door open to reinterpretation of those laws by those in positions of authority to do so and such reinterpretation, of course, is tantamount to change. The situation is somewhat similar to that which prevails in the profession of law where the statement, "The law means what the judge says it means" is commonplace. What the Constitution says, for example, depends to a large extent on the composition of the Supreme Court at any given time. If the term "breakdown of morality" means that there will be no morality, the charge is probably false. Neither this study nor others involving couples practicing co-marital sex, provide any evidence of a lack of a code of behavior. The morality may be different, but it certainly exists, and is quite evident from the data in all of the studies, albeit the code may vary—from the fairly formalized and structured rules for group swinging to the relatively informal basic rule of other types of co-marital sex practitioners—the simple rule, "Exercise judgment and consideration for the other person."

Diminished productivity has long been an argument of those opposed to the practice of hedonism and sexual freedom. The data from this and other studies negate such an argument. The people participating in this study are certainly at least as productive as the average American citizen and many are quite clearly superior. They all earn their living by doing productive work and in the case of some of the women, they are performing the normal functions of housewife and mother as well. Many make contributions to civic, philanthropic, and cultural endeavors. None appear to devote such an excessive amount of time and energy to the pursuit of sex and pleasure that they are relatively useless for any other purpose. None appear to abandon their responsibilities or their various social roles to carry on their sexual activities.

HOW TO DO IT

For those who may consider entering into the co-marital sex contract we have some advice.

1. Communicate. Open and honest communication is an absolutely essential requirement of the co-marital sex contract. Talk and talk and talk about it. Not only in the approach and initiation phase, but throughout the duration of the arrangement. This is no more and no less than is necessary for any good marital relationship.

2. Accept your feelings. Accept the desire for change and variety, both in yourself and your spouse. Be aware of and open to these desires as a normal and predictable part of human life.

Do not assume that such desires somehow derogate either the relationship or your spouse. This attitude should be brought to the surface in the first discussion of the arrangement. The spouse who initiates the first discussion should be prepared for reactions of shock, fear, or anger by the spouse. It is important, therefore, to make clear as soon as possible that the proposal does not stem from deficiency motives—from "I am unhappy," or "You are inadequate." Rather stress the positive feelings about the marriage and indicate that you feel a desire to expand, to have new and different experiences and that you think your partner may have similar feelings or might enjoy such an expansion. Be sure to stress that the object is enrichment of a basically satisfying relationship, not a remedy for one that is failing. It is wise to make a point of stressing positive aspects of the marriage and the spouse, not only at the point of initial discussion, but throughout the existence of the arrangement. We have a theory we call the "more principle." It is like the force that impels the man who has made his first million to continue striving to seek the second million. Obviously, he could rest content with enough money to live in relative luxury the rest of his life without further effort or exertion. It is his knowledge that there is more and that it is attainable that pulls him onward. We feel that if a couple can agree that their motives are based on the "more principle," the co-marital sex contract has an excellent chance of working successfully.

3. *Use persuasion.* At least until the co-marital sex contract has become more common and accepted than at present, the spouse who initially proposes it may anticipate immediate and categorical rejection of the idea by the partner. We do not feel this means the subject must be dropped, although a period of suspension might be useful to allow the initial emotional reaction to dissipate and a more objective consideration to emerge. We feel that as in all marital differences of opinion, some effort to persuade the partner is appropriate. This should not go too far, nor too fast—limits must be gauged in the individual situation; duress, threats, excessive pressure should be avoided. Decisions based on such tactics will be useless because they deprive the arrangement of the mutuality which is neces-

sary to its success. We suggest that the proposer make it clear that this arrangement is not going to be forced on the spouse and will not come into existence unless and until there is accord regarding it. It should be made clear that it is a matter of desire, not a necessity, and can be foregone. This helps diminish the almost automatic resistance that occurs when one feels coerced or "cornered," and allows for a more rational discussion of the pros and cons. If this type of discussion does not emerge by the third or fourth attempt, we suggest the plan be abandoned. In such an instance, the spouse is too rigid or has such strong emotional reactions against it that further discussions would be fruitless and possibly harmful. We feel that a reading of this book and some of the references cited in it by both spouses, either before or after the first discussion, may prepare the ground for easier, more comfortable and more informed discussion.

4. Use the trial approach. It would be nice to believe that once an agreement had been reached, everything would then go smoothly and rewardingly. While this can happen, it is the exception rather than the rule. More commonly, there are unexpected prcblems, disappointments and occasions for reevaluation. Fantasizing potential activities and problems may be useful here. For example, a husband can try to imagine how he will feel watching his wife with another man at a swinging party. Or a wife can try to imagine her reaction to her husband's description of an experience with another woman. However, the only valid test is in the actuality not the fantasy. Therefore, we suggest that an experimental attitude be adopted—a "we'll try it and see" approach. Certainly there should be an exploration and assessment of feelings after the first activity. There may be a desire to drop it. There may be a feeling that while some questions remain, further experience is in order. There may be a desire not to abandon the project but to try a different mode. And of course, there may be sheer delight. Whatever the feelings are, they should be out in the light of day so they can be dealt with appropriately.

5. Ground rules. We feel that ground rules should be established in the beginning subject to future modification as experience may indicate. We cannot offer specific rules as these must be an individual matter according to the couple involved. As a very general rule we recommend that consideration for the spouse and the marriage be given top priority and that reasonable judgment be employed in meeting this priority. Without stating rules, we can specify some areas in which it is advisable to work out ground rules.

A. Time. The couple should have some mutual understanding regarding the expenditure of time in co-marital sexual activity—when, how much time, the limits.

B. Off-limits people. Some people may wish to keep their co-marital sexual activities separated from their usual life—and, therefore, would prefer avoidance of such activities with friends or with people with whom one or both have frequent contact. If this is the case, it should be specified.

C. Disclosure. Whether and to what extent the spouses should discuss their "experiences" with each other is less a problem in swinging than in the independent modes. Some couples prefer no discussion. Others find their marital relationship is enhanced by being able to discuss their experiences with each other. Some in fact, find it most difficult to avoid discussion. Whatever the desire is, it should be openly discussed and a pattern agreed upon.

PUTTING IT IN WRITING

So long as adultery is defined as a crime, as it is at present, a written contract would have no legal standing as a contract to perform an illegal act is not enforceable. We feel that most couples who are capable of entering into such an arrangement would have little need or desire to put it in writing. However, some couples may find such a reduction of the agreement to writing useful, either because one or both spouses are able to express themselves better in writing than verbally, or, simply, as a memorandum that can be referred to sometime later in the event of some disagreement or inability to remember what was said. Therefore, we present the following as a sample of how such a contract might be written.

CO-MARITAL SEX CONTRACT

WHEREAS John Smith, hereafter called "husband" and Betty Smith, hereafter called "wife" desire to expand and enrich their married lives and

WHEREAS both parties feel that sexual activity with others than the spouse will contribute to such expansion and enrichment

THEREFORE, it is mutually agreed that husband and wife shall each be free to engage in sexual activities with others subject to the following terms, conditions, and restrictions.

1. Said activities shall take place only at such times as mutually agreed upon by the parties.

2. Said activities shall not take place with such individuals as are specifically excluded upon request of either party.

3. Said activities shall not be conducted in such a manner as to interfere substantially with meeting the usual marital and familial responsibilities of either party.

4. This agreement and all activities authorized under it shall be terminated immediately upon the request of either party.

5. In the event of termination of this agreement or failure of the activities encompassed within it to achieve the stated goals and expectations of the parties, each party agrees to hold the other blameless so long as each has fulfilled the terms and obligations herein stated.

6. It is understood that this contract deals with an interpersonal relationship and is subject to such modifications as are mutually agreed upon by the parties.

IN WITNESS WHEREOF we have set our hands to this agreement this ____ day of _____ 19__.

_____
Wife

_____
Husband

THE FUTURE

Concerning marriage, some aspects of the future are easy to see: the rules for marriage are changing. That handwriting is already clearly to be seen on the wall. Given the number of options, the nature of the change is less certain. The options include such forms as multiple marriage, communal marriage, term marriage, co-marital sex contract marriages, and, perhaps, other options as yet unknown.

Our prediction is that the co-marital sex arrangement will become a common and accepted marital practice. There are several reasons for feeling that this option will be preferred, although it should be borne in mind that it is possible that several options may exist side by side. That is, in addition to co-marital sex marriages, there may be people who will prefer the term marriage or some other alternative, including the present conventional marriage. There is no critical reason why several alternative forms of marriage cannot co-exist within the same society. However, we feel that for most people the co-marital sex arrangement would be preferred to multiple marriage or communal marriage because it allows for greater intimacy and for the preservation of the basic marital dyad, the basic one-man, one-woman relationship. It also avoids the loss of privacy that is inevitable in group marriage as well as avoiding the greater potential for discord that is present in constant multiple interaction. One-man, one-woman is difficult enough. We also feel that the co-marital sex arrangement will be preferred to term marriages because we feel that people have a strong need to think in terms of a life-long relationship. Perhaps we are incurable romantics but we feel very strongly that what is lost in terms of the feeling "we are together forever" far outweighs the gains to be derived from the knowledge that one is not chained to a life-long commitment. We feel that the gains from the term marriage are to a large extent duplicated by opportunities available through the co-marital sex agreement without the loss of the feeling of permanence. We strongly feel that lovers will continue to want to say to each other, "I will love you forever."

What we see for the future then is a society in which the co-marital sex contract will be practiced openly, without guilt, shame or reproval, without need for concealment, without problems of what to tell the children, and without any feelings that love is thereby diminished. We do not necessarily feel that all couples will conduct their marriage in this manner because for various reasons some may not wish to do so. We also do not feel that all marriages conducted in this manner will necessarily be happy, nor that some will not end in divorce. We do not see it as a cure-all for everything that ails marriage. People will still get married for the wrong reasons, and some people will still find that at some point in marriage it fails to provide for their needs. We also do not foresee this radical change taking place with great rapidity. Social change simply does not occur in that manner and many of the traditional conditioned-in ways of thinking will have to have time to dissipate before such a change could become complete. Yet we believe that this practice will become increasingly prevalent as the years go by and in the not too distant future will become sufficiently common to achieve respectability. When this happens the large majority of the couples who choose this form of marriage, we are convinced, will find themselves happier, will find that their love for each other is enhanced, that their marriage is better, that the divorce rate will drop and that infidelity, of course, as a matter of definition, will virtually disappear. Does this sound too idealistic? We are sure the couples that participated in our study would join us in saying, "It can be done."

Bibliography

Abelson, Herbert, et al., *Public Attitudes Toward and Experience With Erotic Materials. Technical Report of the Commission on Obscenity and Pornography.* Vol. 6, Washington, D.C., U.S. Government, 1970; Response Analysis Corporation, Princeton, New Jersey: 1970.

Bartell, Gilbert D., *Group Sex: A Scientist's Eyewitness Report on Swinging in the Suburbs.* Peter H. Wyden, Inc., New York: 1970.

Berne, Eric, MD, *Sex in Human Loving.* Simon and Schuster, New York: 1970.

Blackwood, Beatrice, *Both Sides of Buka Passage.* Clarendon Press, Oxford: 1935.

Breedlove, William and Jerrye, *Swap Clubs.* Sherbourne Press, Los Angeles: 1964.

Coffin, Tristram, *The Sex Kick.* The Macmillan Company, New York: 1966.

Crawley, Ernest, *Studies of Savages and Sex.* Reprint of 1929 edition, Methuen and Co., London: 1969

Cuber, John F. and Harroff, Peggy B., *Sex and the Significant Americans: A Study of Sexual Behavior Among the Affluent.* Appleton-Century, New York: 1965.

Duvall, Evelyn and Sylvanus M., *Sex Ways—In Fact and Faith.* Association Press, New York: 1961.

Ellis, Albert, *The American Sexual Tragedy.* Lyle Stuart, New York: 1962.

—— *If This Be Sexual Heresy.* Lyle Stuart, Inc., New York: 1963.

Ellison, Alfred, *Oral Sex and the Law.* Academy Press, Inc., San Diego: 1970.

Ford, Clellan and Beach, Frank, *Patterns of Sexual Behavior.* Harper & Brothers, Publishers and Paul Hoeber, Inc., Medical Books, New York: 1951.

Guyon, René, *Sex Life and Sex Ethics.* John Lane, The Bodley Head Ltd., London.

Hunt, Morton, *The Affair.* New American Library, New York: 1972.

Ibert, J.C. and Charles, J., *Love the French Way.* Translated by Marguerite Barnett. William Heinemann, London: 1961.

Kirkendall, Lester A. and Whitehurst, Robert N., *The New Sexual Revolution.* Donald W. Brown, Inc., New York: 1971.

Mantegazza, Paolo, *The Sex Relations of Mankind.* Eugenics Publishing Co., New York: 1935.

Margolis, Herbert and Rubenstein, Paul, *Group Sex Tapes.* David McKay Company, New York: 1971.

Neubeck, Gerhard, ed., *Extramarital Relations.* Prentice-Hall, Inc., Englewood Cliffs, New Jersey: 1969.

Peterson, Joyce and Mercer, Marilyn, *Adultery for Adults.* Bantam Books, Inc., New York: 1968.

Rosenbaum, Salo and Alger, Ian, *The Marriage Relationship.* Basic Books, Inc., New York, 1968.

Rosebury, Theodor, *Microbes and Morals: The Strange Story of Venereal Disease.* The Viking Press, New York: 1971.

Shiloh, Ailon, ed., *Studies in Human Sexual Behavior: The American Scene,* "The Cocktail Lounge: A Study of Heterosexual Relations in a Public Organization," by Julian Roebuck and S. Lee Spray. Charles C. Thomas, Springfield, Ill.: 1970.

Tabori, Paul, *Taken in Adultery.* Aldus Publications Ltd., London: 1949.

Terman, Lewis M., *Psychological Factors in Marital Happiness.* McGraw Hill Book Co., New York: 1938.

Thomas, William and Znaniecki, Florian, *The Polish Peasant in Europe and America.* Dover Publications, Inc., New York: 1958.

Unwin, J. D., *Sex and Culture.* Oxford University Press, London: 1934.